D1051005

A B C

THE WILTON DIPTYCH (LEFT WING): RICHARD II. AND PATRON SAINTS

National Gallery.

A SHORT HISTORY OF COSTUME & ARMOUR

Francis M. Kelly
and
Randolph Schwabe

TWO VOLUMES BOUND AS ONE

DOVER PUBLICATIONS, INC.
Mineola, New York

Bibliographical Note

This Dover edition, first published in 2002, is an unabridged republication of the work originally published by Charles Scribner's Sons, New York, in 1931 under the title *A Short History of Costume & Armour, Chiefly in England, 1066–1800.* The eight original color plates have been reproduced here in black and white. In addition, three double-page spreads from the 1931 edition (Plates VII, XIII, and XX in Volume II) appear as single, full-page illustrations in the present volume.

DOVER *Pictorial Archive* SERIES

This book belongs to the Dover Pictorial Archive Series. You may use the designs and illustrations for graphics and crafts applications, free and without special permission, provided that you include no more than ten in the same publication or project. (For permission for additional use, please write to Permissions Department, Dover Publications, Inc., 31 East 2nd Street, Mineola, N.Y. 11501.)

However, republication or reproduction of any illustration by any other graphic service, whether it be in a book or in any other design resource, is strictly prohibited.

Library of Congress Cataloging-in-Publication Data

Kelly, Francis Michael, 1879–1945.
A short history of costume & armour / Francis M. Kelly and Randolph Schwabe.
p. cm.
Originally published: New York : Charles Scribner's Sons, 1931.
Includes bibliographical references and index.
Contents: v. 1. 1066–1485–v. 2. 1485–1800.
ISBN 0-486-42264-X (pbk.)
1. Costume–Great Britain–History. 2. Armor–Great Britain–History. 3. Costume–History. 4. Armor–History. I. Title: Short history of costume and armour. II. Schwabe, Randolph, 1885–1948. III. Title.

GT730 .K4 2002
391'.00941–dc21

2002025606

Manufactured in the United States of America
Dover Publications, Inc., 31 East 2nd Street, Mineola, N.Y. 11501

A Short History of Costume & Armour

Volume I

1066–1485

PREFACE

THE cordial reception accorded to both editions of their *Historic Costume* has encouraged in authors and publishers alike the hope that the present work too may not lack a welcome. The principle underlying it is essentially the same that governed its predecessor : the primary importance of contemporary art, *rightly apprehended*, to the proper understanding of the evolution of human clothing in past ages. There is no pretence at anything like an exhaustive treatment of the subject, even within the narrow limits to which the authors have—perhaps arbitrarily—restricted their inquiry. Distinctively liturgical, clerical and professional dress has been consciously ignored. So, too, with what may be called secular ritual : coronation and peers' robes, orders of knighthood, official insignia, liveries, and the like : things which early tend to become standardized and to be modified only gradually and imperceptibly over long periods of history. Nor has the dress of the peasantry and working-class been dwelt on. The sections on " civilian " dress deal mainly with the *fashions* of their respective dates ; consequently it is the so-called " upper classes " and their imitators who furnish most of our examples, for it is *their* apparel that incessantly changes with and so most intimately reflects their times. To use a current social shibboleth, costume in olden days was distinctly " class conscious." In the armour section, again, we have heavily stressed the " knightly " element, for this again best illustrates the evolution of defensive attire from the Crusades to the fifteenth-century masterpieces of the armourer's craft, and thence to the decay of the art and its virtual disappearance in the seventeenth century. Armour is here discussed exclusively as the *working-dress* of the warrior ; hence " parade " and tournament equipment is omitted.

Speaking roughly, the period covered extends from the Crusades at one end to the latter end of the French Revolution at the other. Note how throughout this long stretch of time the pace is set, sartorially, by the male sex, and how at length, chiefly through the commercial expansion of England, a *bourgeois* tone creeps into men's fashions in the west ; till by its close the cock-bird, voluntarily stripped of his former fine feathers, is henceforth fitted for an industrial millennium.

Our concern in the following pages is mainly with fashion in England, but we have not scrupled to draw upon Continental sources where these seemed to us aptly to illustrate our point. As pointed out in an earlier work, the general outline of fashionable attire was much the same, and followed the like course of development in Western Europe

(England, France, and the Netherlands). Generally speaking, France was the channel through which the modes of the Continent reached this country. At least in courtly circles the introduction of a fashion usually followed its appearance abroad within quite a short period.

The study of costume has heretofore been associated with dry-as-dust fogies on the one hand, on the other with " period " plays, historical genre-painting, and the like. It is more and more being realized that it has a real practical use in helping art experts to check the *bona-fides* of " old masters " and other alleged examples of ancient work submitted to their critical judgment.

Our thanks are due to the following who have kindly granted us permission to reproduce certain of the subjects illustrated :

The Curator, Barcelona Museum, Plates xxx. and xxxi. ; A. Chester Beatty, Esq., Plates i. and iv. ; R. B. Fleming & Co., Plate xxiii.$_{iii}$; M. Gulbenkian, of Paris, Plate xv.$_{ii}$, from Boccaccio's *Des Cleres et Noble Femmes* ; The Council of the Kent Archæological Society, Plate ii.$_{ii}$, reproduced from *Archæologia Cantiana*, 1880 ; Methuen & Co. Ltd., Plate xxviii$_{ii}$, from *The Armoury of the Castle of Churburg*, by Oswald Graf Trapp ; The Pegasus Press, Paris, Plate xxi.$_{ii}$ *bis*, from *Romanesque Sculpture in France, Eleventh and Twelfth Centuries*, by Paul Deschamps ; Phillips City Studios, Wells, Plate viii.$_{i}$; S. Smith, Lincoln, Plates viii.$_{ii}$, xxvi.$_{i}$; Dr. F. Stœdtner, Plate xxii. ; F. H. Cripps Day, Esq., Plate xxi. *bis* ; The Curator, Rŏmer Museum, Hildesheim, Plate xxvii. ; The Metropolitan Museum, New York, Plate xxviii.

We also wish to acknowledge our indebtedness to F. H. Crossley, Esq., and Brian C. Clayton, Esq., for placing at our disposal their very extensive collections of photographs.

Thanks are also due to J. Pierpont Morgan, Esq., and to the authorities of the British Museum, The Victoria and Albert Museum, The National Gallery, to the Librarians of Trinity College, Corpus Christi College, and St. John's College, Cambridge, for allowing their collections to be drawn upon for illustrations.

In many cases the sources of the subjects have been acknowledged on the plates.

Finally, a debt of gratitude remains to be discharged to Mr. Harry Batsford and Mr. Francis Lucarotti, whose unfailing co-operation has greatly lightened our labours.

F. M. K.
R. S.

CONTENTS

PART I. CIVILIAN

INTRODUCTION

"*Des divergences dues à l'age, à la fantaisie ou à la position sociale de chacun ont toujours coexisté avec la mode générale de l'époque adoptée par le plus grand nombre.*"

HARMAND : *Jeanne d'Arc.*

THE SOURCES.—The materials for the study of costume in the past are of two kinds : artistic and literary. Both are invaluable to the student who would have a real understanding of his subject, but both are not equally easily assimilated. The concrete illustrations afforded by contemporary art in all its branches, although by no means exempt from pitfalls for the unsophisticated novice, are yet easier of general apprehension than the writings of contemporary authors. This is especially the case with the earlier writers. It must be remembered that to contemporary readers, familiar in their daily life with the objects referred to, a precise definition was unnecessary, and that the writer had no inkling of the difficulties he was sowing in the path of the modern commentator. None the less, the student desirous of making the most of his investigations should not neglect this class of evidence. If many passages remain obscure, he will on the other hand, in not a few instances, find text illuminate illustration—and *vice versa.*

While it is perhaps not indispensable for the student to have much knowledge of tailoring, he will find a theoretical acquaintance with the principles of " cut " and drapery of immense assistance in deciphering the naïve productions of the earlier artists. There are several modern costume-books which have devoted considerable attention to such questions. (See BIBLIOGRAPHY.) The solutions they give are generally the result of practical experience. Designers for the stage or film, as well as painters, illustrators, etc., desirous of depicting historical events and personages, can hardly know too much in this way. Indeed, the artist designing an historical cartoon will probably, if conscientious, wish to work from the costumed model, and for this purpose it is advisable for him to be able to have the dresses, etc., correctly made to his orders, and not depend upon theatrical costumiers' " stock."

The artistic material at our disposal is practically endless ; almost daily new stores of information become available in the form of reproductions of every form of art : books are constantly appearing on this or that artist, school of painting, engraving, sculpture, illumination, and what not. Art magazines, illustrated catalogues, even dealers' advertisements, are full of material.

I have already said that the art of the past is strewn with " snags " for the raw inquirer, of which some may fitly be noted here. It is true, for instance, *in a general way*, that the mediæval artist and (to a great extent) his sixteenth-seventeenth century successors dressed the characters of the past in the fashions of their own day, but certain clear-cut exceptions should be pointed out, namely :

(*a*) Christ, His Virgin Mother, and the Apostles are, almost without exception, portrayed in a traditional costume and " make-up " which had become stereotyped many centuries before the date at which our book begins. This tradition has endured, with hardly one important break, to the present day.

(*b*) As time went on (and this is especially notable from the fifteenth century) artists began to aim at giving certain well-defined groups of characters an exotic, or at least unfamiliar, aspect. As a rule these represented pagans, oriental tyrants, and anti-Christian characters generally, for whom they were apt to draw largely upon their imagination. As a result such characters present a fantastic, often hybrid, appearance, due to head-dresses, armour, weapons, etc. (largely born of the artist's fancy), which characterize these figures. His aim is to make them repulsive, ostentatious, and/or ludicrous.

(*c*) There was occasionally an attempt at what may be called " home-made " archæology *in depicting " ancestors " and the like*. This was largely a matter of invention ; but, on the other hand, any fashion that appealed to the artist as sufficiently out of vogue would serve for any preceding period.[1] From *c.* 1500 a highly conventionalized pseudo-classical costume began to be used indiscriminately for the Hebrews, Greeks, and Romans, as a result of Humanism and the Italian culture. More interesting is the occasional delineation in certain works of authentic pieces of armour considerably older than the artist's day. Helmets and other items as early as the fourteenth century (earlier in a few cases) have descended to us, and therefore it is obvious that he too may well have seen them, or contemporary delineations of them, in some armoury, arsenal, or church. This subject cannot be fully developed here, though I venture to suggest it as unploughed soil to the archæologist. A case in point is the unmistakable portrayal of the " pig-faced " bascinet with its pendent "aventail" (*c.* 1380–1420) in works by Memlinc, Hans Holbein the Elder, and Matthias Grünewald (late fifteenth–early sixteenth centuries), of which other contemporary examples could be quoted.

But these exceptions a little practice will ere long learn to discount at sight, when it is no very difficult matter, from observation of ancient works of art and constant checking of one's former data, to collect a very reliable body of knowledge. It is well to build one's conclusions primarily upon examples either definitely dated or whose date can, from internal evidence, be fixed within a little. The student should not allow himself to be *dérouté* by a mere inscription or date which appears

[1] HARMAND, pp. 22–24.

to upset the ideas he is forming: they may well be forgeries,[1] and it behoves him, so far as he can, to verify all data. In conclusion, let him keep his eyes open and either collect illustrations (photos, picture-postcards, reproductions) and—if anything of an artist—make sketches of what he cannot otherwise store in his files. The method of arrangement must be left to the individual; whatever enables him most readily to refer to his collection—which he will find grow amazingly quickly—is obviously for him to judge.

Literary evidence is in rather a different category. A drawing, painting, or carving of its nature, unless of the most primitive technique, conveys a definite impression. Not so the written word. Even the expert commentator on texts is not infrequently reduced to little better than guess-work—quite apart from difficulties of palæography. There are two contradictory strains that infest the whole terminology of costume. To say nothing of particularities of local usage, we find—

(*a*) that certain terms radically change their application with the passage of time; and *per contra*—

(*b*) that an article essentially one and the same (in principle at least) alters its name during its lifetime.

Of the first anomaly the word *Hose* is a good example. At first it designates what we should call stockings or leggings; then it becomes breeches and stockings in one; by the latter part of the sixteenth century it regularly applies to *Breeches*; till by the middle of the seventeenth century reverts itto its original meaning of stockings, which it has retained ever since. *N.B.*—In German it still retains its sixteenth-century meaning.

Of the second we may cite the "pair of *Plates* covered," later known as a *brigandine*, and in its last days as a *coat of plate*.

It is impossible, in view of the vast field of research available, to advise the reader as to literary sources of information. Practically any of the old romances, chronicles, *fabliaux*, are liable to afford him useful material. Nowadays a great number of these are increasingly available in modern type, carefully edited by competent scholars. The French texts should not be neglected considering the close connection between their country and ours for many centuries, to say nothing of Burgundy in its palmy days. With the close of the fourteenth century we can depend more fully on our own native resources, Chaucer, Lydgate, the Paston letters, etc.; the Tudor dramatists and satirists, diarists, writers like Stubbes, Peacham, and Bulwer; later essayists, letter-writers, and biographers, to say nothing of notices in the contemporary news-sheets, give us plenty "to bite on." Wardrobe accounts, wills, and inventories are full of valuable matter. Dictionaries too, and glossaries, had been in use for some time, and one way and another we shall not run short of fuel. Occasionally illustrations accompany the texts.

De Mély and Bishop's *Répertoire des Inventaires imprimés* is an admirable book of reference. It contains detailed references to *published* inventories,

[1] This in a measure applies to armorial devices as well.

French, English, Latin, German, Italian, Spanish, etc., most of which may be read *in extenso* in the original tongues at the British Museum. The *Oxford Dictionary*, with its vast store of contemporary texts, is well-nigh indispensable.

There are a number of ever-recurrent themes in mediæval art, which would of themselves suffice to illustrate the general appearance of certain classes fairly completely down to the fifteenth century.

(*a*) MILITARY.—The Bible was the universal storehouse whence artists drew their subjects. From illuminated Bibles, Gospels, Psalters, and Horæ, we may cite especially the following stock illustrations: Abraham and Melchisedek, David and Goliath, the Massacre of the Innocents and the Resurrection (with the sleeping guards). The various delineations of military saints too, St. George above all, form a perfect gallery of knightly panoply.

(*b*) THE PEASANTRY.—Such subjects as Adam and Eve in their fallen estate, the story of Ruth, and the "Annunciation to the Shepherds," are invaluable, but none are fuller of information than the miniatures in the illuminated calendars, depicting the seasonal occupations: sowing, reaping, ploughing, etc.

N.B.—All the subjects mentioned above, in (*a*) and (*b*), were favourites of the sculptor, who repeated them on church fronts, capitals of columns, etc.; common likewise in stained-glass windows.

Here we must apologize for repeating in substance what we stated in an earlier work. The peruser of old texts must beware of taking every statement *au pied de la lettre*. The element of exaggeration and prejudice, humorous on the part of the satirist, embittered on the part of the moralist, must be watchfully guarded against. Again, the descriptive adjectives cannot be apprehended unless we have some idea of what was the norm or average type at different dates; words such as "long," "short," "loose," "wide," etc., must be judged with allowance for this. What is described as "wide" to-day may be regarded as of average close fit to-morrow. No fashion has ever been introduced but has moved disgruntled Jeremiahs to incoherent fury. When wide, long garments are in vogue they praise the tight and short, and *vice versa*.

A point to remember—and traces of it were visible till late Victorian days—is that people past the meridian of their life adhered (except for formal court wear) to the modes of their youth and prime. Again, the nobility and gentry remote from court circles or the capital would naturally be behind the fashion. Note also that practically throughout the Middle Ages there were two conflicting principles in costume: the dignified, which prescribed long, full robes; and the dashing, which encouraged jauntiness and originality. Often both co-exist or blend; for example, a long magisterial robe will be embellished with *dagges*, *mahoitres*, etc., to bring it into line with the latest town-fopperies. It is worthy of notice that even to this day, for formal full-dress, long, ample outer robes distinguish the liberal professions. "Mr. Speaker," the Chancellor, the clergy, the bar, and university graduates are marked out by " the long robe." So intimately are long garments associated with dignity that in sepulchral monuments and brasses the deceased gentleman, where not clad in armour, is nearly always depicted in his gown.

Such general hints could doubtless be expanded indefinitely ; but perhaps enough has been said, and the rest of this book, supplemented by the student's researches, must fill up the lacunæ.

A SHORT HISTORY *of* COSTUME & ARMOUR

PART I—CIVILIAN

I—" *SHIRTS* "

(1066–1335)

AN old-fashioned theatrical wardrobe mistress within our recollection used to classify all " period " costumes either as " shirts " or " shapes," according to the cut of the main body-garment. " Shirts " were loose and, as she put it, " fitted where they touched " ; " shapes " were (*a*) cut to mould the forms beneath, or (*b*) specially built up ; *i.e.* fit and cut were all-important. Throughout the present chapter the male costume at least belongs to the " shirt " class. The *hose* is practically the only portion that taxes the tailor's skill. For reasons given in our Introduction (p. ix) any attempts to lay down precise dates of changes of cut or explain constructional details must needs be largely based on conjecture.

FIG. 1.

MEN

BODY GARMENTS.—Although contemporary texts afford a more varied nomenclature for these, to avoid controversy it will be convenient here, for current reference, to divide them at the outset merely into *tunics* and *supertunics* ; both were shaped somewhat on the principle of the modern smock or blouse, as was the underlying shirt, and were similarly slipped on over the head. Hence they are uniformly low-necked—often sufficiently to disclose the upper edge of the shirt—with a slit of some six inches down the breast in front, which in wear was closed with a brooch or the like.[1] Less commonly (late twelfth to early fourteenth century) this slit-opening runs diagonally from the side of the neck to the breast or else horizontally along the shoulder. At their first coming the attire of the "Normans"[2] was simple and practical in cut, and so far the Bayeux Tapestry is at one with contemporary authors. Though stuffs with simple "all-over" designs (stripes, circles, dots, quatrefoils, and the like) are found, decoration consisted in the main of deep borders of ornament (woven, embroidered, or *appliqué*) at the neck, wrists, and/or hem, to which was often added—down to the mid-thirteenth century—a similar band round the upper arm [Fig. 2].

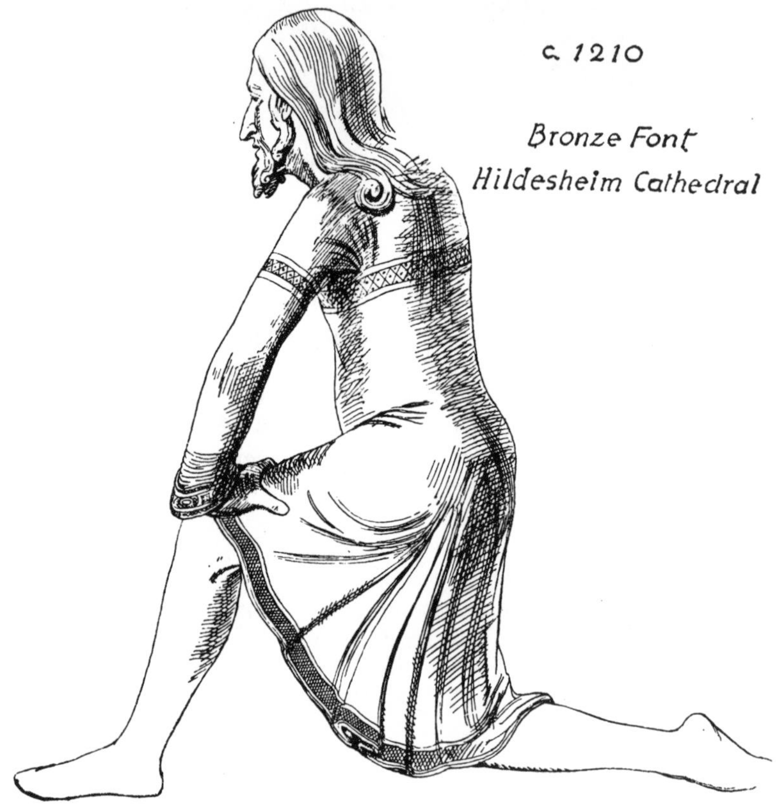

Fig. 2.—The Tunic.

The *tunic* of the Conquest was seemingly cut fairly close to the body

[1] The garments throughout this age are held together by means of brooches, pins, ties, laces, etc. Buttons and button-holes hardly came into vogue till the fourteenth century.

[2] The term is here used loosely to denote the heterogeneous host of adventurers of all nations that followed the Conqueror to England.

A MOUNTED NOBLE

From the Nonantola Gospels, penes A. Chester-Beatty, Esq.

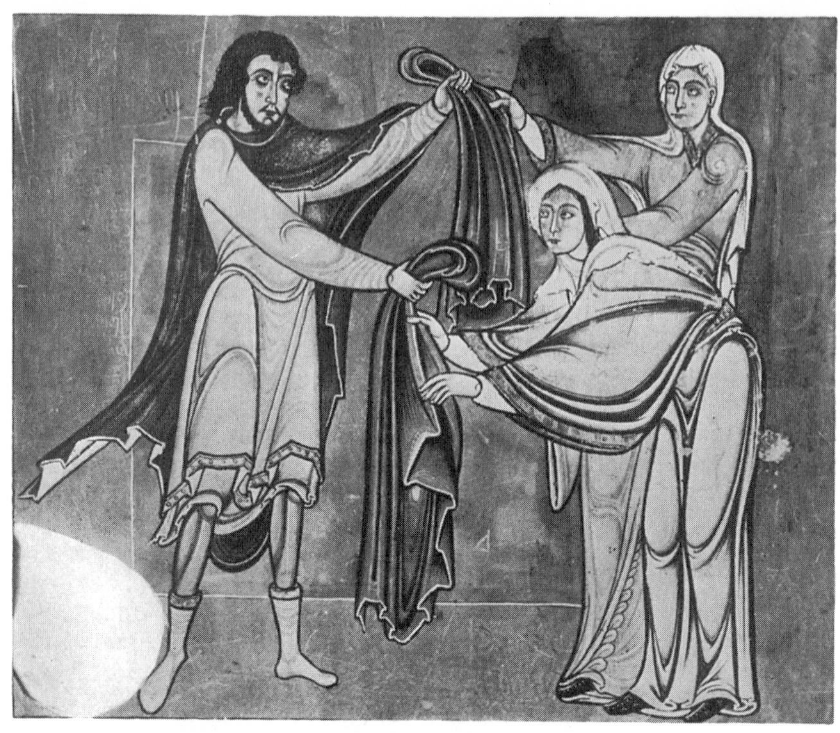

i. ELKANAH GIVES CLOAKS TO HIS WIVES

From Bury St. Edmunds Bible MS., Corpus Christi College, Cambridge.

c. 1180–90

A B C D E

ii. BIRTH AND CHRISTENING OF ST. JOHN THE BAPTIST

Painting in St. Gabriel's Chapel in Crypt, Canterbury Cathedral

[Tunics to mid-leg.]

with full skirts "on the circle," or loose and gradually widening from armpit to hem. The sleeves reach to the wrists, which they fit rather tightly, the upper arm setting easily, the forearm moderately close. For ordinary use throughout this era the tunic fell to the knee [Plates I.; II.; III. ii; IV.; Fig. 2], for full-dress to the ankle [Plates III. i; V. C; VIII. iii; Fig. 1]. The skirt of the short tunic was very generally drawn up, especially at the sides, through the narrow girdle, so as to overhang and conceal it. It might further, for convenience [Plates III. i; VIII. iii; Fig. 1], be slit up at the sides or front. Towards 1100 courtly exquisites wore tunics trailing about the feet, while the sleeves were so widened and lengthened that they hung down sometimes a foot beyond the hand [Fig. 1], to free which, for action, they were turned up from wrist to elbow — how kept in place can only be guess-work — in a deep cuff. After about 1160 these exaggerations die out: the longest tunics just clear the ground, the fullest sleeves stop at the wrist. In the last years of the twelfth century appears a variant of the tunic which remains typical of the whole of the thirteenth: body and sleeves are cut in one piece, the latter narrowing outward *from the waist* to a narrow cuff.

FIG. 3.—*Garde-corps.*

SUPERTUNIC. — To the end of the twelfth century this is merely a wide-sleeved, loose-bodied upper garment cut on the circle.[1] On state occasions it allowed some six inches at least of the tunic to show below the hem. Soon after 1200 appears a variety, cut, like a monastic scapular, in one piece, and hanging down from the shoulders to mid-leg fore and aft, the head being slipped through a hole in the centre. It widened from shoulder to hem, and the open sides might be caught together on the hips by clasps or stitching; commonly also it is slit up in front well-nigh to the fork. Between 1225–1250 appears another form which lasts through the century, and has been identified with the *garde-corps*

[1] It can generally only be identified, apart from the underlying tunic, where it is so cut as to reveal the sleeves, neck, or skirt (Plate II. i) of the latter.

[Plate xxiv. ii ; Fig. 3]. This is a very loose frock to the ankle or mid-leg, whose distinctive feature is the *very* wide, long sleeves, gathered at the top, where they have a short slit lengthwise in front to allow the arm to pass through ; in which case they hung idle almost to the knees. Often it was worn with a hood. About the last forty years of the period

Fig. 4.—The *Garnache*.

under review two other forms of supertunic occur, to last well into the following age. One is a loose frock with deep armholes and *short* hanging sleeves ; the other is the *garnache*,[1] a development of the scapular type, in which the upper part widens out beyond the shoulders and hangs

[1] Note the peculiar *lapels* at the breast-opening in Fig. 4 ; these recur in male gowns throughout the fourteenth century.

cape-like to the elbow, not unlike the sleeves of our "Inverness" coats [Fig. 4]. The sides might be sewn together or left open. Where the supertunics are unconfined at the waist and closed at the sides, *fitchets* (vertical pocket-slits) make their appearance, about the middle of the thirteenth century; their object was to give access to the purse and other objects worn at the girdle that confined the tunic beneath. From about the last third of the twelfth century occur supertunics lined with fur, by the name of *pelissons*.

Cloaks.—These are simple wraps, either rectangular or semicircular, the shortest reaching below the knee, the longest to the ankle, and fastened either over the breast or over the right shoulder by means of a brooch or a cord [Plates I.; II.; III.; IV. A; V. C; VIII. iii]; to the edges of the

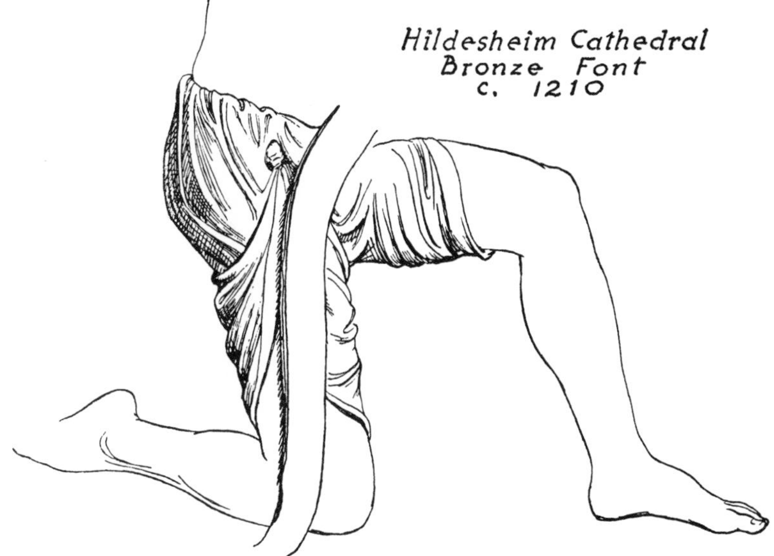

Fig. 5.—Breeches (showing method of adjustment).

more courtly cloaks were often sewn metal eyelet-plates through which the cord ran, and could be tightened or relaxed *ad lib*. One twelfth-century mode of attachment consisted of a ring sewn to the right-hand upper corner of the cloak, through which the stuff of the opposite edge was pushed and knotted. Voluminous circular wraps, like the South American *poncho*, with a central aperture for the head and armslits, occur from *c.* 1300.

Leg-wear.—The principal leg-coverings prior to *c.* 1150 were the *breeches* (Fr. *braies*, Lat. *braccæ*), which at this date much resembled our pyjama trousers, being fastened like these by a running string at the hem. They reached to the ankle at least,[1] were for the most part of linen,

[1] It is likely that on occasion the more tight-fitting sort, like the hose, ended in a stirrup or loop passing under the foot, recalling the "strapped" pantaloons of the early nineteenth century; some perhaps had feet attached.

and, among the well-dressed, were cut to fit the leg, from above the knees downward, pretty closely (like the Indian *jodhpurs*, or old-fashioned Scots trews). Only common folk wore loose trousers unconfined. Possibly they may have been at times of thin cloth ; at any rate at this period they are often of bright colours. As an alternative to the close fit, not infrequently they were caught in to the leg from knee to ankle by cross-straps [1] [Plate I.], or a kind of puttees ; or tight, shaped *hose* were drawn over them to the knee. These generally are topped with an ornamental border, probably fashioned as a garter. There is much needless confusion in costume-books between *braies* (breeches) and

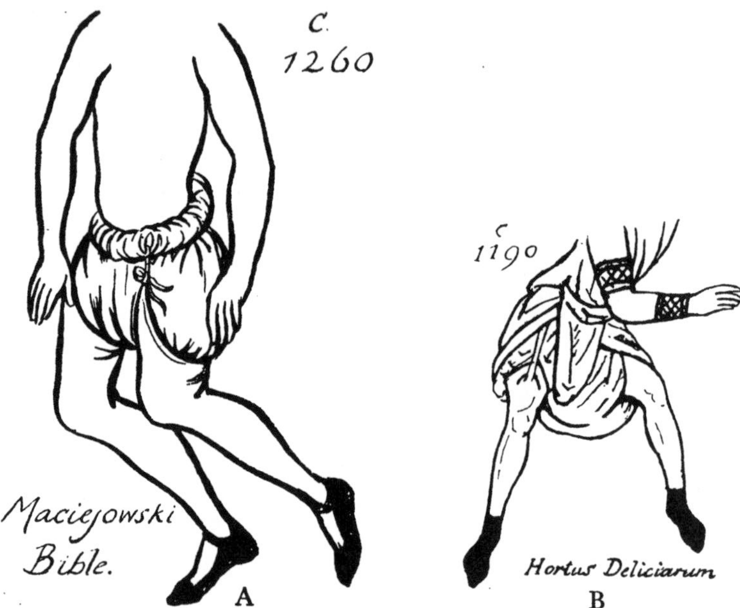

FIG. 6.—Hose drawn up and tied over Breeches.

chausses (hose). In a word, the former, *whatever their length, always reach from the waist down*, while the latter are *primarily* stockings or leggings. From *c.* 1150 the breeches are shortened to the knee and henceforth become a mere linen underwear.[2] The *hose*, on the other hand, develop into tall, tailored stockings of elastic stuff, carefully fitted to the leg and knee. They widen out at the thigh, and the shortened breeches are tucked into them. The tops of these long hose are cut to a point in front, at which they are tied up by a cord or thong to the *breech-girdle* (Fr. *brayer, braïel*), *i.e.* the running string that confines the breeches at the waist [3] [Plates

[1] Cross-bands and "puttees" vanish early in the twelfth century ; a variety of the former, reaching right up the leg, reappears in rare instances *c.* 1200.

[2] At first the hose reach up to the knees only, a fashion of which examples are found well into the thirteenth century [Plate III. ii ; Fig. 7, C].

[3] This running string was exposed at intervals to allow of this attachment [Fig. 7, A, B]. The purse, keys, etc., could also be slung from it out of sight.

c. 1170

i. THE OLD AGE OF DAVID

Victoria and Albert Museum.

c. 1170

ii. DAVID AND THE LION

Victoria and Albert Museum.

A B

THE SCOURGING OF CHRIST

From a Saxo-Thuringian Psalter, penes A. Chester-Beatty, Esq.

[? Whether the band of ornament at the knee may not be in the nature of a *garter*. Cf. Plates IX.–X.

Note in B decorated border of hose into which breeches are tucked, also tie of hose and curious foot-wrappings.]

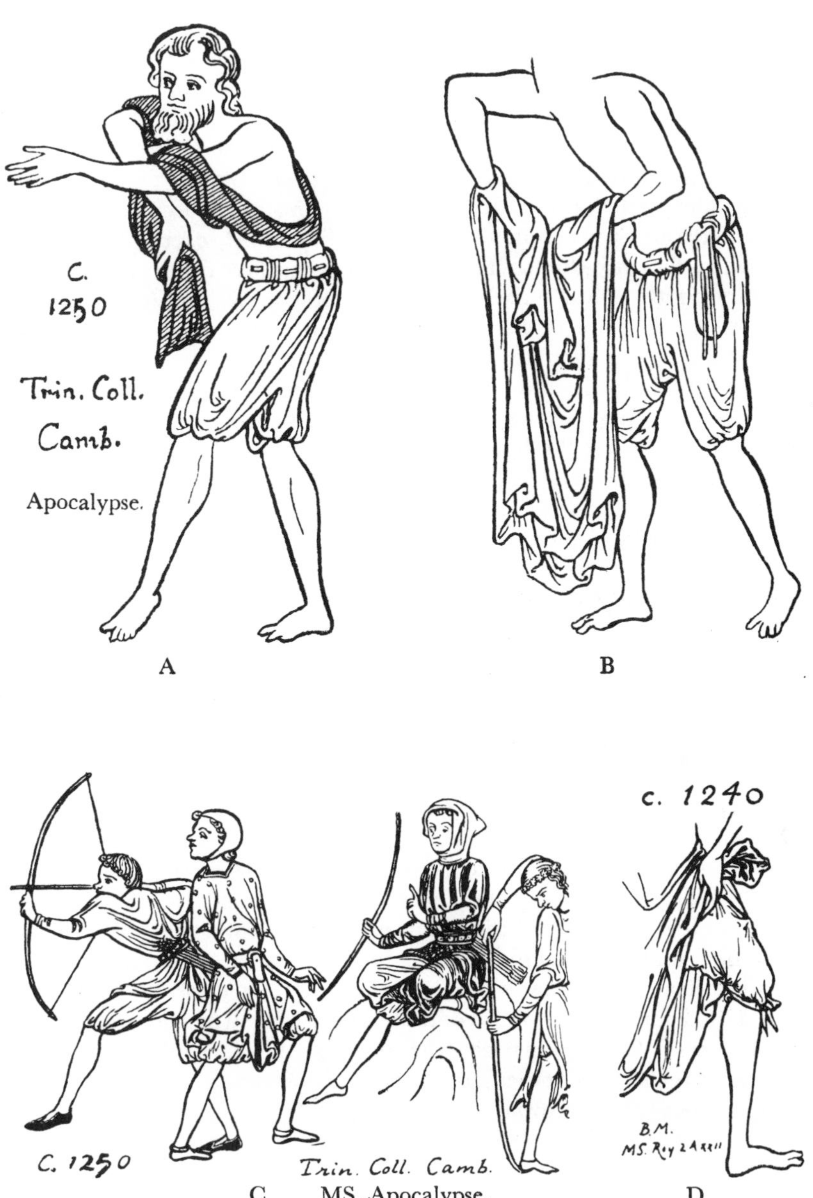

FIG. 7.—A, B, and D, Breeches ; C, *ditto* with short Hose.

V. B; VI. i, A; Fig. 6]. It is next to impossible in many cases to decide whether these early hose cover the feet or only have "stirrups" as before described. It would seem, however, that by the last third of the twelfth-century footed hose, with thin leather soles attached, for *wear without shoes*, were in use [Plate III. i]. (For fuller discussion of the *braies* down to the middle of the fifteenth century, see HARMAND, pp. 78–97.)

HEAD-GEAR.—It should be noted here once for all how general was the habit of our ancestors down to the end of the fourteenth century of walking abroad bareheaded, and *per contra* how widespread till a much later date the practice of retaining the hat indoors. Till about 1125, hats and caps seem to have been little used, excepting, perhaps, the hood for travelling. The *hood*, from the last third of the twelfth century, is *the* characteristic head-wear of the Middle Ages: a plain pointed cowl, more or less easy-fitting and ending in a short cape or gorget about the shoulders. Mostly it was closed all round, less commonly open in front, and fastened with a clasp at the throat. The point later develops into a long tail or *liripipe*. About 1300 first appears the habit of converting the hood into a kind of cap or kerchief by inserting the head into the facial opening, the gorget and peak projecting fore and aft, or sideways, and the facial opening was turned up or rolled to form a brim, when the gorget stood upwards in a cockscomb-like bunch of folds. From the second quarter of the twelfth century a limited assortment of hats and caps appears. We find forms almost identical with the present-day Basque *béret*, first popularized for both sexes by Borotra of tennis fame [Plates VIII. iii; XXIV. ii, A, B]; others recall the Victorian "polo-cap," mostly with rolled or turned-up edges. Most of these, like our bérets, end at the top in a kind of short stalk. The Phrygian cap shape of the Saxon era survives till *c.* 1200. Hats of the "wideawake" type (the classic *petasus*) are also worn, especially for travelling, with low crowns and wide brims; these often had cords attached, by which they might be slung at the back. The brim in the course of the thirteenth century begins occasionally to be turned up at the back (more rarely in front). The hat is frequently worn over the hood. Finally we may mention the *coif*, a close-fitting caul of linen enclosing the hair and ears, and tied under the chin, commonly used as an under-cap, beneath another head-dress [Plates VI.; XXIV. ii, A]. It appears before 1200, and lasted far into the fourteenth century, after which it was retained by lawyers. As often as not the men of the eleventh to thirteenth centuries went bareheaded, or wore at most an ornamental fillet or chaplet about their brows.

FOOT-GEAR.—Most shoes and boots were more or less pointed. For the most part the shoes of the eleventh century reached up to the ankle [Plates I.; III. ii, etc.]. Of the long curly toes cited by most writers as a typical mode under Henry I. and Stephen, contemporary art gives us little if any evidence.[1] From the twelfth century we often meet with

[1] We can only point to the seal of Richard, Constable of Chester, as an example of extravagantly long twelfth-century "piked shoon."

shoes cut away over the instep and fastened in front of the ankle by a brooch or strap and buckle [Fig. 6, A] ; the high shoes were at times slit down the sides or in front. Otherwise they are shown as closed up to the ankle, and presumably laced up the sides like the boots ; such closed shoes were not infrequently by " the better sort " decorated with ornamental bands recalling the earlier sandals [Plate II. ii]. Yet another type of shoe, cut low in front and high at the heel, appears in the late twelfth century.

Boots or buskins, reaching well up the calf [Plates II. i ; IV. A], and laced up the inside, generally with turn-over coloured tops, are pretty common throughout the twelfth century, but lose vogue early in the thirteenth. From about 1220, the shoes, like the rest of the attire, were very simple in cut.

UNDERWEAR.—The *shirt*, as now, was of linen, and not very different in cut from what it remains to this day. Among the rich it had bands of ornament at the neck and wrists. It is often visible above the top of the tunic and on the forearms. Of the *braies*, which from the middle of the twelfth century become mere underwear, we have already spoken.

HAIR.—For the most part the Normans at their coming into England were close-cropped and clean-shaven. The *moustache*, on an otherwise shaven face, was sufficient of a rarity to provoke comment. A peculiarly Norman feature was the shaving of the occiput up to the ears. Within a short time fashion ran to the opposite extreme : hair and beard were grown as long as possible [Fig. 1], and elaborately curled and braided, and this fashion lasted to about the middle of the twelfth century. A fashion characteristic of the whole twelfth century consisted in parting the long hair on *both* sides, the centre locks being brushed forward fringe-like on to the forehead. About 1180–1210 the hair is often worn of moderate length, as is the beard. For the remainder of our period men's fashionable hairdressing followed the " bobbed " mode so popular in latter-day feminine circles immediately after the War : it formed a deep fringe on the forehead, and was docked squarely or turned up in deep roll-curl below the ears. There was a strong tendency towards shaven faces, but short, full beards with moustaches were not uncommon.[1]

ACCESSORIES.—Of these, the most important is certainly the girdle or belt. At the time of the Conquest this would seem mostly to have been a plain thong, band, or cord fastened in front. As often as not it seems to have been concealed by the overhanging folds of the tunic. About the middle of the twelfth century the girdles have grown more ornamental ; occasionally *c.* 1170–1190 we meet with narrow sashes, knotted in front with hanging ends [Plate II. ii, C, D] ; and from the last quarter of the century

[1] At *no* period of the Middle Ages did the combination of a moustache *with shaven cheeks and chin* enjoy any degree of favour in England or France. Till a very much later period it was regarded as a barbarous custom. In armour the beard is, of course, hidden by mail, but where the upper lip is unshaven its presence may safely be assumed. Cf. the effigy of the Black Prince at Canterbury with his other " portraits," with chin unarmed, revealing his beard.

onward the fashionable girdle is very long, with one end hanging far down in front, the buckle and mounts being highly ornate. It formed the carrier for the purse [Fig. 7, B], keys, and other indispensable odds and ends. The girdle might be worn over either tunic or supertunic ; where both garments were in wear, usually over the former and under the latter. [*N.B.*—The *gardecorps* and *garnache* are never confined at the waist.] For greater safety, the purse, etc., were sometimes attached (out of sight) to the waistband of the *braies*. It should be noted that to the end of the Middle Ages the sword was not normally worn with civil attire, even the dagger scarcely so occurring before *c.* 1300. Even " knights " rarely carried weapons in everyday attire.[1] Princes or their representatives on particular occasions (especially when sitting in judgment) might gird on a sword, but mostly nursed it sheathed, with girdle attached, as an Indian rajah does his tulwar. The sword was only carried when actually needed ; even then it was mostly kept out of sight. Exceptions to this rule were apt to be sternly checked by the authorities. Wallets or pouches, varying from plain bags to increasingly ornate and elaborate purses of varying size, were slung at the belt (or, more secretly, at the breech-girdle—*vide supra*), and served the same purpose as our pockets. Jewellery includes rings, brooches, clasps, and the like, often affixed as ornamental fastenings to the garments. Ornamental circlets of precious metal were commonly worn about the brows of great nobles. Plain or slightly ornamented staves were sometimes borne as walking-sticks. A mode which is met with *very occasionally* from about the last third of the twelfth century is that of " dagging," that is, slitting up the edges of the garments into " dags " or tongues. It is apparently rather a German mode, and here was restricted to the hem of the tunic and supertunic and the gorget of the hood.

WOMEN

" The Queen of Spain has no legs " : an axiom followed in polite society throughout the Middle Ages, and indeed much later. Little more than the tips of the toes is ever visible below the dress of women of any social pretensions in the art of the age. The division into bodice and skirt is also quite foreign to mediæval fashion. With the exception of the exaggerated sleeves that prevailed chiefly in the first half of the twelfth century, the dress was picturesque, dignified, and simple in cut throughout this period.

BODY GARMENTS. — Corresponding to the tunic and supertunic respectively we have what I propose to term the *kirtle* and *surcoat*. Most of the forms of the male equivalents are adopted, with but slight modification, for both of these. *Pelissons*, too, are in common use throughout the period under review. Characteristic of extreme feminine fashion between

[1] The popular notion of the mediæval " knight " as one whose days were lived in *cap-à-pie* armour, and of the gentry as bristling with arms like so many Anatolian brigands, is pure " Wardour Street " romance.

A B C D E

OLD TESTAMENT SCENES

From the Maciejowski Bible, penes J. Pierpont Morgan.

A B C

i. THRESHERS (BREECHES AND HOSE)

A B C

ii. A GARRISON SURPRISED

Both from Maciegowski Bible, penes J. Pierpont Morgan.

[Note (B) padded *cuishes* and (C) *ackton*.]

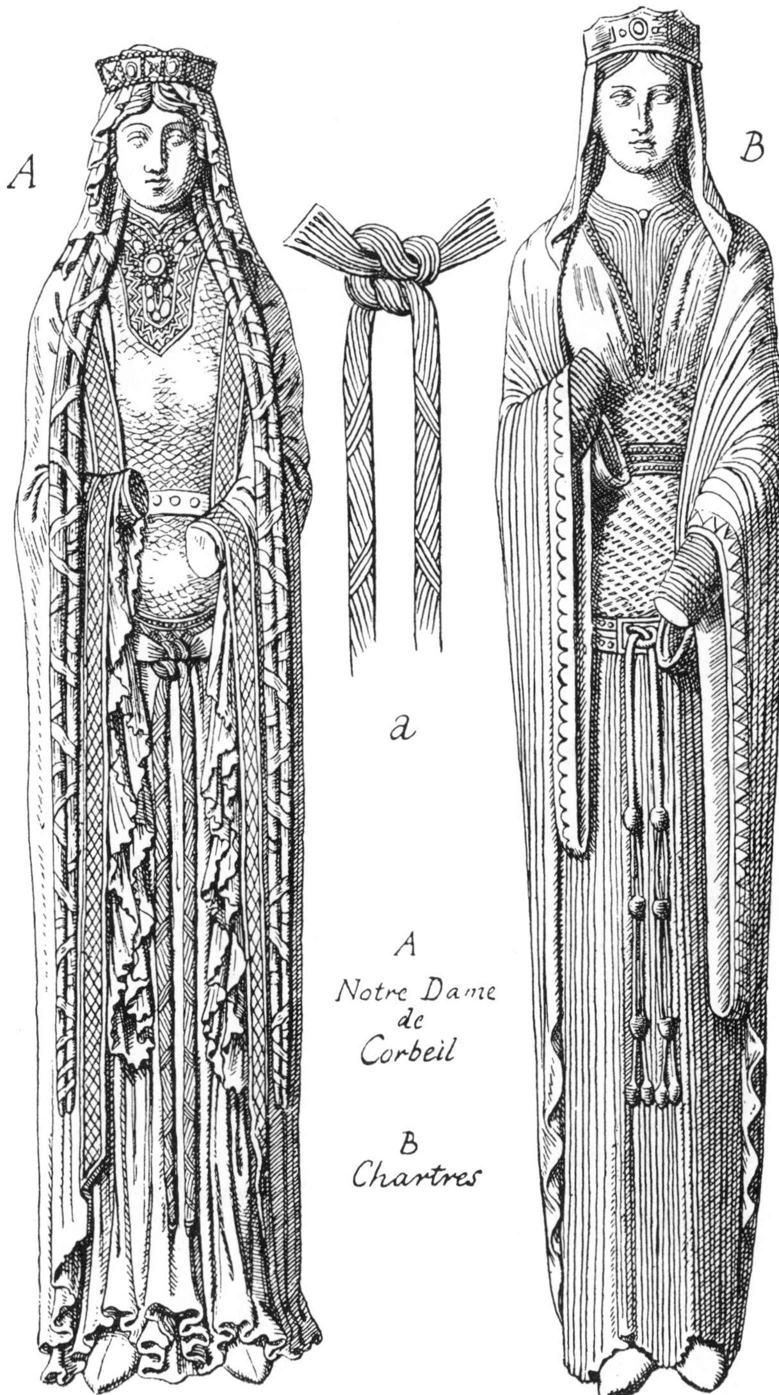

FIG. 8.—Mid-twelfth-century Noble Dames.

c. 1125 and 1170 are gowns whose upper part is of skin-tight fit to below the hips, whence they fall in close folds to the ground, forming a regular train behind [Figs. 8, 9]. Whether anything corresponding to the modern stays was known thus early seems more than doubtful, though there is definite evidence that the close fit is the result of tight lacing, mostly down the back. It would certainly appear that such gowns were made of a fine and elastic material, at least as regards the upper part corresponding to the modern bodice, perhaps akin to a close, sleeveless jersey.[1] It is not impossible that, in default of a regular busked corset, close bandages (almost surgical in character) worn beneath the gown, assisted the effect of the tight lacing. In some carved examples we almost get the impression of a very wide sash, closely wound after the manner of a bull-fighter's *faja*, worn *over* the gown. Whatever the material, the folds often have a crimped or gauffered appearance that recalls the early Ionic *chiton* of the Ancients. This appearance characterizes the first half of the twelfth century, and contrasts with the heavy "Doric" draperies that preceded and followed it, and which it never drove from the field. The other distinctive features of extreme feminine fashion at this date are two: first, the exaggerated prolongation of all parts, which was at times such an encumbrance that the draperies had to be shortened by tying them up in knots; secondly, the abrupt widening of the sleeves below the elbow into a kind of exorbitant streamers trailing sometimes as low as the ground [Figs. 8, 9].[2] These modish exaggerations scarcely outlast the middle of the century, and vanish before 1200.

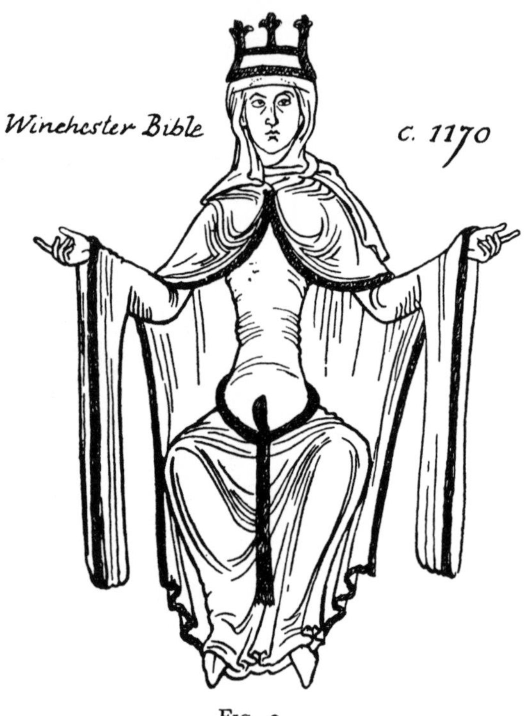

Fig. 9.

[1] There are those who would see in this a separate garment worn *over* the gown (a "jumper"), but this seems pure guesswork. The "honeycomb" pattern, so often shown on the bodice-part, suggests some kind of *smocking* [cf. Fig. 8].

[2] Not to be confounded with the very wide *funnel* shape that is found throughout the period under discussion, and reappears towards 1400.

Except for the *invariable* length of their draperies, the feminine body garments of the whole rest of this age differ little in other respects from those of their lords. After *c.* 1300 appear the first hints of *décolletage*, and towards 1320 first appears what soon afterwards became *the* feminine *robe d'apparat* of the whole of the later Middle Ages : the so-called " sideless gown." It is a mere development of the sleeveless surcoat slit from shoulder to hip [Fig. 10] : it is distinctly low necked, the part in front of the slit being markedly reduced in width and connected with the full back by mere shoulder-straps. The side openings might be square-cut or rounded, the latter form presently becoming general.

FIG. 10.—Veil and Wimple.

CLOAKS. — These, in general, are similar in cut to those worn by the men, but in most cases trailed on the ground, and were nearly always fastened loosely by an adjustable tie or cord over the breast[1] [Plates II. ; V. B ; VIII. i, ii ; Figs. 8, 9]. A variety of the male *poncho* form (but prolonged into a train behind) has the fullness at the sides apparently caught forward and fixed in front of the shoulders, so as to overlap the fore-part, giving somewhat the illusion of two distinct garments—a cloak over a loose surcoat—the side folds being slit for the passage of the tight-sleeved arms. A kind of small cape or hood seems to have been commonly worn with it.

LEG-WEAR.—The breeches or *braies* were peculiar to the male sex throughout the Middle Ages. Many " good stories " of that era depend for their humour on this fact. The covering of the ladies' limbs was limited to *hose* : mere stockings to above the knee, fastened there by plain ties or garters.

HEAD-DRESS.—Of coverings for head and neck there is a fair variety, and nothing, the hair alone excepted, so differentiated the sexes. The simplest and most general, dating back to remote times, is the *veil* [Plates II. ; V. B ; VIII. ; Figs. 8, 9, 10, 12], a mere strip of material (mostly linen or thin stuff), either rectangular or " on the circle." It is placed on the head so that one straight edge overhangs the forehead, the rest

[1] It seems to have been a general habit to pass a finger over this cord.

lying over the neck and shoulders at the sides and back. This is the simplest usage, although from the beginning the ends could be draped *ad lib.* across the throat or round the shoulders. It was often confined by a circlet or fillet at the temples. In public at least, women of rank nearly always went veiled down to the second quarter of the twelfth century. In one form or another, the veil is more or less in vogue to the end of the Middle Ages. About the middle of the century occurs the *barbette*, a wide band of linen that passes under the chin, the ends being pinned together over the crown [Fig. 11]. The *wimple*, a linen covering for throat and bosom, appears *c.* 1190 ; it frames the face, being pinned up to the hair above the ears or on top under the veil, and is commonly tucked inside the neck of the dress ; usually it veils the chin [Figs. 10, 12]. About 1220 the fillet round the temples develops

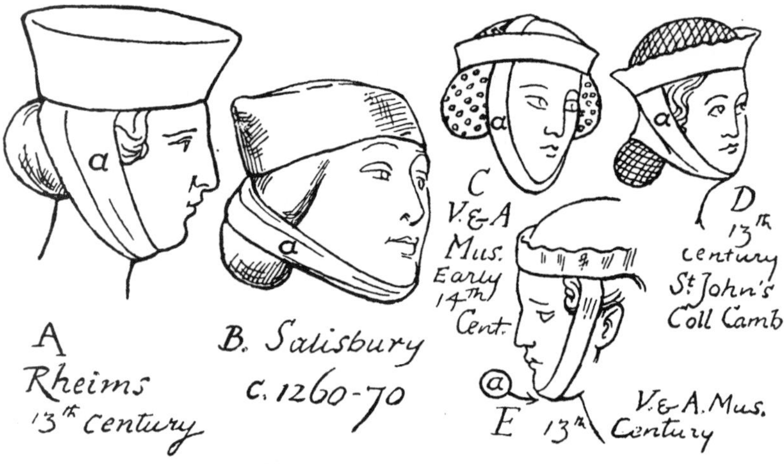

FIG. 11.—(*a* : barbette).

into a tall band of stiffened linen worn in conjunction with the barbette, and shaped like a pill-box [Fig. 11]. Sometimes it seems to be worn over what resembles a "polo cap." The coronet is worn by noble dames inside this "pill-box," whose upper rim from the middle of the century is often gauffered. At first cylindrical, this presently widens at the top, and by *c.* 1290 is lengthened sideways to an elliptical section.[1] It is very generally worn independent of the veil and pinned to the side hair.

From the middle of the thirteenth century the hair is generally gathered into a network bag or *crespine* [Plate VII. ; Fig. 11, C, D], forming a bulging mass at the back or (from *c.* 1270) hanging in a great boss over either ear (a mode that outlasted the fourteenth century).

[1] Occasionally one end of the *barbette* is passed through the "pill-box" and allowed to hang down to one side. The elliptical form followed the vogue of a *wider* hairdressing.

A B C D

BAND OF DEEP RED VELVET EMBROIDERED IN GOLD, SILVER, AND COLOURED SILKS. EARLY XIV CENTURY

Victoria and Albert Museum.

c. 1300

i. STATUE ON WEST FRONT, WELLS CATHEDRAL

c. 1300

ii. "QUEEN MARGARET," LINCOLN CATHEDRAL

c. 1240

iii. QUEEN MARGARET, LINCOLN CATHEDRAL

A B

i.

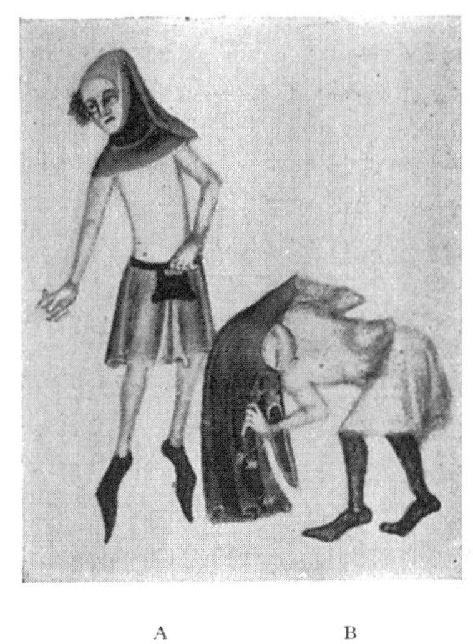

A B

ii.

A B

iii.

A B C

iv.

FOURTEENTH-CENTURY SCENES

All from Luttrell Psalter, c. 1340, British Museum.

[Note (iii. A) arrangement of braided locks in a "ramshorn," and (iv. C) garters with hanging ends.]

FOOT-GEAR.—This is practically always hidden by the long robes o₁ the ladies, the tips of the toes being the most that is visible. The evidence goes to show that both sexes were shod alike.

HAIRDRESSING.—Concealed below the veil at the beginning of the century, the hair makes an almost sensational appearance among the highest classes between *c.* 1120 and 1150, being parted in the middle and arranged in two long tails, either braided into plaits, twisted with ribbon, or enclosed in cases of silk bound with ribbon [Fig. 8]. These generally hung down in front and (length being a fashionable desideratum) were often eked out by means of false hair, tow, or other devices, reaching down to the knee or lower, and ending in ornamental ferrules. They are worn in conjunction with fillets and light veils. Hair simply flowing unconfined over the shoulders or in a single braided tail behind is not unusual throughout the period, chiefly for young girls on ordinary occasions [Plate v.]. From the close of the twelfth century the hair,

FIG. 12.—Veils and Wimples.

so far as it is visible, is arranged in plaits, and variously coiled into chignons or coronets. A very typical fashion from *c.* 1275 to the end of the fourteenth century was to coil the plaits in a spiral " bun " like a snail-shell over either ear—as is still to be seen to-day [1] [Plates VII.; IX. i. A, iii, A; Fig. 12, B].

UNDERWEAR.—The women's chemise differed in no particular from the shirts of the men, except that it always reached to the feet. It had the same ornamental borders and bands of embroidery. The *braies* were exclusively the prerogative of the male sex.

ACCESSORIES.—Between *c.* 1125–1175 occurs a form of girdle apparently reserved to ladies of the highest rank for State occasions. It consists of a flat ornamental belt, whose ends, crossed at the back of the waist, were brought forward to below the hips. To either end of the belt was

[1] By Mr. Herbert Norris aptly termed " ramshorn."

attached a long knotted and tasselled plait of silk; these, loosely knotted together, secured the belt and hung far down in front [Fig. 8]. The presence, from the late thirteenth century, of *fitchets* (cf. p. 5 *ante*) in female attire suggests that the chemise was often girt beneath the gown. Jewellery was much alike for both sexes.

II—" *SHAPES* "

(1335–1380)

DURING the eleventh, twelfth, and thirteenth centuries the costume of both sexes, broadly speaking, retained something of the simplicity and flowing lines of the antique, modified at intervals by the influence of Byzantium and the East. The exaggerations noted in the first half of the twelfth century [cf. Chapter I.] were but a transient phase ; after, as before, the forms in vogue are on the whole graceful and dignified. With the second quarter of the fourteenth century the general character changes, but not till after the accession of Richard II. do we meet with any of those marked eccentricities of cut that distinguish the later Middle Ages.[1]

Most of the forms found in the late thirteenth century occur throughout the fourteenth, but now begins the vogue of " shapes " [cf. p. 1]. Stateliness had hitherto been the prime object of aristocratic attire ; side by side with this ideal now arises the cult of jauntiness. The dress of the younger generation aims at accentuating the underlying physique, and tailoring begins to be an art. It is conspicuously the age of *buttons* (Plate XII.).

MEN

BODY GARMENTS.—Although long, full robes continued to be worn by the elder men and for special occasions, the trend of fashion is increasingly in favour of short, tight garments, designed to show the legs, sheathed in long hose, to the best advantage. Over the shirt was worn the *gipon* or doublet, and over that again was commonly donned the *cote-hardie.* The former had tight sleeves adjusted to the fore-arm by a close-set row of small ball-buttons from elbow to wrist. The tight-fitting body was more or less padded throughout, particularly at the breast, where after *c.* 1350 it swelled out to a marked convexity in front. It was laced or close-buttoned (like the fore-sleeves) down the front, and was made increasingly shorter as the hose grew longer, till by the close

[1] It is noteworthy that though Edward II. and his favourites have left a name for wild extravagance in apparel, contemporary art has recorded for us no grotesque deformations of outline such as are met with in the twelfth century and after 1390. Their foppery was presumably shown in excess of ornament, costly material, possibly even in the *manner* in which their finery was worn.

of the period it barely covered the hips. It was a distinctively *waisted* garment, with tight skirts which now begin to be cut independently of the body. Moreover, it now begins to take over from the *braies* the duty of bracing up the hose (*vide infra*, p. 19). The *cote-hardie* from the first was buttoned or laced tightly over the gipon, at first as far as the waist, where it flared into a loose skirt open in front [Plates IX.–XI. *passim*]. From about the middle of the century it was fastened in front down to the hem [Fig. 13, etc.]. The sleeves till *c.* 1350 covered the arm to the

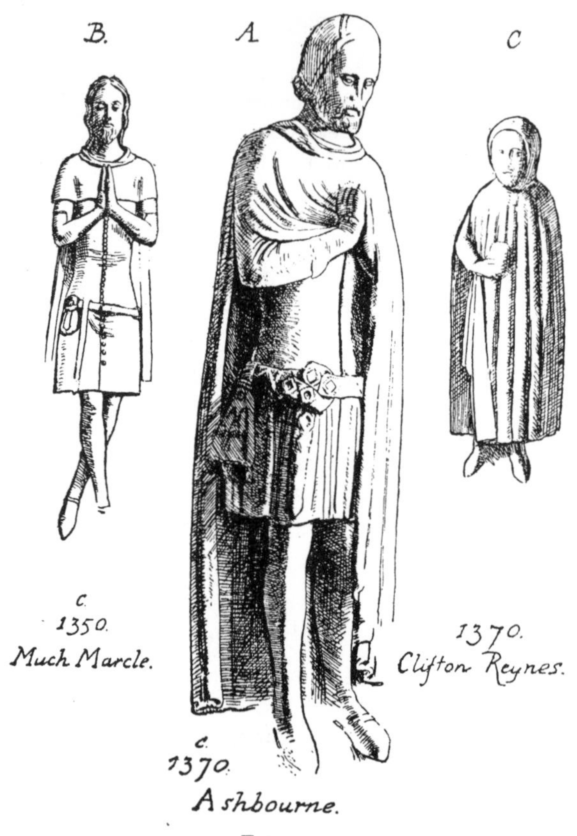

FIG. 13.

elbow, whence they hung loose in a tongue-shaped flap [Plates IX. i, B; X. iv, B], which was then generally replaced by a *tippet*, *i.e.* a broad band of stuff (generally white), whereof one end encircled the arm above the elbow, the other flying free in a streamer three or four feet long [Plate XIII. i, G; Fig. 13, B]. The skirts of the *cote-hardie* in the course of the century tend increasingly to be *dagged*, *i.e.* slit up in pendant strips, tongues, or leaf-like motives. At first reaching as far as or just below the knee, after *c.* 1360 the *cote-hardie* uncovers the thigh more and more. The gipon in the third quarter of the century is often worn uncovered

i.

ii.

iii.

A B

iv.

EVERYDAY AMUSEMENTS

From Luttrell Psalter, c. 1340, *British Museum.*

[Note in (i.) hose braced up by a button or brooch; in (ii.) and (iii.) the hose are apparently gartered at the knees.]

i.

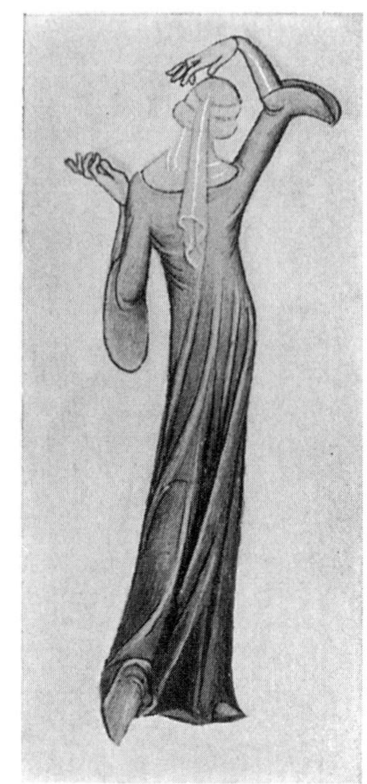

ii.

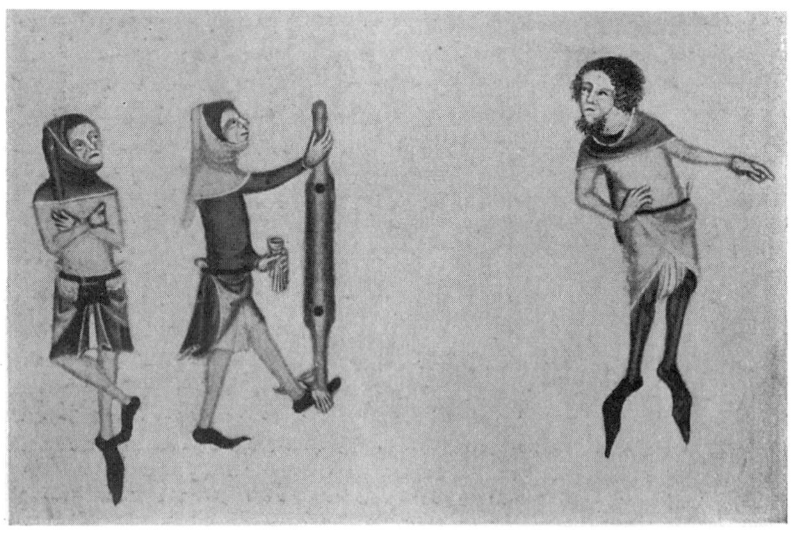

A B C

iii.

EVERYDAY LIFE

From Luttrell Psalter, c. 1340, British Museum.

[Note (i.) fullness of boot at small of leg, caught together by buttons or clasps.]

[Plate XII. E]; it reaches at most to mid-thigh. When worn under the *cote-hardie*, its presence is betrayed solely by the close sleeves at the forearm; these from *c.* 1360 are prolonged almost to the knuckles. As before, there is no vestige of a collar to any of the body garments; indeed, they are all cut lower than ever at the neck.

It is difficult to say at what precise date shoulder-tippets or capes make their appearance *independently of the hood*, but it seems fair to date them from early in this period. They, too, are often dagged.

CLOAKS.—These are, for the most part, long, cut "on the circle," and secured by a clasp or (very commonly) by several round buttons over the right shoulder [Plate XII. A; Fig. 13, A, C]. As the front part was commonly flung back over the left shoulder [Plate XII. C], costly linings lost nothing of their effect.

LEG-WEAR.—Not, perhaps, till after 1350 is there any essential change to note in this department, but then the character of the *hose* alters. They are not as yet united to form "tights," but they fit tightly right up to the fork, and are pierced along the top edge with eyelet-holes through which are passed and knotted a series of *estaches*,[1] or strings, affixed to the inside of the gipon. By the end of the period the hose are cut to reach the hips, to their eyelet-holes correspond similar eyelets along the skirt of the gipon, and both garments are united by *points*, or short tagged laces, knotted on the outside of the gipon.

HEAD-GEAR.—The hood remains in essentials as before, except that the *liripipe*, or tail at the back, develops in length and breadth. The kerchief-like method of arrangement described on p. 8 continued in vogue with the higher classes, though not very common till after 1370 [Plate XIII. i, D, E], when the liripipe tends to be twisted about the head turbanwise. The "skirt" or collar of the hood being often dagged, the cockscomb effect of the whole was enhanced. Throughout this period, however, the hood is, as a rule, worn normally [Plates IX. ii, B, iv, C; XI. iii, A, B; Fig. 13, C]—*i.e.* as a cowl covering head, neck, and shoulders—the edges of the face-opening often turned back to disengage the face. Often, when not immediately needed, it is simply cast over the shoulder. The *coif* continued unchanged [Fig. 13, A]. Modifications of some of the hats and caps already described in the preceding period are worn throughout this and the succeeding age. They were worn alone or over the hood. The wide-awake or "petasus" type had a low round or tapering crown, to which the brim was often caught up behind, and projected in a peak in front, or *vice versa*. Another form in vogue *c.* 1325–1350 has a high, domed crown, and a close turn-up border or rim. The broad-brimmed variety often had strings attached by which it could be slung behind the shoulders.[2] Soft, low hats, with rolled or "pork pie"

[1] HARMAND, p. 126 *et passim*; this monograph is invaluable for its wealth of detail concerning the mediæval hose, their evolution, construction, and mode of attachment.

[2] Note that throughout this period men as often as not went bareheaded out of doors, the hood being frequently thrown back on the shoulders.

brims, were also worn, and even the older *béret*-form occurs. It is towards the middle of the century that we first meet with *plumes* attached to the wide-brimmed, high-crowned hat. One or two tall feathers—peacock or ostrich—stand up in front of the crown, attached at the base by a jewel, brooch, or ornamental socket. These were commonly dyed and spangled.[1] Ornamental hat-bands already begin to appear. Ornamental fillets or chaplets over the bare head are still in favour.

FOOT-GEAR.—Boots or buskins [ever since *c.* 1200] remain exceptional in mediæval art prior to *c.* 1400. The few examples we do meet with characterize mounted travellers or huntsmen ; they reach up to the thighs, are shaped to the limb, and laced, buckled, or buttoned in to the small of the leg at the side. Where they were not specially shaped to the leg, the fullness below the knee was caught back from the front to the outside of the leg and hooked or buckled down in a broad fold [Plate XI. i]. The shoes are for the most part simple enough in cut, though often rich in material or ornament. They reach to the ankle in most cases, and are laced down the inside ; others are low-cut in front, with a strap and buckle at the ankle. They were often exceedingly ornate, being covered with reticulated, diapered, and floral designs, either embroidered or perforated. All foot-gear worn by the better sort fits the foot closely, and has more or less pointed toes, which after 1360 tend increasingly to a tapering " piked " shape.[2] The vogue of soled hose (these throughout followed the current fashion in toes) in lieu of shoes continued to the close of the fifteenth century.

UNDERWEAR.—From now onward till after the middle of the fifteenth century the body-linen, being entirely hidden from view, is wholly utilitarian and devoid of ornament. The *braies* (divorced henceforth from the hose) from *c.* 1340 shrink to the dimensions of our bathing-drawers ; they fasten with a running string at the waist.

HAIR.—The " bobbed " coiffure described in the last chapter lasted till about the middle of the fourteenth century. After this the hair is generally parted down the centre, and hangs level with the chin or lower ; at other times it is cropped fairly close all over. Though clean-shaven faces occur throughout this epoch, beards and moustaches grow in general favour : they tend to a " Vandyke " or forked type, and the cheeks are commonly shaven. Long beards with whiskers are chiefly favoured by the elderly.

ACCESSORIES.—The belt or girdle henceforth assumes great importance [Fig. 13]. The metal mounts are often highly ornamental. The *gipsière* or pouch, increasingly elaborate in design, is regularly attached to the

[1] Plumes, though not infrequent in the fourteenth and fifteenth centuries, were far less popular previous to the Renaissance than the " Romantic " or Wardour Street school of antiquaries would like to suggest.

[2] Throughout the Middle Ages the fashionable cut of boots and shoes strongly emphasized the natural distinction between left and right, the point being in the continuation of the big toe ; hence, shoes correctly cut on mediæval patterns (excepting the grotesquely elongated rat-tail points in vogue at certain dates) are unexpectedly comfortable in wear.

belt (clerks substitute, or add, the penner and inkhorn), and behind it (vertically or horizontally) is affixed a dagger, often long and broad, the only weapon regularly carried with civil attire throughout the Middle Ages; it is suspended from the belt to one side [Fig. 13, A, B], or directly in front, this last mode being characteristic of the last third of the fourteenth century. The dagger is also worn independently, attached to the belt by a cord. The long hanging end of the girdle is often twisted and looped after the style of the Garter. Highly characteristic of courtly circles from *c.* 1360 on is the *knightly girdle*: a broad band of metal plaques, without visible fastening,[1] *encircling the hips* [Plate XII. C, E]. This particular type of girdle also regularly accompanies the knightly panoply in the field, when it carried the sword and dagger. At this period the nobles and their households begin as a regular thing (isolated examples occur from the twelfth century) to introduce heraldic motives into their apparel; this was often wholly or partly party-coloured, generally in accordance with the principal tinctures of the owner's armorial shield, and embroidered with his bearings, badge, etc., a fashion especially prevalent throughout the fourteenth century. Even the "counterchanging" of the shield is suggested in aristocratic civil fashions, producing oddly variegated colour schemes, the legs and arms often contrasting with the body, and with each other.

WOMEN

Body Garments.—Women in this period wear close-fitting tight-sleeved gowns or *kirtles*, over which is commonly worn a *cote-hardie* resembling that of the men in the close row of buttons down the front, and the close elbow sleeves with pendent flaps [Plate XI. ii] or tippets [Plate XII. B] (cf. p. 18). It was still commonly made with *fitchets* (cf. p. 5). Both kirtle and *cote-hardie* are markedly *decollétés*, not infrequently baring the point of the shoulder, and are cut to mould bosom, waist, and hips; sometimes they are laced at the back. The sleeves of the kirtle, like those of the male *gipon*, are close-buttoned from elbow to wrist, and from *c.* 1360 extend mitten-like to the knuckles. Towards 1360 the so-called "sideless" surcoat develops the form that it was to retain practically unaltered throughout the Middle Ages [Plates XII. D; XIV. ii, B; Figs. 15, 16]. From now on it is generally lined and/or edged with fur and full at the back, while the elliptical side-openings encroach upon the front till it is at times a mere narrow fur-edged band connecting shoulders and hips. Made very low-necked, mere shoulder straps of fur unite back and front.[2] A *placard* or shaped stomacher of fur often fills the space in front between the side openings. Down the centre-front to hip-level runs a broad jewelled and buttoned band. The openings are

[1] From its position it is plain that it must have been in some way firmly fixed upon the gipon or the cote-hardie, quite apart from the brooch or buckle that clasped it in front: presumably it was hooked to the garment.

[2] How it was prevented from slipping off the shoulders must be guess-work.

wide and reach well below the hips round which they reveal the jewelled hip-belt (see "knightly girdle," p. 21), confining the kirtle or *cote-hardie* worn underneath. Between the side-openings the front is, presumably, fastened down to the under-garment,[1] moulding the underlying figure; the hind part often hangs free from the shoulders [Plate XIV. ii, B]. (*Note.*—In its completed form the sideless surcoat became and remained

FIG. 14.

essentially a robe of State.) Apart from this, however, the feminine surcoats for the most part are alike in being loose, waistless, and ungirt; sleeves show the same variety as in men's attire, or are non-existent. Short *pelissons*, too, are worn still fairly commonly.

CLOAKS.—These are loosely fastened across the breast by ornamental

[1] A German MS. of 1334 at Cassel shows undergown and sideless surcoat, still united, stripped from the person as a single garment.

A

B

C

D

E

From his tomb in Westminster Abbey.

THREE SONS AND TWO DAUGHTERS OF EDWARD III.

[Note "fitchets" at B.]

A B C D E F G H

i. AN EXHORTATION

A B C D

ii. A CORONATION

Both from Brit. Mus. MS., Royal 20, c. vii., Chroniques de St. Denis (*c.* 1395–1400).

tasselled cords [Fig. 14, A], which pass through brooches or clasps affixed to the edges of the cloak. They are rarely worn except on State occasions. Otherwise they take the form of mere wraps, sometimes hooded, and are used only for travelling or in very severe weather.

LEG-WEAR.—The feminine *hose* retained the form of stockings gartered above the knee. There will henceforth be no occasion to refer to the coverings of the lady's limbs, which were exposed to view only by accident.

HEAD-DRESS.—No particular novelties appear before *c.* 1350. Till that date the veils, wimples, etc., are disposed with the hair to give the face somewhat the outline of an inverted triangle or wide V. Sometimes

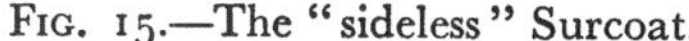
FIG. 15.—The "sideless" Surcoat.

FIG. 16.—"Sideless" Surcoat.

the ends of the wimple are pinned *under* the side-plaits of hair. After that date ladies of rank much affect a kind of frame consisting of a fillet or metal band, setting low upon the brows, from which depends from the temple down either cheek an open-work tube through which the plaits of hair are drawn up, emphasizing the square contour of the face. Noblewomen on State occasions surmounted this frame with their coronets (which in this case were fashioned to fit the side-tubes). Small folded veils were commonly pinned to the crown of the hair, whence they floated freely behind ; such veils are often the only covering for the hair. A new form of veil appears *c.* 1350 (and lasted well into the fifteenth century), which for convenience may be termed the " ruffled veil "

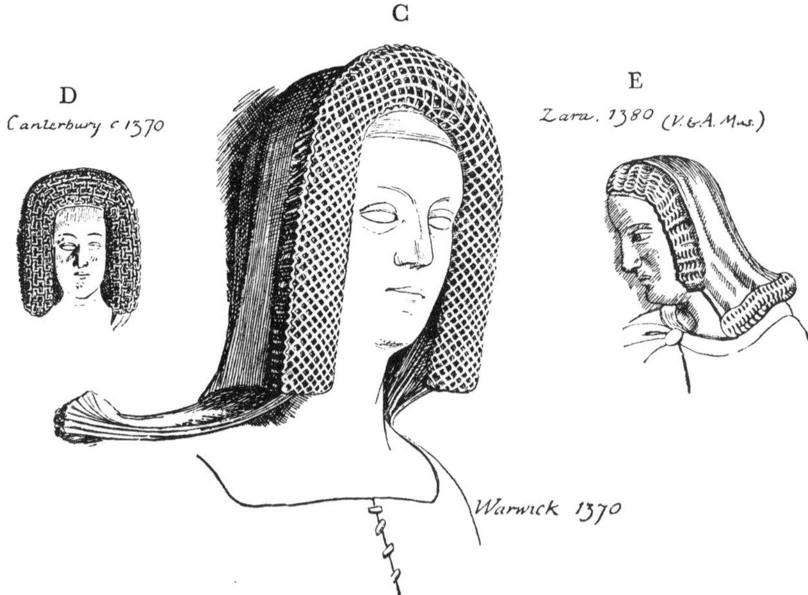

FIG. 17.—B to E show the "ruffled" Veil. B (a German instance) shows the straight edges pinned together in front and clearly explains construction of some examples.

[Figs. 14, A; 17, B–E]. It is composed of several semicircular goffered layers of fine linen. It is placed on the head with the straight-edge foremost and the curved edge hanging on the shoulders. The front edge frames the face closely as far as the angle of the jaw,[1] with a ruff-like or honeycomb border (not unlike the quilled caps still sometimes worn by our old countrywomen). From the jaw down the plain straight-edge flows free and plain to the shoulders to meet the curved back-edge, which often has a similar ruched border throughout. In some of these veils the ruching in front only extends from temple to temple. Hoods and hats after the masculine model might be worn by ladies for travelling and sport. Otherwise the use of the hood is rather bourgeois; women, in contrast to men, commonly wore it wholly open in front (*i.e.* from the chin down). The hair-nets or *crespines* persist right through this period.

FOOT-GEAR.—This, as before, followed the masculine lead.

HAIR.—This plays a capital part in the costume of the period. The plaits coiled spirally over the ears continue their vogue, but from about 1340 the courtly fashion is so to dispose the plaits that the face is framed between two vertical braids. Most coiffures of this period are secured by a narrow fillet round the head level with the ears.

ACCESSORIES.—Jewellery grows richer and more profuse for both sexes alike in the fourteenth century, in the form of buttons, clasps, rings, buckles, brooches, and the mounts of girdles, pouches, and ranged from plain wrought-iron, brass, or copper, up to gold and silver, often set with precious stones. The belts in particular are richly dight with metal. Ladies borrowed from their lords the knightly girdle or hip-belt, often just visible through the openings of the sideless surcoat; likewise the use of pouches *with daggers attached.* Nor were they less forward in turning heraldic elements to account in adorning their apparel.

[1]Hence some kind of tape or tie under the chin seems postulated at this point.

III—*HOUPPELANDES; HIGH NECKS, WIDE SLEEVES, AND DAGGING*

(1380–1450)

WHILE most of the features typical of costume in the last part of the period just reviewed recur in a measure till after 1420, between 1380 and 1390 a number of fashions evolve more eccentric than any yet described, entirely altering the aspect of the modish world. Side by side, or combined with ultra-tight garments, is adopted an extravagance of superfluous material and a reckless profusion of dagging. A number of German elements are imported to which are presently added a number of Franco-Burgundian novelties. In fact, now actually begins that era of fantastic creations popularly associated with "mediæval" costume.

MEN

BODY GARMENTS.—The *gipon* at first remains practically unaltered, except that it now reaches merely to the hips, and that it tends to a rather high waistline above which the breast is padded to a globose profile [Plate XV. ii, E]; *c.* 1410 to 1450 it is generally laced up.

The great novelty (for both sexes) is the *houppelande*, a high-necked gown, fitting closely to bust and shoulders, and for the rest cut on the lines of a wide funnel, so as to fall in massive tubular vertical folds; the vast sleeves are likewise mostly cut funnel-shape [1] [Plates XIII. ii; XVII. B, C]. It has a high collar, buttoned right up to the ears, and expanding at the top like the neck of a decanter, so that the head rests on this border as later upon the Elizabethan ruff [Plates XIII.; XIV.; XV. i], this ruff-like impression being often enhanced by the dagging of the edge. The collar often rises above the ears behind, like an incipient hood. The skirts are slit up in front or at the side. The length varied: some *houppelandes* (and these the more ceremonious) trailing on the ground, while others reached to the ankle, calf, or just below the knee. Dagging was the height of fashion; every border (including the slits of the skirt) was apt to be so adorned. Sometimes the dags were an added trimming affixed in overlapping, scale-like rows.[2] The folds of the gown are

[1] Sleeves of this type still form part of the habit of the Benedictine Order; *c.* 1390–1415 they were often prolonged at the back almost to the ground.

[2] One characteristic form is a kind of falling epaulette-fringe [Plates XIII. ii, D XIV. i, A, B, E].

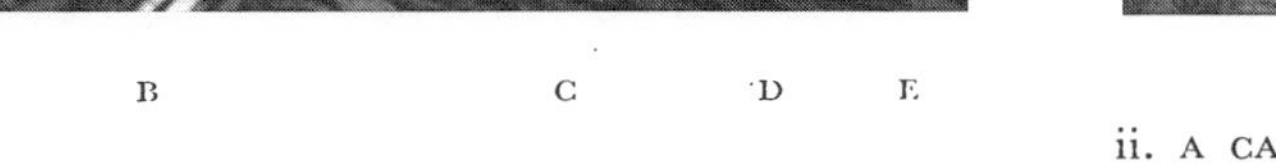

i. A BETROTHAL

ii. A CAVALCADE

Both from British Mus. MS., Royal 20, *c. vii., Chroniques de St. Denis* (*c.* 1395–1400).

[Note roundlet cap of i. C, D and ii. B, and cf. Plate XVII. A. Enlarged and bent upward at the sides. these formed the basis of the later "heart-shaped" head-dress, XVIII. C.]

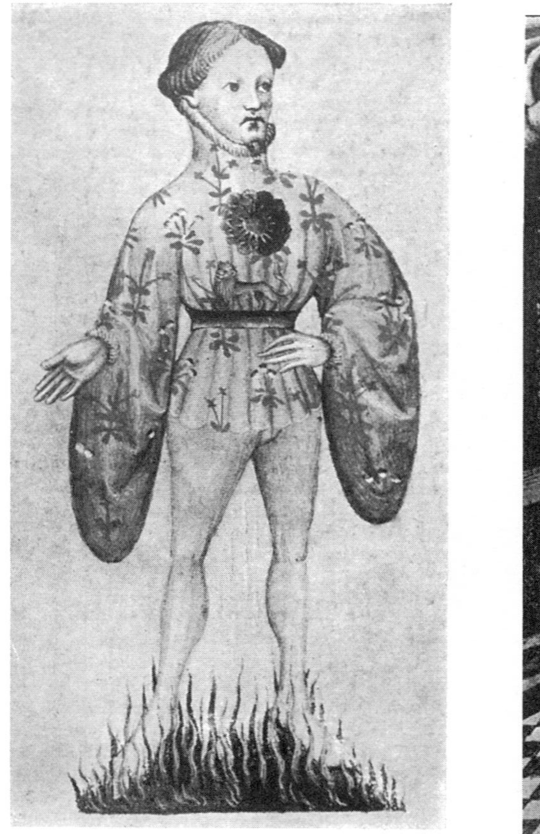
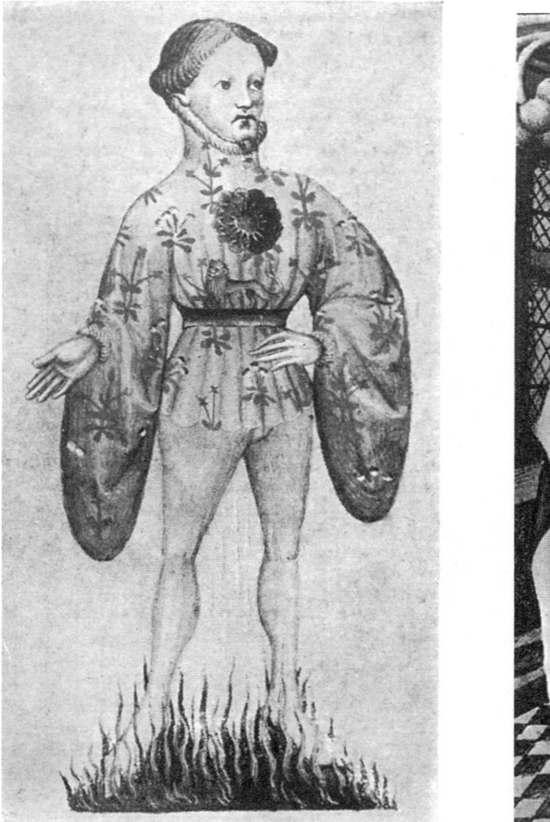

i. FIGURE FROM JOHN FOXTON'S "COSMOGRAPHY, A.D. 1408"

Trinity College, Cambridge.

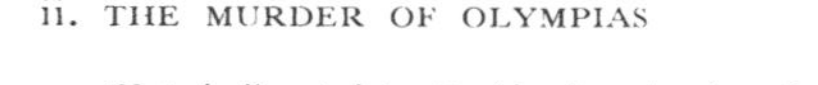

A B C D E

ii. THE MURDER OF OLYMPIAS

From Boccaccio's "Des Cleres et Nobles Femmes" MS.

[Note in ii. E *points* attaching hose to gipon.]

generally caught in and arranged more or less symmetrically under the girdle. All these robes of the houppelande class are cut on the same principle so far as the body is concerned; the apparent differences are all of detail, namely, the sleeves, the position of the girdle, the cut at the neck, and the length. Although the high expanding collar is found down

FIG. 18.—Heinrich Urech 1397 (sepulchral slab at Nordhausen.—*From Creeny*).

to *c.* 1420, by 1410 it tends to be lower, narrower, and open at the throat; another variety about the same time forms a deep revers lying flat upon the shoulders. From *c.* 1425 the collar shrinks back to the shoulders, and is low with rounded corners, opening a little way down the breast in an open V. Linings and borders of fur are greatly affected to the houppelandes.

After *c.* 1420 the slit-up skirts lose much of their vogue, and are uncommon after *c.* 1440, the gown being close all round. A curious effect is sometimes produced in the 'thirties and 'forties by buckling the usual girdle well down upon the hips, whereby an unsightly fulness is produced in the houppelande. The exaggerated funnel sleeve is found in State apparel till close on 1450, but about 1405 appears the

FIG. 19.—Hermann von Werthere † 1395 (sepulchral slab at Nordhausen.—*From Creeny*).

"bagpipe" sleeve, whose cut will be best understood by reference to Plate XV. i. This type gradually loses favour from the 'thirties, at which period come in wide sleeves slit down in front so that the arm in its undersleeve could be thrust through the slit, as in Plate XVII. A. From *c.* 1450 on the sleeves are made both wide and long, as in a modern dressing-gown, or, again, they are wholly open in front so as to hang loose from the shoulders. From the second quarter of the fifteenth century the folds of the gown are arranged in a group of formal pleats tacked down at the waist fore and aft.

The cote-hardie is closely buttoned down over the gipon in the last quarter of the fourteenth century. It now borrows from the houppelande its various forms of collar and sleeve; in addition, just before and after 1400 it has sleeves close-buttoned down the forearm, extending trumpetwise from wrist to knuckle. (Fig. 18 shows a pointed long-sleeve, with similar

Fig. 20.

bugle-cuffs.) Furthermore, from *c.* 1405 on it, too, is very commonly arranged in a group of pleats fore and aft. It is now rarely buttoned, the mode of fastening it, when shaped to the waist, being mostly invisible (? by hooks and eyes at the back, under one of the pleats). From *c.* 1390 to 1410 the bucks often wear it excessively short, barely covering the fork, in fact [Plate xv. i]. It then lengthens again, till by the second quarter of the fifteenth century it mostly reaches to the knee.

The *gipon* from *c.* 1420 borrows the collar from the houppelande and cote-hardie (when the latter become low-necked), and has close sleeves to the wrist, at first with a spreading cuff to the knuckles, from *c.* 1420 ending at the wrist. It is visible at the neck, at the breast and forearm, so far as uncovered by the upper garment. It has a row of eyelet-holes along the lower edge, for attaching the hose.

CLOAKS.—Except with peers' robes and those associated with knightly orders, the cloak is rarely worn from 1400 on by the upper classes, except for travelling and in emergency. The shoulder-cape (independent of the hood) is a favourite vehicle for dagging, but dies out *c.* 1430. Though cloaks proper fall out of modish favour, their place from *c.* 1425 is not infrequently supplied by garments of the heraldic *tabard* class, made to slip over the head ; one form in favour in the 'thirties and 'forties is sleeved on the lines of the modern " Inverness " cut short at the knee.[1]

LEG-WEAR.—From now on the hose become what we should call " tights," *i.e.* they unite into a single garment covering the person from hip [2] to toe. The *codpiece*, a kind of small bag covering the fork in front, now makes its appearance, and persists till the last quarter of the sixteenth century. Along the upper edge runs a series of eyelet-holes corresponding to those at the base of the gipon, to which the hose are attached by *points*—short, tagged laces—threaded through these holes and knotted in a loop outside the gipon.[3] The toes followed the current fashions in footwear ; when long-pointed, they were stuffed with tow. Party-coloured hose, except for livery, rather lost favour between *c.* 1420–1470.

HEAD-GEAR.—The evolution of the age-old hood in this period reaches its most interesting stage ; hitherto it had preserved its primary utilitarian character, however varied its mode of wear or the ingenuity of the wearer. It is now indifferently worn as a cowl (capable of being pushed back at will on the shoulders), or with the head inserted in the opening of the cowl, and the gorget and liripipe draped or twisted about the head *ad lib.* into a kind of turban. A favourite style *c.* 1390–1410 is to twist the liripipe turbanwise round the temples, the gathered folds of the dagged gorget falling over it like the comb of a Minorca fowl [Plate XIV. ii, A]. These various arrangements requiring time and skill, a new " ready-made " form evolves towards 1420 ; the *chaperon* [Plate XVII. B]. The main feature of this is the *roundlet*, a padded circlet resembling a miniature motor-tyre, to whose inner circumference are sewn a gathered " skirt " and a long streamer, modelled respectively on the gorget and liripipe of the hood. The " skirt " (gorget) flops over the *roundlet* in a bunch of folds, the iripipe hangs down to one side, or is draped about the shoulders. When momentarily discarded the *chaperon* with its skirt was slung behind the shoulder and balanced in front by the liripipe [4] [cf. Plate XVI. i, A, and Fig. 21]. The chaperon is *par excellence* the typical head-gear of the first half of the fifteenth century, and maintained its supremacy till *c.* 1460,

[1] The front part is commonly caught down by the girdle, while the full back hangs loose, cloakwise ; it derives from the *scapular* and *garnache* (p. 4).

[2] They do *not* as yet reach up to the *waist*. The codpiece was essential, as tailors knew nothing of " dressing " right or left.

[3] To " truss the points " is the old term for thus bracing up the hose.

[4] In an atrophied form it still survives in the " hood " of the robes of the Order of the Garter.

c. 1460

A B C

i. MARRIAGE OF KING LOUIS OF NAPLES AND SICILY TO PRINCESS YOLANDE OF ARAGON

Froissart's Chronicle Harl. MS. 4379, fo. 126, British Museum.

c. 1400

ii. ADORATION OF THE MAGI

Add. MS. 29433, fo. 67, British Museum.

A

B

*

C

"COUNTS OF HOLLAND" (STATUETTES)

Photos : Victoria and Albert Museum *Amsterdam Museum.*

[NOTE.—C retains the distinctive features of A.D. 1395–1405. In B the liripipe has been broken away

A

B

C

"COUNTESSES OF HOLLAND" (STATUETTES)

[NOTE.—A shows most of the features of *c.* 1410.]

Photos: Victoria and Albert Museum *Amsterdam Museum.*

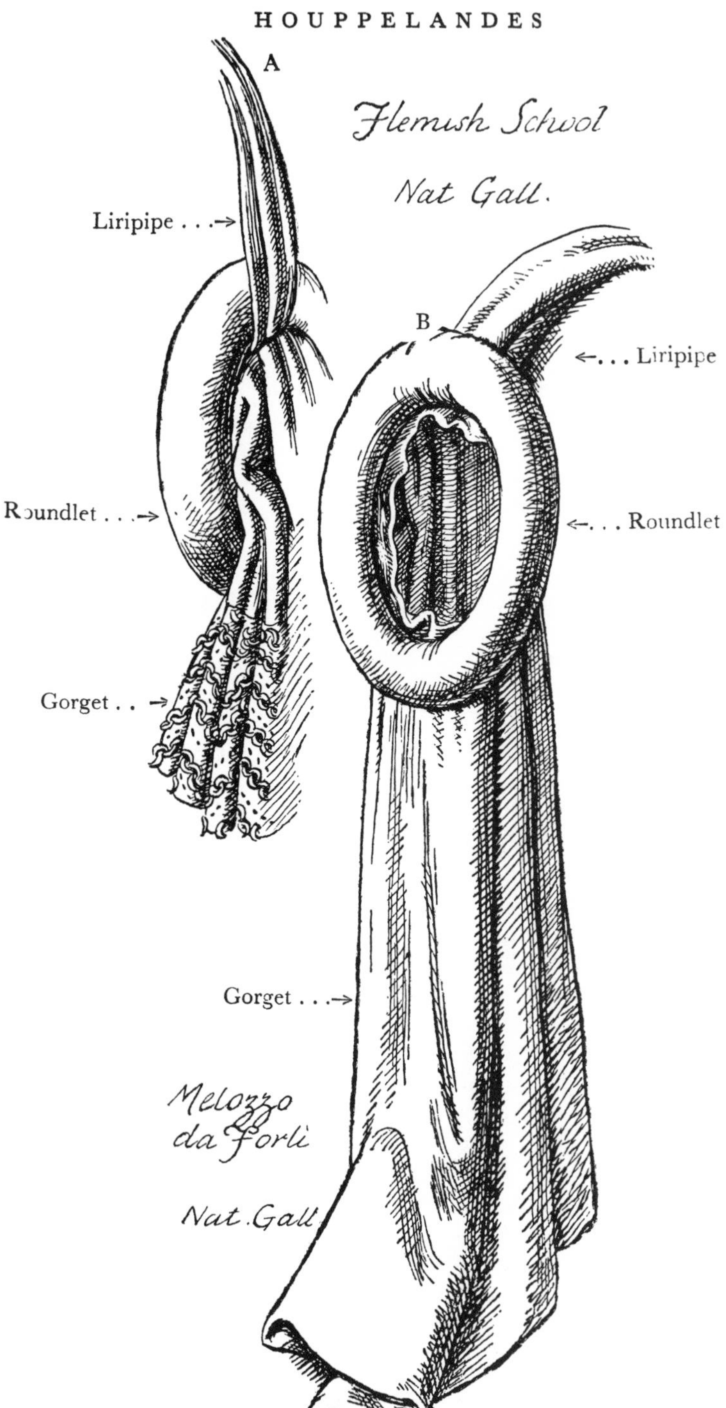

FIG. 21.—Chaperons (slung over shoulder) :—A, Outside view ; B, Inside view.

when it was gradually relegated to the professional classes and graver *bourgeoisie.* Note that the chaperon and the turbanwise hood may be worn *over* a second cowl-like hood. Except for travelling, sport, etc., hoods become plebeian after *c.* 1450. Other head-dresses worn *c.* 1394–1415 were a tall cap with a "topper"-like crown and turned-up or rolled brim [Plates XIII. ii, B; XIV. i, E; XV. ii, E], and another whose bag-shaped crown sags forward over the brim like a "Phrygian" cap or Spanish peasant's "gorro" [Plate XIII. i. C]. Various hats of the wide-awake type appear, notably a form with down-turned brim and bell-top. Another, chiefly affected by princes, has a four-lobed upturned fur brim. By the 'thirties the linen *coif* (cf. p. 8) becomes the badge of clerics and lawyers, but a trifle earlier is introduced a close caul or skull-cap of various materials not covering the ears, but reaching well down to the nape; this may be worn under any of the others specified. Brooches, medals, or jewels may be worn in the roll or turn-up of chaperon, hood, or cap, or in the band of the hat. A head-dress common to both sexes and peculiar to the beginning of the fifteenth century is a kind of open roll of stuff, encircling the brows like a coronet—in fact, an independent *roundlet.* It is often covered with dagged material, the effect recalling a wreath of oak-leaves [Plate XIV. ii, B]. It is often worn also over the bascinet when in armour.

FOOTWEAR.—Towards 1395 the pointed toes are prolonged into exaggerated "pikes" like toothpicks. By *c.* 1410 these lapse from favour, and for the rest of the period the shape approaches the normal; though the "piked shoon" reappear in the 'forties. Most shoes of the period are closed up to the ankle. From about 1400 on we also find buskins reaching to the calf, generally laced or clasped tight to the leg, more rarely bagging loosely. For riding and travelling, long boots reaching well up the thigh are worn, and towards 1450 are widely adopted by fashionable men for pedestrian use.[1] These among the upper classes moulded the limb closely, being laced or buckled at the side; or the fullness below the calf caught back and buckled as before (cf. p. 20). Towards 1450 the tops have a coloured turnover. Somewhere about this period the vamp of the boot begins to be cut separate from the leg. *Pattens* or thick wooden undershoes, strapped over the boot or shoe, were worn to raise the feet clear of the mud.[2]

UNDERWEAR.—This is generally invisible. At most some shirts, furnished (*c.* 1430–1450) with a close collar, show a narrow line of white above the collar of the gipon.

HAIR.—The hair in the last quarter of the fourteenth century is mostly parted in the centre and flows along and full to the level of the jawbone, but about 1395 comes in a new *coiffure*, in which the loose ends of the hair are curled outwards in a thick roll round the nape, just covering the tops of the ears and tapering to nothing in the centre in front [Plate XVI.].

[1] I am unable to say whether the French foppery of wearing *a boot on one leg only* ever obtained here.

[2] Well shown in Van Eyck's portrait of Arnolfini in 1434 (Nat. Gall.).

The roll appears to have been dressed over a pad or fillet, often decked in front with a jewel surmounted by an osprey. Towards 1410 comes in a very unsightly development: the "bowl" crop, *the* typical masculine mode between 1410 and 1450 [Fig. 22, A]. The head is shaven at back and sides to *above* the tops of the ears, and the hair is brushed outward from the apex of the scalp, forming a kind of shaggy skull-cap. Examples of the older modes and of hair merely short-cropped all over also appear throughout. Towards 1450, in a few cases, the "bowl" is abandoned, and the hair, brushed away from the apex, forms a straight fringe all round, partly covering the ears [Fig. 22, B]. Beards, pointed or forked, are found up to *c.* 1410, but from *c.* 1400 the cheeks are mostly shaven and the beard dwindles, often to a pair of small chin tufts. Even these

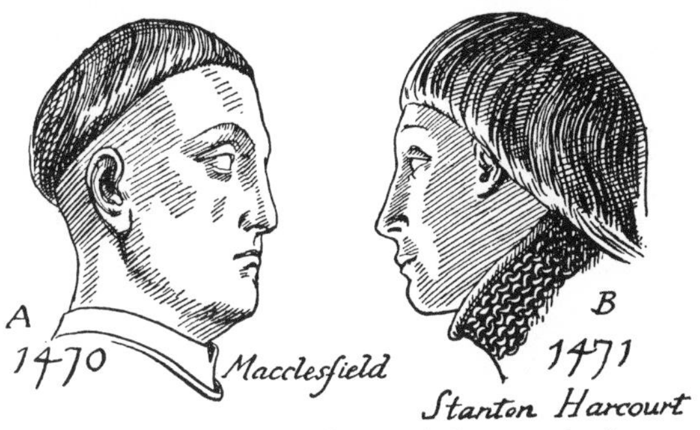

Fig. 22.—A, "Bowl" crop (a late survival).

are rare from *c.* 1415, and from the 'twenties till the second quarter of the sixteenth century all self-respecting faces are clean-shaven.

Accessories.—The girdles show no essential changes from those of the preceding age. The "knightly girdle" (metallic hip-belt) is worn over the *cote-hardie* up to *c.* 1410. A fashion pretty common between *c.* 1400 and 1420 was an ornament of folly-bells suspended by narrow chains from the girdle; at other times they are attached to a baldrick (shoulder-belt), or from a collar about the shoulders. At this period comes in the fashion for both sexes of jewelled collars; they commonly bore personal devices, and in that case marked the partisans of this or that political or social leader. Finger-rings were nothing new, but at this date they became more elaborate and profuse. The pouch and dagger worn at the girdle were often of imposing dimensions and elaboration.

WOMEN

Body Garments.—The close-fitting kirtle, the cote-hardie, and the sideless surcoat last without essential change into the second decade of the fifteenth century, the low necks likewise. Soon after 1400 the ladies adopt and adapt the *houppelande*, at first almost unaltered, even to (at times) the high, spreading collar [Fig. 25, B]. Most masculine types of sleeve occur in female attire (the type seen in Plate xvii. A seems reserved to men). The feminine houppelande is mostly belted high up under the breasts, rather in Empire style [Plate xv. ii; Fig. 23]. The high collar grows rare after *c.* 1415, its place being taken by a broad square collar (often of fur) lying flat on the shoulders, often with a slight **V** *décolletage* [Figs. 23, 24, 27, B]. In the 'forties the *décolletage* deepens in a wide **V** to the girdle in front and behind, bordered with the aforesaid collar or a broad lapel of the "roll collar" type. In front the kirtle or undergown, just visible in the opening, partly masks the exposed bosom. For state wear these robes trail over the feet and sweep the ground in a train behind. Graver dames wear loose full-skirted gowns, reaching up to the neck, and often ungirt, the upper parts covered by the *wimple* or *barbe* (*vide infra*, p. 45), the sleeves of comfortable width. *Note.*—

FIG. 23.

FIG. 24.

A "high stomach" (literally) was produced, presumably, by underpads.

CLOAKS.—Full and long (cut "on the circle"), these are an important item of female attire on ceremonious occasions. They fasten loosely across the breast with cords or jewelled bands. More close-fitting cloaks often with hoods and capes are sometimes used for travelling.

HEAD-DRESS.—Up to *c.* 1400 we find no very striking innovations. The various net-like coverings develop into boss-like structures at the sides, at first hemispherical, then (from *c.* 1400) more or less in form of truncated cones or box-shaped [1]; the earlier forms are placed above the ears, but from *c.* 1410 increasingly they cover them completely. These are often surmounted by a richly ornamented padded roll or circlet [Fig. 25, B], shaped to the underlying structure [Fig. 27, B], as

FIG. 25.

was the coronet of great ladies when worn in this conjunction [Fig. 25, A]. The point to notice is that most feminine headwear of the fifteenth century entirely conceals the hair. In the first quarter of the century width appears the main object, in the second, height gradually supplants this ideal: we have, expressing these phases respectively, the "horned" coiffure and the "heart-shaped." Fine veils of gauze, often stretched over wires, are variously adjusted to all these head-dresses. The "butterfly" form appears in England from *c.* 1450. A head-dress worn throughout the fifteenth century and later by elderly dames and widows is the old mediæval nun-like veil in heavy material. The heart-shaped head-dress frequently borrows the male liripipe and "skirt," plain or dagged.

[1] To describe these lucidly *and* concisely is very difficult. The reader is referred to illustrations *passim*: Stothard, Hollar, Boutell, and other works on effigies and brasses, as well as to those in almost any costume book. But—*verify dates.*

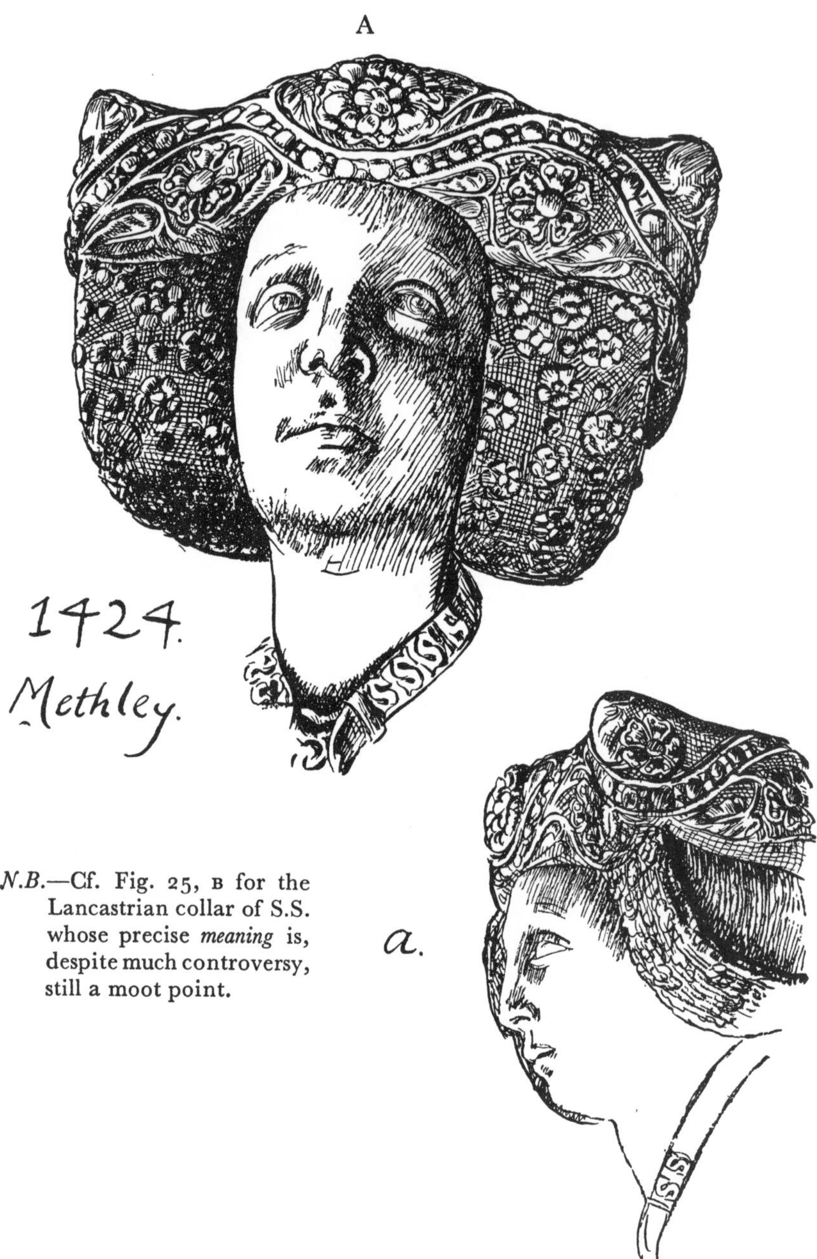

N.B.—Cf. Fig. 25, B for the Lancastrian collar of S.S. whose precise *meaning* is, despite much controversy, still a moot point.

Fig. 26.

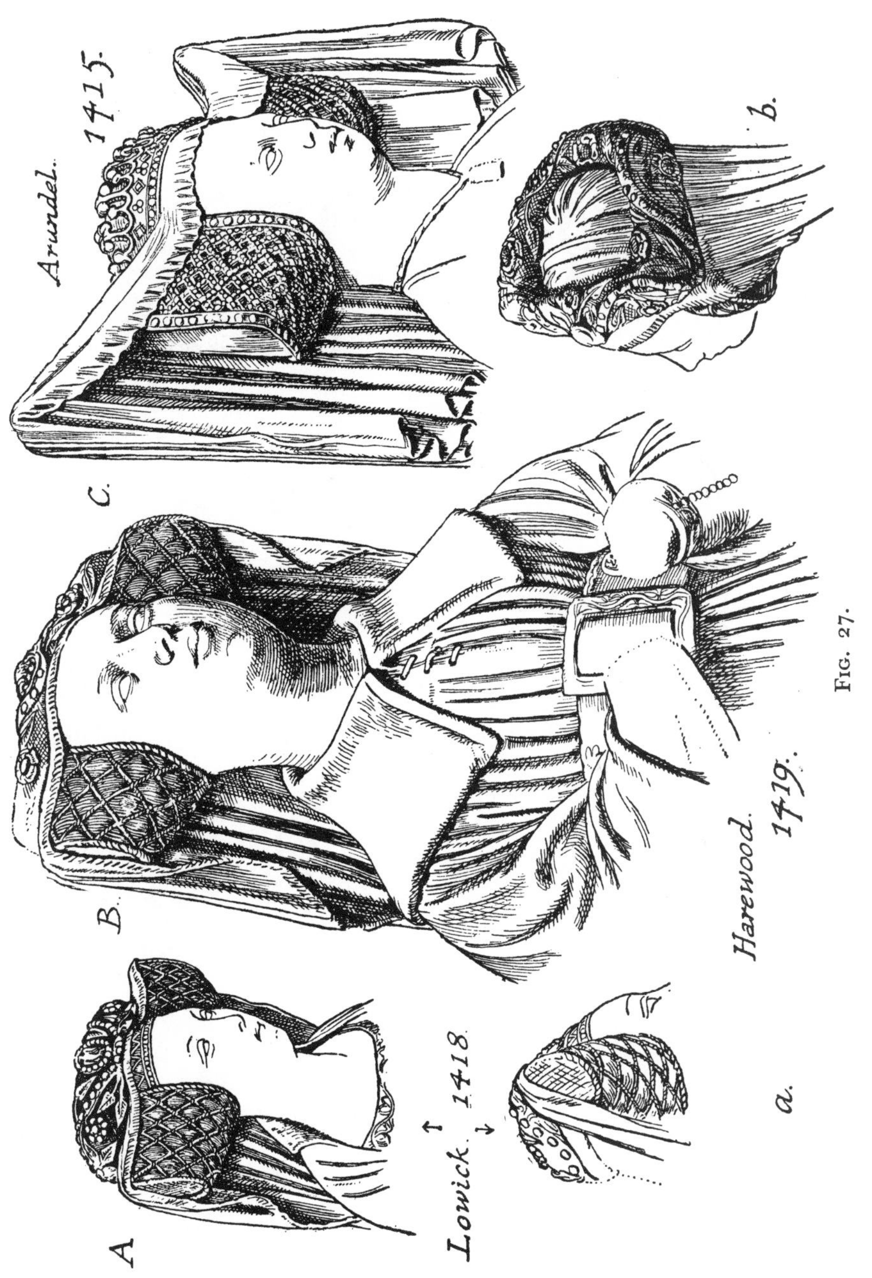

FIG. 27.

Hoods and hats after the male type are at times worn for travelling sport, etc.[1]

FOOTWEAR.—Ladies rarely wore boots ; otherwise their footwear was as under MEN.

UNDERWEAR.—Not visible.

HAIR.—Brides, queens at their coronation, and children wore their hair flowing freely on their shoulders. Till *c.* 1420 quite young girls often did the like. Otherwise throughout this period the hair is not only carefully concealed under the head-dress, but the forehead and temples are shaved, and the eyebrows plucked to a mere thread.

ACCESSORIES.—Same as for men. Note, however, how, by those entitled to wear them, coronets are variously adapted to fit the underlying head-dresses.

[1] The typical feminine hood was cut like the men's, but left open at the chin and throat.

IV—*BURGUNDIAN MODES*

(1450–1485)

THE model for courtly manners and fine living in Western Europe was the sumptuous court of the Dukes of Burgundy. It had begun to be so indeed by the middle of the first half of the fifteenth century, and by 1450 its supremacy was paramount, and so remained for the next thirty years or so, to be succeeded by a distinct Franco-Italian element. The Burgundian influence in English fashion was largely strengthened by the alliance between Burgundy and the house of York. It was another age of foppish eccentricity.

MEN

BODY GARMENTS.—Particularly typical of the age under review are long sleeves gathered and grotesquely padded out and upward at the shoulders, especially in the 'sixties and 'seventies. These padded shoulders appear to have been known (in France, at least) as *mahoitres*.[1] The gipon has now become a *doublet*, the *cote-hardie* is supplanted by the *jerkin* or *jacket*; while *gowns*, long or short, are but modifications of the *houppelande* [Plate XVI. i, A; Fig. 28]. *Mahoitres* are common to the two latter. The doublet, with its padded breast, fits close to the trunk, has a rather high collar open in front, and reaches at most to the hips. The sleeves are for the most part close to the wrist; towards 1480 they are slit ("*slashed*") across (a fashion that developed in the sequel) at the elbows, and (sometimes) at the shoulder, to show the fine linen of the shirt bulging out in a limp puff. In the latter part of the period the doublet sometimes opens down the breast, over which it may be loosely laced, affording a further glimpse of the shirt. The *jerkin* reaches sometimes to mid-thigh, sometimes barely covers the hips. The sleeves might narrow to the wrist, but are increasingly made long and roomy (*not* gathered in to the wrist), and are frequently slit down the front seam, so that they may be allowed to hang free behind the arm [Plate XIX. A]. Another form is full, and gathered to the wrist, slit lengthwise, and loosely laced across, showing the sleeve of the shirt. The hanging sleeves are often looped together at the back so as to be out of the way [Plate XIX. C].

[1] The effect is often akin to the ballooning shoulders in vogue in the 'thirties and 'nineties of the nineteenth century.

FIG. 28.—Brass of John Luneborch, † 1474, at Lübeck.

A B C D E F

FROM "CHRONIQUES DU HAINAULT" *Bibl. Roy. Brussels M.S.*, 9243.

[Note in B falling draperies of head-dress, borrowed from male *chaperon*, at D "fez"-like cap and beaver hat slung over shoulder by a scarf (*liripipe*).]

A B C

A BANQUET

Brit. Mus. Royal MS., 15 *E iv.*, *Anciennes and Nouvelles Chroniques d'Angleterre*, *fo.* 134.

[Note long "piked shoon," also (C) hanging sleeves of jerkin twisted together behind. In England the conical "steeple" herein rarely exceeds the truncated form of (B).]

Some jerkins have pleats radiating from the waist symmetrically disposed, sewn and padded (also found in the close gowns, *c.* 1450–1470) ; others are open in front in a deep V to the waist.[1] Though both long and short gowns are still worn closed all round, the tendency grows to have them open all the way in front ; though this opening often fastens up with hooks and eyes, a double-breasted set being not unusual. They might be girt or unconfined. Lapels and broad falling collars, chiefly of fur, are frequent. Irrespective of the length of the gown, the slit sleeves often hang to the calf of the leg [Plate XIX. A].

Garments of the tabard class (*vide* p. 30, *supra*) are comparatively rare.

CLOAKS.—If anything, these are less common than in the preceding age (*vide* p. 30, *supra*).

LEGS.—The *hose*, " trussed " as before, reach from about 1475 *up to the waist*. Codpieces continue.

HEAD-GEAR.—In the 'sixties the *chaperon* gradually loses favour in polite circles. The old *liripipe* survives, however, till *c.* 1480 in the form of a long scarf attached to the brim of the beaver hat, the free end being often knotted or tasselled to act as a counterweight when the hat is slung behind the shoulder [Plate XVIII.*bis* D]. Hats are worn in great variety : high crowned or low, with brims narrow or broad ; some are conical, others, again, have crowns akin to our " toppers " and " bowlers." Although more showy textiles were employed, felts and beavers (no novelty) were in great favour. Plumes are not rare ; either a tall upright ostrich feather in front or a pair standing up at the back, attached by a medal or jewel. The hatband is often of jeweller's work. Caps of felt are seen, almost identical with the Oriental fez (even to the short stalk on top) ; by the ultra-modish these are often elevated into regular sugar-loaves. After 1475 comes in a low cap rather like our father's " smoking caps," with a deep " pork-pie " turn-up fixed with a jewelled brooch. In the 'eighties a wide section of the brim in front is cut away, and the gap laced across by silken or gold cords.

FOOTWEAR.—The toes, sharply pointed in 1450, in the 'sixties and 'seventies are prolonged into immense needle points [Plate XIX.]. From *c.* 1480 these lose favour, and by *c.* 1500 vanish for ever. The toe of the shoe is now clumsily splayed out at the ball of the foot, whence it narrows abruptly to a short, obtuse point. Otherwise the boots and shoes are practically as in the last chapter, except that the latter are often slit down at the sides and rise up to a point in front of and behind the ankle. The very tall boots, with turnover tops, are in great favour. *Pattens* are much worn.

BODY LINEN.—The shirt, now increasingly made with a neck-band, begins in this period to make something of a show at the throat, the breast, and the openings of the sleeves. Embroidery in black and red silk, or gold thread, comes into favour towards the end of this era ;

[1] Actually it is at times difficult to distinguish jerkin from doublet, owing to the custom, now becoming general, of wearing *stomachers* (vest-pieces akin to our " dickies ") and separate sleeves attached by (mostly invisible) points.

chiefly on the neck-band, into which the shirt is gathered in close pleats.

HAIR.—All faces are shaven. The "bowl" crop is *démodé* after 1460. The later cuts already described persist throughout this period. Another style comes in *c.* 1465, much favoured by exquisites: the hair is allowed to grow freely, overhanging the forehead and, at back and sides, reaching almost to the shoulders.

ACCESSORIES.—There is nothing particular to add to the remarks on this heading in the last chapter.[1] Walking sticks appear more generally than hitherto, but are still little more than plain staves of varying length, sometimes with a round pummel.

WOMEN

BODY GARMENTS.—There is little change to record in these: indeed, there would be something of monotony in the lines of the female figure, but for the touch of variety in the head-dress. Chiefly to be noted is the alteration in the outline of the *décolletage* of the upper gown, which in the 'sixties is generally rounded, and from *c.* 1480 is cut square, almost

FIG. 29.

baring the shoulders; from this date, in fact, the line across the bosom tends to show a slight upward curve. The tubular folds of the *houppelande* rather lose favour, and the upper gown in the last years of this era often moulds the bust closely in the old *cote-hardie* manner. Long tight sleeves widen out from the wrist to a squarish cuff.

[1] It should be unnecessary to point out that the *decoration* of the various objects reflects the æsthetic taste of the day; too wide a field to enter into within our limits.

Cloaks.—As in Chapter III.

Head-dress.—This lends chief distinction to the feminine contour of this age. Indeed, towering head-dresses, grotesquely out of proportion to the rest of the figure, are the keynote of the age, more especially

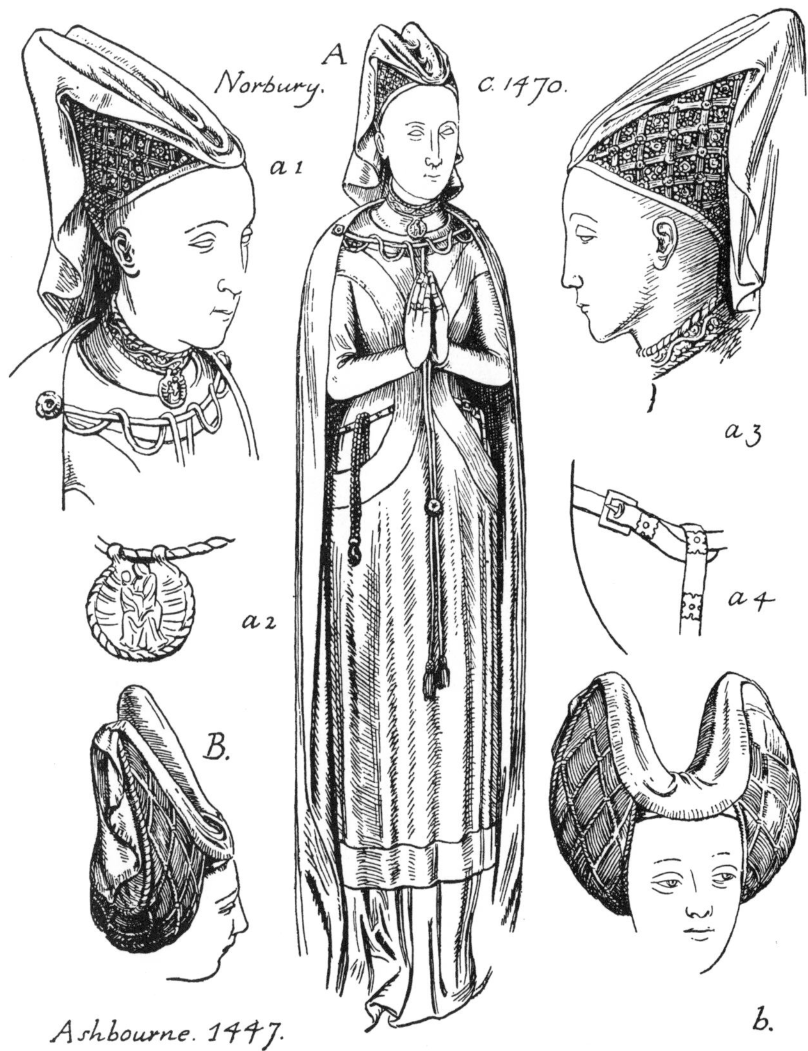

Fig. 30.—" Horns " and " Hearts."

between 1460 and 1480. Most of these are accompanied by voluminous gauze veils, which are apt to be borne up and out by an understructure of fine wires. All these great head-dresses are worn tilted back at an angle of forty-five degrees. Some are shaped like beehives or waste-paper baskets [Plate xvi. i, c]. The gauze " butterfly " head-dress,

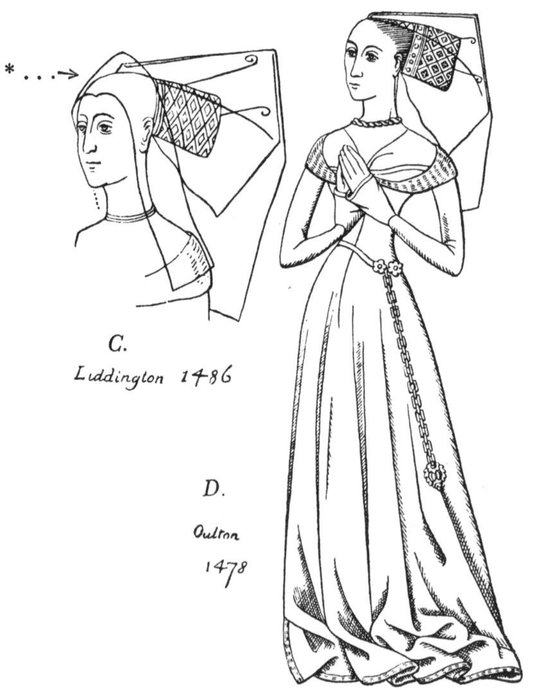

FIG. 31.—The " Butterfly " Veil.
In D the long frontlet (*) prefigures the Henry VII. hood.

in high favour from the 'fifties to the 'eighties, is mostly mounted over a foundation of this shape. Another highly characteristic form of the 'sixties and 'seventies is the *hennin*, or steeple-cap. To what extent this, at least in its fullest development, ever gained a real vogue *in England* seems to me—*pace* most costume-writers—questionable. It would, on the evidence, appear to have been essentially a Franco-Burgundian mode. It appears neither on English effigies nor brasses (which *per contra* freely record the horned, heart-shaped, butterfly, and similar forms pretty freely). So far as it is recorded at all in purely English art,[1] it appears only in a markedly truncated form [Plate XIX. B].

The nun-like veil of the Middle Ages had never been abandoned. In the fifteenth century, made of dark stuff, it was distinctive of widows; with it went its old companion the wimple, transformed from *c.* 1400 into the *barbe*, a kind of linen bib attached to a narrow chin-band, and forming small vertical pleats in the centre. Ladies of high rank wore it covering the chin, others beneath. Turban-like head-dresses occur—first seen *c.* 1400—sometimes mere rolls through which the hair hangs down unconfined. Most of the loftier forms of head-dresses show a small U-shaped black loop in the centre of the forehead [Plate XIX. B]. This is *not*, as so often stated, a lock of hair; a mere glance at contemporary paintings settles that. Probably it served to adjust the tall cap to the head. Hoods creep into favour *c.* 1480.

FOOTWEAR.—As for men.

HAIR.—This is for the most part wholly concealed. Where the head-dress, as is usual with the foundation of late butterfly veils, is tilted to the very back of the head, the hair on the brow and temples is often shown strained back from the face [Fig. 31, D].

ACCESSORIES.—*Vide* last chapter.

[1] The wife of Sir John Doune of Kidwelly in Memlinc's portrait appears to be attired *à la mode de Bourgogne* in consonance with the modes of the court to which her husband was accredited, and other exceptions appear to be on a par with this.

Complete "Gothic" Armour (German) *c.* 1480–1490 showing Component Parts.

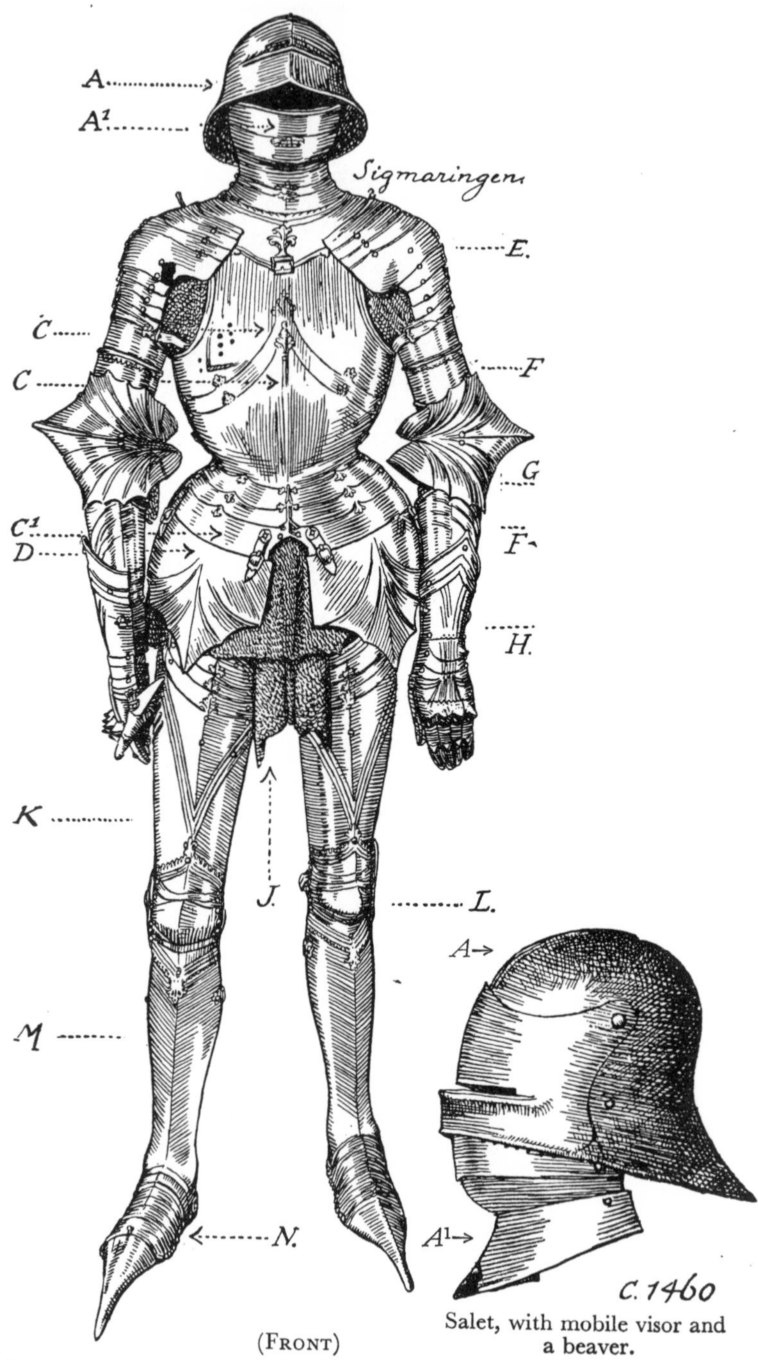

Salet, with mobile visor and a beaver.

(Front)

A, Headpiece (*salet*); A¹, Beaver; C, Breast; C¹, Fauld (or paunce); C², Back; C³, Culet or hoguine; D, Tasse; E, Pauldron; F, Vambrace;

COMPLETE "GOTHIC" ARMOUR (GERMAN) *c.* 1480–1490
SHOWING COMPONENT PARTS.

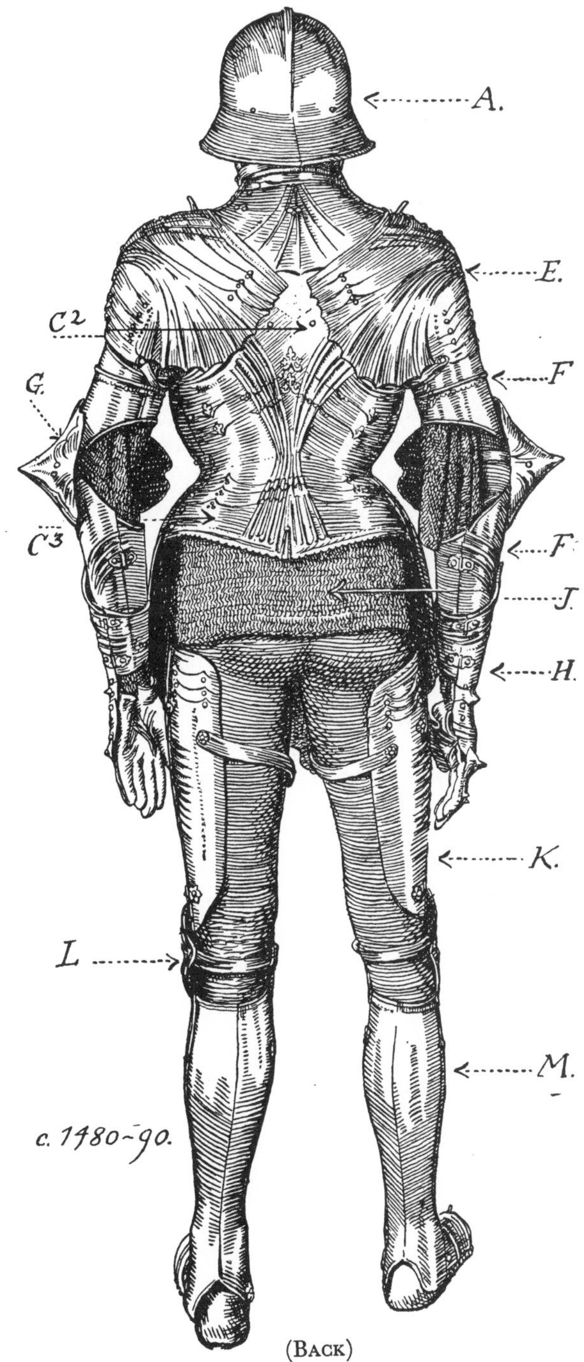

(BACK)

G, Coutere; H, Gauntlet; J, Coat of mail (*haubergeon*); K, Cuish; L, Poleyn; M, Greave; N, Sabaton. *Note.*—C, C[1], C[2], C[3], compose the CUIRASS.

PART II—ARMOUR

(1066–1485)

IN the Middle Ages and as long as armour was a living thing, the term *mail* denoted exclusively a defence of rings interlinked as in the modern women's steel purse [Plate XXI. *bis* i]. Only by a *late* poetical licence did the term come to be used of armour at large. "Chain-mail" is a mere modern pleonasm; "scale-mail" and still more "plate mail," sheer nonsense. Meyrick's at one time generally accepted categories [1] —"ringed," "mascled," "trelliced," "rustred," etc.—may henceforth be dismissed as fictions: so far as they were not pure inventions, they were based on a misconception of passages referring to the so-called "chain" mail, whose antiquity and ubiquity are even now insufficiently recognized. Mail was in use in Western Europe centuries before the Crusades. So far from mail being imported from the East as a consequence of the Crusades, we are expressly told that it was the *First* Crusaders who brought it to Constantinople *on their way to* the East. In twelfth to thirteenth century art, where Christian warriors confront Moslems, it is the former who wear mail, the latter scales or plates. Nor does mail seem to be at all convincingly rendered in Oriental art of any age.

It can only be regretted that the famous Bayeux Tapestry [Plate XXI.] should have so preponderant a standing as evidence of the military equipment of the days of the Conquest. And this for four reasons:

(*a*) It has been exploited and illustrated *ad nauseam* in practically all the works on costume and armour, although—

(*b*) The actual date and original provenance have in recent times been the subject of the most diverse opinions on the part of antiquaries.

(*c*) At best (*i.e.* in its presumed original state) the "tapestry" must have been of a crude and summary character.

(*d*) Little or no account has been taken *in costume-books* of the alterations due to shrinkage, wear and tear, and arbitrary restorations.[2]

[1] MEYRICK, Sir Samuel Rush: "On the Body Armour anciently worn in England" (*Archæologia*, xix.). Meyrick, long venerated as *the* final authority on armour, was responsible for disseminating a number of gross misconceptions, not yet wholly dispelled.

[2] On this point, see DAWSON, Chas., F.S.A., *The Restoration of the Bayeux Tapestry*, London, 1907.

i. FROM JEAN MANSEL'S " FLEUR DES HISTOIRES "

Bibl. Roy. Brussels MS. 9232.

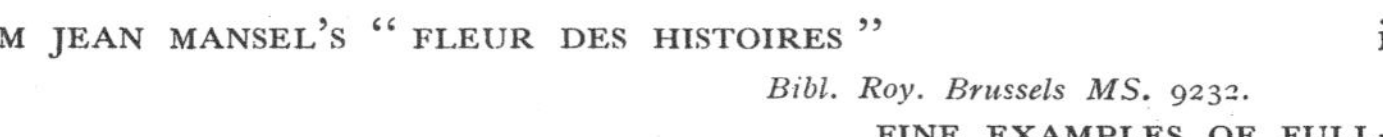

ii. FROM " HISTOIRE DE CHARLES MARTEL "

Bibl. Roy. Brussels MS. 9.

FINE EXAMPLES OF FULL-DRESS COURT ATTIRE

[In (ii.) note tall " fez "-like caps, *mahoitres*, and slashed sleeves.

c. 1110–18

i. FONT IN ST. BARTHOLOMEW'S CHURCH, LIÈGE

c. 1128

ii. ANGOULÊME CATHEDRAL (FRONT).

WILLIAM OF NORMANDY AND HIS STANDARD-BEARER

From Bayeux Tapestry.

[N.B.—The *chausses* are mere leggings, leaving the feet unarmed; the armour is MAIL.]

With all deference, however, to Messrs. Marignan, Lefèvre des Noëttes, Belloc, and others, the evidence, as carefully weighed by competent antiquaries, appears definitely in favour of a date and place at which, at least, the facts and traditions of the campaign were thoroughly alive (whether or not the work was commissioned, as seems likely enough, by Odo, Bishop of Bayeux, brother of the Conqueror, and one of the protagonists of the battle of Hastings (*d.* 1097)). As such it is a " star witness," and the only graphic one to the material facts, and we are bound to refer to it—with caution against too literal an interpretation of its crude conventions—in conjunction with other evidence of the period.

Mail Period

(TO *c.* 1250)

At the time of the Conquest the defensive armour of the heavy-armed horseman (mostly a knight) consisted of a HAUBERK (or BYRNIE), HELM, and SHIELD ; for offence he was armed with LANCE, JAVELIN, SWORD, and—often—MACE. The hauberk reached about to the knees, and was slit from hem to fork in front and behind for convenience in the saddle. It is possible that this slit skirt *may on occasion* have been laced or tied round the thigh. It comprised a hood or COIF-DE-MAILLES, covering the head and neck, with wide sleeves to the elbow ; in a few cases the forearms of the chiefs were covered to the wrist with under-sleeves, and their legs with leggings of defensive fabric [Plate XXI.].

At least among the best-armed warriors, these defences certainly appear to have been habitually of MAIL.[1] SCALE armour was also assuredly in use, and various combinations of padding, quilting, and leather-work, perhaps reinforced with metal in the form of studs, etc. Padding and quilting must, almost certainly, have very early been used under the mail defences, and (with leather) as the main body-armour of the common (foot) soldier. The helmet at this date is a conical cap mostly with a NASAL [Plate XXI. ; Fig. 32], and sometimes a neck-guard. The shield of wood covered with leather or hide, and with a border, UMBO (centre-boss), and other reinforcements of metal, and carried by means of a GUIGE and ÉNARMES,[2] has the outline of a large " kite," curved to the body ; less often is convex and circular. The lance, with its pennon, is not unlike that of a modern lancer, the javelin or throwing-spear has the head singly or doubly barbed. The SWORD has a massive plain cross-guard (QUILLONS), a spherical or quoit-shaped PUMMEL, and a long broad blade with obtuse point. The mace is a mere stout cudgel, or has a lobated metal head.

[1] MAIL = a network of interlinked rings. I use the term exclusively in this, the only correct, sense.

[2] *Nasal :* a bar-like projection from the helmet-rim down over the nose. *Guige :* strap for suspending the shield from the shoulders. *Énarmes :* loops by which the shield is gripped and guided.

This general description holds good till well into the twelfth century. The archers, by the way, carry short bows which they draw not, as later, to the ear, but *to the breast*, the arrows being carried in a quiver.[1] About 1100–1130 there is a general tendency among the knights to lengthen the hauberk to the calf of the leg, but by the middle of the twelfth century the hauberk shrinks upwards to the knees once more. Wide sleeves to the wrist also appear on seals, but towards 1150 these are generally tightened to the forearm, and from the last quarter of the century continue in bag-like gloves with a separate stall for the thumb alone, although examples of the full elbow-sleeves occur, even for the "knights," well into the thirteenth century. The mail-hose or

FIG. 32.—"Knights," Eleventh to Twelfth Centuries.

CHAUSSES become fairly common after *c.* 1150, till by *c.* 1190 they are general. These are braced up by a strap connecting with the breech-girdle beneath the hauberk. Two varieties occur :

(*a*) A shaped strip of mail laced behind the leg and under the sole, a form in vogue till *c.* 1280 [Fig. 32, C].

(*b*) From the close of the twelfth century onward they are shaped like the contemporary civilian HOSE with feet.[2]

[1] Till the thirteenth century, archers, as a rule, are without defensive armour.

[2] In the Bayeux Tapestry and the thirteenth-century Douce MS. Apocalypse Bodleian, Oxford) are shown footless mail leggings worn with leather shoes.

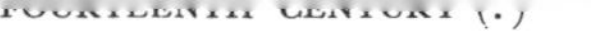

i. PART OF A PIECE OF MAIL

Penes F. H. Cripps-Day.

ii. THE GUARDS AT THE SEPULCHRE. (CAPITAL IN THE CHURCH AT ST. NECTAIRE.)

FROM SILVER SHRINE OF CHARLEMAGNE

Cathedral, Aachen.

The "Phrygian-cap" helm of the pre-Conquest form—*i.e.* with horn-like crown curving forward—continues in use till the last decade of the twelfth century; but from *c.* 1150 the tendency is to a round-topped or ovoid crown. How early the cylindrical, flat-topped crown and the mask-like face-guard perforated with SIGHTS and VENTS (apertures for vision and breathing) first appeared *in England* is difficult to determine with accuracy, but both occur on the second seal of Cœur-de-Lion (1198 or earlier), and were probably introduced at least as early as the Third Crusade [1]; they grow general after 1200. The seal already

FIG. 33.—The *coif-de-mailles*, with its *ventaille* buckled (B) or laced (C) into position and (D) loosened for comfort.

shows us a fan-like crest (our earliest pictured instance) on a helm *enclosing* the head, features unique at this date. Till after 1210–1215, the face-guard is affixed to a plain flat iron cap, reaching down over the temples only. (See vignette on title-page from seal of Gerard de St. Aubert, 1199, also Plate XXII. F, G.) After that date evolves the completest head-piece hitherto known [Plates XXIII. i and iv, XXIV. iii, A]. Such

[1] A confirmation by Richard I. in 1198 of a grant earlier bestowed upon one Alan Basset is made over his second seal, expressly because the first royal seal had been "*in aliena potestate dum capti essemus.*" Richard, captured in 1192 and ransomed in 1194, was then re-crowned at Winchester, which was doubtless the occasion when this second seal was struck. The flat-topped helm with face-guard likely enough appeared in the Third Crusade, since it figures on French, Flemish, and German seals dating from 1192–1199.

helms, presumably padded inside, were worn over the *coif-de-mailles*, itself drawn up over a padded and quilted ARMING COIF [Plate XXII. C]. At times the outline of the mail over the head [cf. Fig. 33, D] suggests that this under-cap was of the nature of certain hitherto unexplained head-pieces, seen in the Wells and Temple Church sculptures [Plate XXIII. ii]. These appear to be close-fitting hoods or caps of leather or padded work, reinforced about the temples with a slightly projecting roll, often leaving little more than the eyes, nose, and mouth uncovered—not always

FIG. 34.—A shows the *chapel* with strings for attachment ; B, padded arming coif ; C, gamboised cuishes ; D, schynbaldes.

even the latter. Such details are rarely in evidence in contemporary art, yet common sense seems to suggest they must have been far more general than this would tend to show. Were mail worn *immediately* over chin and cheeks, not only would it bruise them unbearably, but every blow or thrust would be liable to shatter the underlying bones.

Let us sum up, then, the armour of the close of the twelfth century, since in all essentials it remained unchanged from *c.* 1190 to 1260 [Plates XXII.–XXIV.]. It consists of the hauberk, with coif, sleeves, and gloves attached, all in one, and CHAUSSES.[1] The sleeves, CHAUSSES, and COIF

[1] We have arbitrarily applied the French form *chausses* (=hose) to leggings *of mail*, as opposed to civilian hose.

mould limbs and head pretty closely. All these are—among the better class warriors—generally of mail. The term "HELM" from now on designates the cylindrical closed head-piece and its later derivatives. Round or ovoid head-pieces also occur, and presently closer-fitting steel-caps (BASCINETS) are worn under the cumbrous helm. Another form of head-piece (CHAPEL DE FER) is a close kinsman of the modern "tin hat," and this, with variants, continues in use till after 1500 [Plate XXIV.; Figs. 34, 36].

The kite-shaped shield lasts till well-nigh 1200; but, from about 1180, the arched upper edge is increasingly flattened down, at first with rounded corners, but eventually becomes an elongated, reversed triangle about the last years of the century (although the rounded basal angles are found till *c.* 1220–1230). From that date it is superseded by the flat-iron or "heater" contour. The shields down to *c.* 1180 are of great length (sometimes reaching down from shoulder to foot); later of large dimensions, but rarely extending much below the wearer's knee.

ARMING

The method of putting on and adjusting the armour is worth noting, if one would understand the real nature of the equipment. Both the art and literature of the period need to be carefully sifted, and the evidence of both, where possible, confronted for this purpose; such evidence being casual and widely scattered. After the various under-garments (*vide infra*) had been adjusted, the hose were either laced on (see above) or drawn on like waders, being then attached by thongs or suspenders to the breech-girdle; the hauberk was then pulled on over the head. Out of action the COIF-DE-MAILLES was allowed to fall back on the shoulders [Plate XXII. B, E], while the fingerless gloves dangled loosely from the wrists, being slit up the palms to allow of this. But in battle the COIF DE MAILLES and gloves were drawn over head and hands, and secured about the temples and wrists respectively by laces or straps. One side of the hood formed a loose mail lappet (VENTAILLE [1]), which in action was wrapped across throat and chin and laced, tied, or buckled to the hood over the opposite temple; when undone it left chin and throat exposed; occasionally, too, the face-opening was tightened by a running lace. Similarly the chausses were gartered or laced below the knee to minimize the drag of the mail over the patella [Plate XXII. D]. Only a careful scrutiny of numerous effigies, etc., will reveal such details, too often omitted as insignificant by the ancient artists. Indeed, miniatures—and, still more, seals—are generally too small or too summary in treatment to allow of their representation. This is especially so previous to mid-thirteenth century.

[1] I have used this French term here of the lappet of the *coif-de-mailles*, restricting the old English form AVENTAIL to the so-called "camail" of the fourteenth-century bascinet.

MILITARY UNDERWEAR

Exactly at what date defensive underclothing, as apart from the indispensable " breke and eke a sherte," came into use is difficult to determine. Obviously something stronger than the ordinary tunic and hose would be needed to counteract the shock transmitted from mail to body. Between the hauberk and tunic was certainly (and probably from a very early date) interposed a padded and quilted jacket (GAMBESON, or ACKTON). No doubt extra stout hose were worn under the mail chausses, and, though contemporary art seldom betrays these intimate details, the literary evidence reveals not a little. Thus we find reference to collars of stout stuff (padded ?), wadded shoulder-caps, and (apparently) defences (whose nature is not specified) for knee-cap and shin. The GAMBESON (or ACKTON) is discernible from a fairly early date. We also hear of a leathern body-garment known as a CUIRIE, which may have been of CUIRBOULY (an exceedingly tough preparation of boiled leather), which seems fairly early to have been, in part at least, reinforced with plates of metal. There is evidence that prior to 1189 plates of tempered steel were worn *under* the hauberk, and what looks like a CUIRASS of sorts, of leather or steel, buckled together at the side, appears *over* the hauberk in effigies apparently not later than 1260–1280.[1] Gamboised sheaths (CUISHES) for the thigh appear about the middle of the thirteenth century (apparently pulled on over or independent of the mail chausses) [Plate VI. ii, B], and very soon are reinforced with knee-cops (POLEYNS) of iron and/or cuirbouly.

SURCOAT

Although the Winchester Bible (*c.* 1170) shows us sleeveless gowns or frocks worn over the body-armour, this appears to be altogether exceptional, and not till *c.* 1210 do these outer coverings of textile stuffs occur in art with any frequency. I am inclined to think heraldry to have been the real incentive to these outer garments. The older school thought the surcoat was introduced to mitigate the heat of the eastern sun striking on the armour of the Crusaders. This is now discredited, and it is suggested (on the strength of a passage :

" Gay gowns of grene
To keep their armor clene
And were hit from the wette ")

that the purpose was to act as a sort of primitive mackintosh. A moment's consideration of mediæval effigies, etc., should suffice to negative this suggestion. The early surcoats—even if we suppose them in some sense waterproofed, for example by painting, oiling, or waxing—are so widely open at neck and sides as to give rain, snow, or mist free access to the

[1] Cf. *Pre-Gothic cuirasses of plate* (APOLLO, July 1930, pp. 37–43).

c. 1240

i. WEST FRONT, WELLS CATHEDRAL, *c.* 1230.

c. 1240

ii. LEATHER UNDERCAP, *c.* 1240

iv. HELM

c. 1250

iii. KNIGHT IN MAIL FROM TEMPLE

i, ii, iv. WEST FRONT, WELLS CATHEDRAL
iii. TEMPLE CHURCH EFFIGY

i.

ii. A B C

iii. A B

ROMANCE OF ALEXANDER

i. and iii. from Romance of Alexander MS., O. 9. 34, c. 1250, ii. from Medical MS., O. 1. 20. All in Trin. Coll. Camb. Liby.

[Note latticed, quilted CUISHES of iii. A; the latticed design perhaps indicates a reinforcement of crossed straps.]

mail of back, breast, and flanks, while leaving head and limbs entirely exposed. The use of the surcoat is roughly coeval with the rise of heraldry.[1]

The lance shows no essential change in form, but the manner of handling it alters early in the twelfth century. In the Bayeux Tapestry many knights still wield it (as in earlier days) freely at arm's length, as the desert Arabs yet do wield it ; but by *c.* 1130 at latest the importance of couching the lance under the oxter, bending well forward in the saddle and galloping full tilt at the foeman—in fact, making warrior, steed, and lance a combined shock-unit—was universally realized. The javelin, though not discarded, fell into the background. The sword underwent no essential change except that the branches (QUILLONS) of the cross-guard from *c.* 1110 showed a growing tendency to curve inwards towards the blade, the blade to taper, and the PUMMEL sometimes took a mushroom or " Brazil-nut " shape. From 1066 to *c.* 1160 the sheathed sword was usually attached to a girdle *under* the hauberk. The mouth of the scabbard protruded through a slit on the left hip of the hauberk [Plate xx. ; also Bayeux Tapestry, Brit. Mus., Cotton Nero, C. iv.].[2] From *c.* 1170 the sheath was attached to a diagonal sword-belt connected with a waist-belt, worn outside the hauberk.

The cross-bow was in pretty common use as early as the First Crusade (1096–1097), and though prohibited as " hateful to God " by Innocent II. in 1139, received a fresh lease of favour under Richard I. (who died by one), and grew in favour thenceforth, without ever in England seriously challenging the vogue of the long-bow.

[*Note.*—Early in the twelfth century we meet with occasional *impressionistic* attempts better to represent the texture of mail than by a powdering of circles, cross-hatching, and the like crude conventions. By the last quarter of the twelfth century these are general and fairly ingenious, and become perfected in the course of the thirteenth century.]

i. "*Mixed*" *Armour*

(EARLY PERIOD, 1250–1350)

From 1250 to *c.* 1310 there is little if any change apparent in the *general* outline of the armed knight. The CUISHES of GAMBOISERIE (quilted and padded work) are generally visible, usually reinforced by POLEYNS (knee-cops) of iron or *cuirbouly*, and, the hauberk being presently shortened to mid-thigh, we frequently get a glimpse of the GAMBESON or ACKTON (generally quilted vertically as are the cuishes) peeping out from below it. The closed, flat-topped HELM remains the chief knightly head-piece. It would appear to have been secured on the head by thongs or laces. Between 1280–1290 it is prolonged to rest on

[1] Down to *c.* 1320 the surcoat is loose and hangs in folds to below the calf. It is slit up to the fork fore and aft for convenience in the saddle.

[2] The idea obviously was to protect the belt from being severed ; equally obviously this method was soon felt to be more a hindrance than a help.

the shoulders, projecting some way down over the breast, the top being either rounded, or more commonly tapering from the SIGHTS upwards to a sugar-loaf crown [Fig. 36, A, B]. The tapering is most marked in front. Some knights, presumably fearing danger less than discomfort, fought armed only in a lighter steel skull-cap (BASCINET) or a CHAPEL [Fig. 36, C], or even contented themselves with the coif of their hauberk, to which Matthew Paris shows a kind of iron mask (perforated for sight and breath) affixed to cover the face. Others—and this is particularly true of the whole fourteenth century—wore the HELM over the BASCINET. From old French romances it seems clear that attempts to adapt some kind of movable visor to the BASCINET itself were being made as early as the close of the thirteenth century, thereby affording as much protection as the great HELM, without its cumbrousness. But the latter held its own in the battlefield till the introduction, about the last quarter of the fourteenth century, of the HOUNSKULL or "pig-faced" bascinet [Plates XXVIII., XXIX. ii] relegated it to the tilt-yard.[1] By the close of the thirteenth century the helm was secured to the wearer's girdle by a chain, which soon after *c.* 1310 was attached to a circular plate or rosette on the breast, probably affixed to a concealed BREAST-PLATE beneath the surcoat, and similar BREAST-CHAINS were attached to the pummel of sword and dagger, the object in all three cases being to prevent helm or weapons being dropped or lost in the mêlée. When not in immediate action, the helm was carried at the saddle-bow, or slung over the shoulder.

C. 1330

Gresford.

FIG. 35.

From the latter part of the thirteenth century the hood of mail was divorced from the hauberk, and lost its movable flap or ventaille. Early in the fourteenth century the mail-hood was increasingly replaced by the AVENTAIL, a curtain or tippet of mail, laced to the edge of the bascinet, to protect neck and chin.

There is evidence in contemporary romances that, besides metal

[1] Actually to jousts and tournaments. The earliest actual *tilt* appears to date 1429, in Burgundy. In it the jousters rode along an intervening barrier.

POLEYNS, greaves or shin-guards (BAINBERGS, SCHYNBALDES) were worn directly over the mail chausses as early as the thirteenth century, but their actual appearance in effigies, brasses, etc., seems hardly earlier than *c.* 1315; though isolated examples may be found in MSS. as early as *c.* 1260 [Fig. 34]. They become common in effigies, brasses, etc., between 1320 and 1330 [Plate XXV. A and C]. *Closed* GREAVES are mentioned in France as early as 1302, and appear on the monument of William de Valence, 1323, in Westminster Abbey. By the middle of the century they are general. The so-called BANDED MAIL appears in art *c.* 1270–1280, and is found up to *c.* 1370–1380.[1] About the same time appear those curious shoulder-guards known as AILETTES, which are seen down to *c.* 1340 [Fig. 36, C].

Towards 1320 appear gutter-shaped plates of metal protecting the outside of the upper arm (RERE-BRACES), and upper side of forearm (VAMBRACES), and metal caps covering shoulder and elbow, the bend of

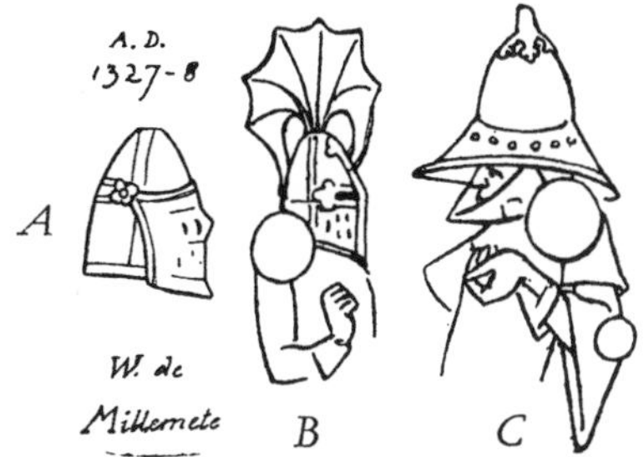

FIG. 36.—A and B, Helms (B, crested); C, Chapel and Beaver.

the arm being guarded by a circular metal plate, and the armpit similarly [Plate XXV.]. At the same time, to the schynbalde was adjoined a defensive vamp or shoe, of articulated LAMES, known as a SABATON. Sometimes, about the same date, the sleeves of the "banded" hauberk end at the elbow, and from beneath them projects a VAMBRACE of ALWITE (*vide infra*, p. 62 *note*) or scales, *enclosing* the forearm; vambraces of scales also appear. From the beginning of the fourteenth century, if not earlier, the contemporary inventories mention PLATES or PAIRS OF PLATES, as armour for the trunk, apparently in this case meaning small, rectangular, overlapping plates of metal riveted to a foundation, or (more commonly, till the middle of the century) *covered* with leather or canvas, in some cases faced with velvet, silk, etc.; in fact, analogous to what later was known as a BRIGANDINE.[2] By the last years of this period (*i.e.* towards 1350) the limbs are already fully encased in steel.

Down to 1310–1320, the knightly surcoat hangs in loose folds to the calf of the leg, is slit fore and aft almost to the fork, and open from the

[1] Various suggestions have been made as to its structure. If it represents anything more than ordinary mail, the late J. G. Waller's suggestion seems the only one that will hold water, namely, that it represents mail reinforced by thongs threaded through alternate rows of rings.

[2] See BUTTIN: *Guet*, pp. 17–46.

shoulder to the hip on either side [Plate XXV. A]. Subsequently it is cut short in front, level with the hips, and often made to lace or button at the sides, the hind-skirt retaining its old length, a form found in the second quarter of the century [Fig. 37].[1] About the 'forties comes in a form laced or buttoned tight to the trunk in front, at sides or behind,

FIG. 37.

as far as the waist, with a full-draped skirt, slit laterally or fore-and-aft, and reaching to within a few inches of the knee.

We have alluded (p. 57) to the defences of PLATES (or BRIGANDINE-work) already worn between surcoat and mail. About the 'forties (although possibly introduced earlier and concealed by the long haber-

[1] There seems no particular reason for calling this form a " cyclas."

A. SIR WM. FITZRALPH, *c.* 1320, PEBMARSH, ESSEX.

B. SIR HUGH HASTINGS, 1347, ELSING, NORFOLK

C. SIR JOHN D'AUBERNON, JUN., 1327, STOKE DABERNON, SURREY

BRASSES

[NOTE.—C shows so-called "banded" mail.]

i. THE FALL OF PRIDE ("HAUBERK OF PLATE")

From Sub-Dean's stall, Lincoln Cathedral (choir).

ii. MINIATURE FROM POEMS OF CHRISTINE DE PISAN, *c.* 1415

Brit. Mus., Harl. 4431 *fo.*

[NOTE.—The two bascinets and aventails (a and b) in the second figure are lined throughout with quilted red silk.]

geon and gambeson), we first become aware of studded CUISHES, presumably of leather [Plate XXV. B]; which studded design may quite possibly indicate underlying plates. It is at first but a glimpse of them that we perceive above the leather-and-metal POLEYNS. Combined with vertical bands of metal (iron, steel, or LATTEN), these studs over leather are common defences of the legs and arms (*c.* 1350–1380). GAUNTLETS—as distinguished from mail or scaled gloves or MUFFLERS—begin to develop from *c.* 1320. At first they are varied and individual (evolutionary) tentatives on the road to the fully developed gauntlet. The BASCINET, with laced-on, interlinked AVENTAIL, develops from *c.* 1320 [Plates XXV. B, C, etc.]. Generally it is visorless, being worn in action under the great HELM, though as early as *c.* 1347 [Plate XXV. B] at least attempts at movable visors are found; *c.* 1300–1330 helms, too, with movable (pivoted) face-guards appear [Fig. 36, A], but seem to have had but brief success. From the last quarter of the thirteenth century the great shield—which in use reached from wearer's mouth to knee—shrank to a more marked heater-shape of reduced proportions, and could be moved more readily to ward off a blow [Plate XXV.; Fig. 35].

At this point it may be well to call a halt and summarize the equipment of the "knight," as it had developed by the middle of the fourteenth century. And be it noted, as M. Buttin has very pertinently pointed out, that this is pre-eminently the period of "superimposition"; *i.e.* of defensive armour accumulated in layers, one over the other.

The knight, then, having donned hose and close gipon of some strong material, proceeded to the arming of the legs. Chausses of mail were still, and indeed up to close on 1370, in wear. Over these were drawn close-fitting gamboised CUISHES, generally reinforced at the knees with POLEYNS of CUIRBOULY, iron or LATTEN, or of a combination of these. By the close of the period these cuishes (of leather) are sometimes shown as studded, which seems to indicate BRIGANDINE-work. The shins are generally reinforced from *c.* 1320 by SCHYNBALDES of CUIRBOULY or solid metal, prolonged into laminated SABATONS [1] to cover the feet. Even as early as the 'twenties, we occasionally find close greaves *enclosing* the limb from the knee down. Over these were strapped the rowelled spurs. Next the warrior donned his padded ACKETON, generally quilted in vertical lines, as commonly were the cuishes [Plate XXV. A]—these latter at the beginning of the century were sometimes covered with brocade or embroidery. Then came the HAUBERGEON of mail. This probably had, as a rule, a more or less high collar (STANDARD) of mail (the old continuous COIF was out of vogue). It reached just below the hips; the sleeves were either close-fitting to the wrist, or reached a little down the forearm. In the former case REREBRACES of ALWITE or CUIRBOULY protected the outside of the upper arm, and similar VAMBRACES the forearm; the shoulder and the bend of the arm being partially guarded by

[1] The date of the earliest references in English to SABATONS negatives the theory that it applies specially to the broad-toed variety (unknown till end of fifteenth century). SOLERET in English is rare and late.

plates of metal in the form of discs, lion's heads, etc.[1] Beneath the shorter mail-sleeves the forearm was encased in a *closed* vambrace of metal [Plate xxv. c], or merely by the sleeve of the acketon. From *c.* 1280–1340 we also find AILETTES used to protect (?) the shoulders. The HAUBERGEON of this period often hangs down in a point in front. Over the haubergeon was worn the HAUBERK, a term now commonly transferred to a defence of riveted PLATES, probably even by this date equipped with a larger rectangular or elliptical PLASTRON over the breast, to which were affixed the suspensory BREAST-CHAINS (*vide supra*, p. 56). Over all the knight laced or buttoned his armorial SURCOAT or GIPON, sometimes padded or GAMBOISED, and usually ensigned with his armorial bearings. This was generally perforated on the breast to let pass the aforesaid breast-chains, by which helm, sword, and dagger (and sometimes scabbard, or mace) were attached to avoid their loss in the mêlée. The BASCINET, with its AVENTAIL affixed, was next put on. The knight was then fully equipped, with the exception of the HELM (worn till nearly the close of the century *over* the bascinet), the gauntlets (from now on independent of the hauberk), and the shield. These were only donned at the last moment when actually moving into action. Till then the gauntlets were hung (by loops) from the sword-guard, the helm and shield slung over the shoulder, more rarely at the saddle-bow. The gauntlet-cuffs, of elastic metal, opened at the inner side of the wrist, and could be tightened there by straps and buckles. They were lined with leather gloves. The long, loose surcoat of the thirteenth century had been girt at the waist by a narrow strap or a cord, the sword being independently suspended by a broad diagonal belt. Although the documents give no information on the point, it seems self-evident that such belts must have been securely fixed over the surcoat (presumably behind the right thigh ; otherwise in action they would inevitably have slipped down). For offence the " knight " bore sword, dagger, and lance (which, by this date, begins to develop a definite grip), occasionally a MACE, a MARTEL, and at times also an ESTOC or " foining-sword," used exclusively for thrusting (in fact, a hand-to-hand substitute for the lance) and carried at the saddle-bow, unlike the ordinary (cut and thrust) ARMING SWORD, which was girt to the person.

Whereas the outer body-armour is not infrequently discernible in German effigies, in French and English monuments this rarely happens, owing to the all but universal use of the armorial surcoat. At the most—and even that is exceptional—we get a glimpse of it at the side openings or hem of the surcoat.

The hat-shaped CHAPEL continued in pretty general use. CRESTS were in the main restricted to the great helm [Plate XXVII. ; Fig. 36, B]. Notable are tentative efforts to introduce solid plate gorgets (cf. the eponymous figure and that of Almeric St. Amand in the Hastings brass,

[1] From some of the pictorial and still more the carved " documents," isolated attempts appear to have been made to inlay plates of metal in the mail, instead of buckling them over.

Elsing, Norfolk), which, however, do not seem to have "caught on" for a full half-century later [Plate XXV. B; Fig. 36, C]. From the outline of effigies and brasses alike it would seem that the solid cuirass, sharply cut into the waist, was not in vogue till the ensuing epoch.

The lesser warriors, who formed the bulk of the infantry, were a hetorogeneous crew so far as their armament went. They were unprotected as to the nether limbs, and usually contented themselves with body-defences of leather or quilted work, sometimes partially reinforced with metal, in the form of studs, scales, or portions of mail. Their heads were covered with chapels or skull-caps of metal or leather, reinforced with metal. Hoods and tippets (= capes), of mail or scale-work, were also worn, with or without a helmet. They carried circular convex shields; the BUCKLER, peculiar to the English middle-classes till well-nigh the end of the sixteenth century, appears as early as the thirteenth century. It was a small circular shield, with a single énarme, about the size of a large pot-lid, *wielded at arm's length to parry the enemy's blows.*

These lesser men carried short spears or javelins, long dagger-knives (or short swords), and/or a variety of HAFTED WEAPONS, many of them derived from agricultural implements. The names of many of these have been preserved to us; but, at this early date, it is difficult with confidence to identify such terms with weapons delineated in contemporary art. The pole-axe so effective at Hastings in the hands of Harold's house-carls, remained in vogue and was a favourite weapon subsequently of knights fighting on foot. It was not as yet elaborated, but a mere axe-head set upon a long shaft (reaching, when grounded, to the bearer's shoulder or thereabouts).

OTHER WEAPONS

The FAULCHION, much used in the thirteenth to fourteenth centuries, was a very broad, scimitar-like, single-edged sword, broadening towards the point. Sometimes the edge alone was curved, at others the whole blade had a backward curve. The BATTLE-AXE, too, figured largely in the field. The MACE, with a relatively simple head of metal, was increasingly favoured by knights; a cruder kind, of hard wood garnished with spikes, being used by the foot-soldiers. The Bow, which played so leading a rôle in the rout at Hastings, became steadily more popular, especially after it had been improved on the model of the Welsh bow. It was from the thirteenth century, and remained till well into the sixteenth century, *the* characteristic arm of the English yeoman, who as a long-bowman remained by universal acclaim its supreme exponent. It had by 1300 or earlier attained its typical length of about six feet, the arrow being a "cloth yard" long, and discharged from the ear. *Per contra* the CROSS-BOW, though in use till the sixteenth century, never in England gained the favour of the rank and file, its greater power and range not, in the opinion of our bowmen, atoning for its slow rate of discharge and general cumbrousness. The skilled bowman could loose off his sheaf of arrows while the arbalister was firing a single bolt.

ii. "*Mixed*" *Armour*

(LATE PERIOD, 1350–1400)

i.e. to the full development of ALWITE[1] (Fr. *harnois blanc*)

There is no very marked development obvious in the third quarter of the fourteenth century. The general outline of the figure, however, tends more and more to betray an underlying waisted CUIRASS (*i.e.* back and breast) of solid metal. The BASCINET, which till *c.* 1350 had been low-crowned, rather full about the ears, and with an obtuse or even globular apex, now grows increasingly taller and more pointed [Fig. 39]. It is by no means certain that what appears to be a mere armorial GIPON in monuments, etc., may not in many cases actually represent armour *faced with material.* Probably, too, from the waist downward (there are occasional suggestions of this in certain effigies), the abdomen and loins were, more often than is suspected, protected in a measure by a FAULD (or PAUNCE) of plates or lames; though this is very rarely in evidence till *c.* 1400. The arms and legs from now on are generally guarded by ALWITE. Even by the close of the preceding epoch the POLEYNS had received bilobed or heart-shaped extensions on the outer sides, forming some slight extra guard for the bend of the leg. From now on they begin to be equipped with extra plates above and below, overlying CUISHES and GREAVES. Alternatively they have the leather

FIG. 38.—Brass of Sir Ralph de Knevynton, Aveley, Essex. 1377.

[1] I use this term instead of "plate" armour, to avoid confusion with the defences of overlapping splints (LAMES), rectangular scales, and the like, all in old texts described as "plates." On the other hand, the old English ALWITE, like the French *harnois blanc*, applies specifically to armour composed in the main of large solid plates, only the articulations being guarded by movable lames.

RITTER VON STEINBERG, †1397

Römer Museum, Hildesheim.

[N.B.—The armour procured from Germany by Thomas Mowbray for his abortive duel (1398) with Bolingbroke may have been of this type.]

The trunk is here armed in a velvet-covered BRIGANDINE.

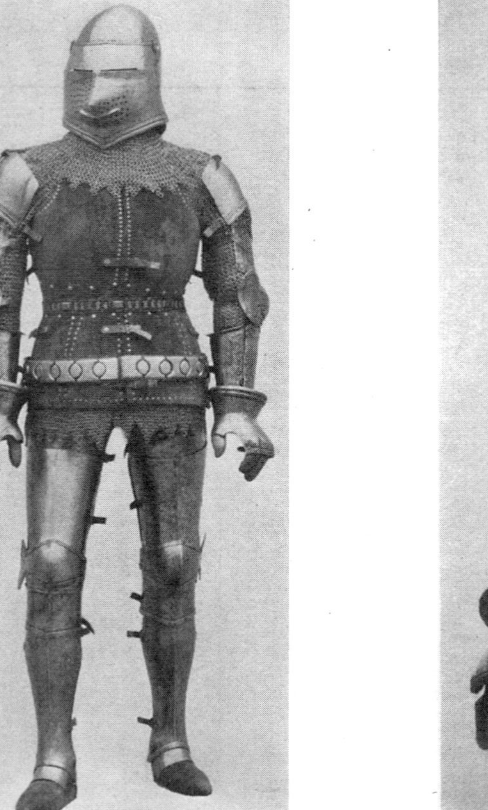

[Note early LANCE-REST projecting from cuirass in front of right armpit; also at top centre of breast-plate the *lisière d'arrêt*, a V-shaped bar riveted there to deflect an upward thrust.]

i. COMPLETE SUIT OF ARMOUR (COMPOSITE). ITALIAN, *c.* 1400.

Metropolitan Museum, New York.

ii. ARMOUR OF A BAILIFF OF MATSCH. (WORK OF THE MISSAGLIAS, MILAN.) *c.* 1390

Schloss Churburg, Tyrol.

[N.B.—These may give some idea of the type of armour furnished by Galeazzo Visconti, Duke of Milan,

FIG. 39.—The Bascinet and Aventail. *a* shows their union by a lace running through staples ; *c*, a primitive Beaver.

lining projecting below the knee in an escalloped, vandyked, or leaf-shaped fringe. From the advent of the shortened, close-bodied surcoats, the waist-belt had been generally discarded, the broad sword-belt retaining its former place in the present period. From about 1360 comes in the *cingulum militare,* as it has been termed, so characteristic a feature of knightly equipment from now on to the middle of the fifteenth century; that broad *hip*-belt of goldsmith's or ornamental metal-work (often enamelled and jewelled), formed from a series of decorative plaquettes, jointed together or mounted on leather [Plates XXVI. i; XXVII.; XXVIII. i; Fig. 40]. From their position, low down upon the hips, these belts must have been hooked or otherwise fixed upon the gipon, and invisibly clasped in front. From them now depend the sword and dagger, vertically upon either hip. As already mentioned (p. 21, *ante*), the upper nobility of both sexes soon adopted this mode when in ceremonial mufti, although they did not retain it so long as the military. The great crested helm continued to be worn over the bascinet in battle till about 1380, after which date it was relegated to the tournament. The bascinet was now regularly worn independently with a visor, of which the HOUNSKULL or so-called "pig-faced" type is most characteristic between *c.* 1380–1420 [1] [Plates XXVIII.; XXIX. ii]. The breast-chains of the preceding generation vanish *c.* 1380. The AILETTES had dropped out *c.* 1330. CUIRBOULY, plain or reinforced with metal, continued in use side by side with steel and LATTEN, all three being used for body and limb defences. In the effigy (*c.* 1380) of John, Lord Montacute—or Montague—(Stothard, pl. 94), the breast (though ensigned with his armorial bearings) has a distinct keel or vertical ridge down the centre, such as we rarely meet with till the breast-plate of the "Gothic" period, and (apparently) laminations at the waist.[2] Latten was not only used by itself to form portions of the harness, but, more especially throughout the fourteenth and fifteenth centuries (if not indeed as early as the thirteenth), for the ornamental borders to the "white" harness [Fig. 40, B]. It seems a gratuitous assumption that the highly ornamental POLEYNS, etc., of the late thirteenth and fourteenth centuries *must* have been of cuirbouly; the metal workers of that age show in other departments of their craft their competence to turn out elaborate decoration, embossed, engraved, inlaid, and enamelled. The Knevynton brass (Aveley, Essex—Fig. 38) shows a "hauberk" of peculiar construction. It is apparently covered with leather or textile stuff, the nature of the underlying metal being indicated by the arrangement of the exposed studs (rivet-heads). The plastron or breast appears to be made of three longitudinal plates, the two outer recalling the heraldic "flanch" or "voider"; the later GUSSET of plate may, perhaps, be regarded as a descendant of this. Below the

[1] There were those who fought bare-faced (*i.e.* in *un*visored bascinets), such as the famous Sir John Chandos. To this habit and to his overlengthy *parement* (surcoat) he owed his death.

[2] Note that Montacute's armorial outer garment, laced down one side, is *hinged* on the other.

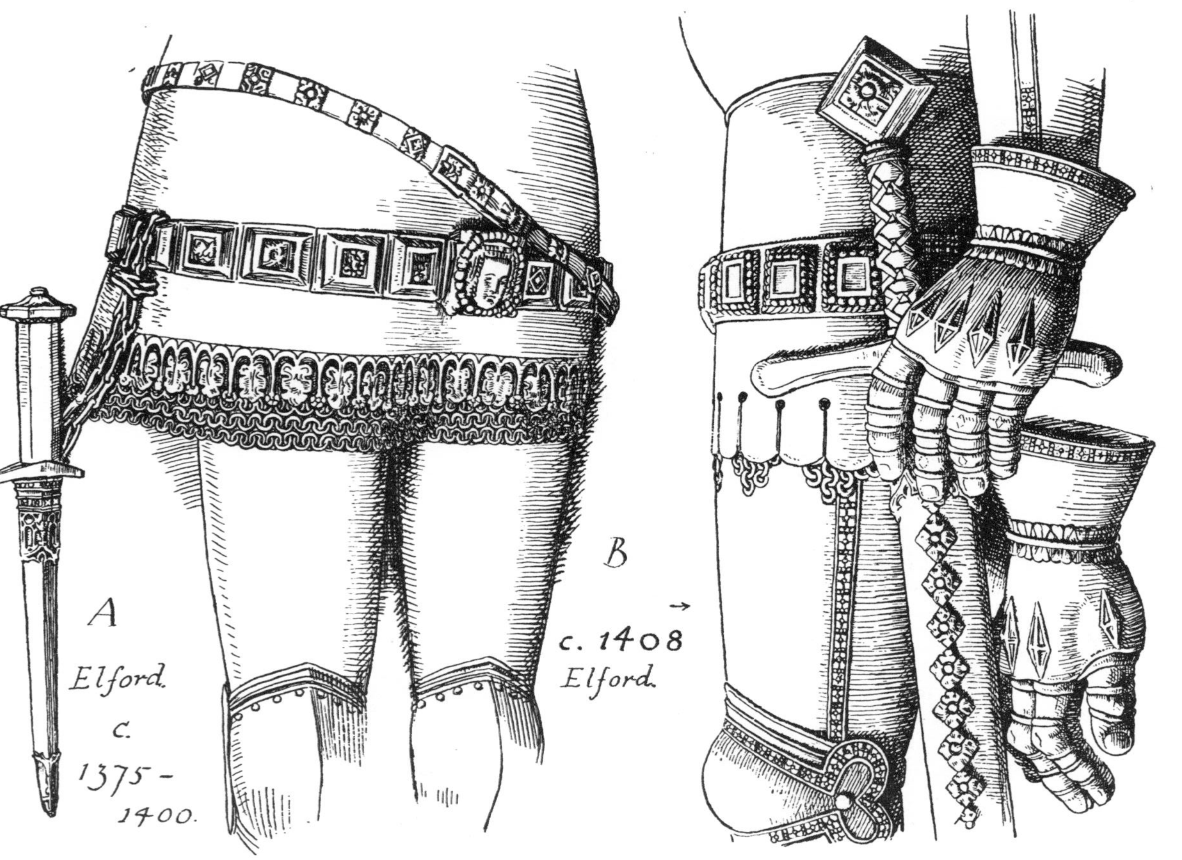

FIG. 40.—Knightly Girdles.

Note in A, attachment of dagger and ornamental fringe of surcoat; in B, the decoration of plates by engraved borders, etc., of latten, and the fine, typical gauntlets.

waist this seems continued by a skirt (FAULD or PAUNCE) of brigandine-work (?). This example is the more noteworthy because a *unique* breastplate covered with velvet preserved in the Bavarian National Museum, Munich, is constructed on very similar lines, though in outline more of Gothic type. (It is there attributed to the early fifteenth century.) Although the sleeved HAUBERGEON persisted in use, there are indications that independent pieces of mail attached to the acketon and hose were beginning to be used, instead of the complete coat of mail, wherever the cuirbouly or " white " harness left the joints exposed : the bend of

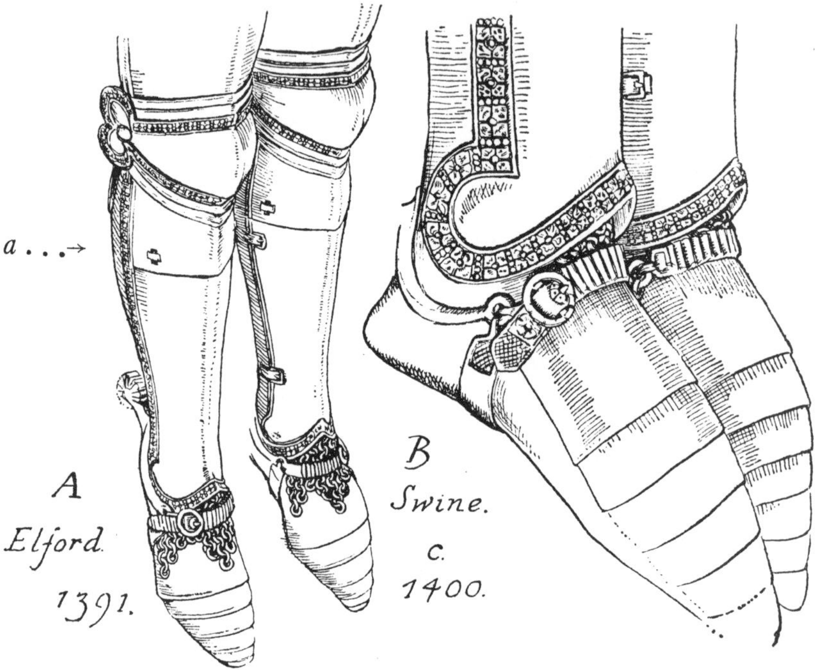

FIG. 41.—Note mail at instep, and attachment of greave to flange of poleyn by sliding rivets at *a*.

the arm, the armpit, the ham, and—this is peculiar to the late fourteenth century—an interval left above the instep between GREAVE and SABATON. A point to be borne in mind is that (except in certain sixteenth-century armours exclusively intended for foot-combats in the lists) the CUISHES *at all periods* leave the back of the thigh exposed, an essential to a proper seat in the saddle, where the rider's position more or less protected that part.[1] The effigy of Sir Guy de Bryan (*c.* 1390) at Tewkesbury (STOTHARD, pl. 96 and 97) is unique in having the legs covered with mail chausses, over which are worn metal poleyns ; a narrow vertical band of metal reinforces the front of the thigh, another the shin, two more the outer

[1] Some slight extra protection to the *outer* side of the thigh was given from *c.* 1360 by a hinged flange or plate.

side of the thigh and leg respectively. These appear to be embedded in or permanently affixed to the mail.

It is in this period that the armourer begins to give earnest of that astonishing mastery of his material and practical adaptation of form to the warrior's needs that distinguished the best products of the fifteenth and early sixteenth century, and still stirs the connoisseur to wonder and enthusiasm. We now first hear of "proof," *i.e.* of submitting armour to severe tests of its capacity to resist the diverse weapons used in the field.[1] We are now well on the way to that technical "sleight of hand" which enables the hammerman to graduate the thickness of the metal according to the importance of the part covered and its relative liability to hurt. Another point, quite apart from the relative thickness and the temper of the material, is the provision of "glancing surfaces," *i.e.* the fashioning of surfaces so as to *deflect* a hostile point or edge. Italy was rapidly becoming the headquarters of the finest armours [cf. Plate XXVIII.]. It is at this period that the famous Missaglia family of armourers at Milan appears. The HOUNSKULLS (bascinets) on Plate XXVIII. are fine examples of the armourer's craft towards 1400. Grotesque as it appears (incidentally, *when the visor is raised*, it is strikingly picturesque), the "pig-face" is an uncommonly efficient defence. The sharp-beaked visor and the high-pointed crown afford an attacking weapon the minimum of purchase, and their mere shape is grim and sinister.

The shield was soon to be largely discarded by the knightly class, as the armourer's craft makes the "white harness" independent of such adventitious aid. Very shortly we shall find the harness in general more strongly made on the left side than on the right, for the mounted men charged each other left side to left side, the lance being aimed *across* the horse's neck. The latest forms of the shield vary considerably from the "heater" shape. It had long been used as a LANCE-REST, and now a deep indent (BOUCHE) in the dexter top corner allowed the lance to be more securely couched.

The close of the fourteenth century witnessed a revival of an old fashion (see *ante*, pp. 8 and 32) in civilian footwear; the inordinate prolongation of the pointed toe. In armour this fashion was not as yet carried to the extremes that sometimes occur in the fully developed "Gothic" armour. Such, at least, is the conclusion suggested by the effigies, etc., of the period. The well-known effigy of the Black Prince at Canterbury displays SABATONS ending in elongated "pikes," but moderate enough compared with those presently worn at Court.

It is to be noted that the DAGGER does not become a regular feature of knightly accoutrement till the middle of the fourteenth century. Where not attached directly to the hip-belt, it was either hooked by the sheath into the body-armour on the right hip or slung from a cord or chain. A very usual form, both in military and civilian circles, was the BALLOK KNIFE (moderns term it a "kidney dagger"),[2] a type that

[1] For the question of armour-proof throughout the ages, see BUTTIN: *Épreuve.*

[2] LAKING: *Record of European Armour.*

persisted till the sixteenth century, and whose modern analogue is the Highland dirk (*skean-dhu*). It is hardly feasible in the space at our disposal to describe in detail the various forms of sword and dagger (the chief differences lying in the shape and decoration of the hilt and blade). A contrivance of German origin in fourteenth-century swords is a double flap of leather (Fr. TASSETTE), set over the junction of the QUILLONS with the GRIP, the object being to prevent rain from entering the sheath. Its place is presently taken by a shield-shaped plate, decorated with heraldic or other motives, fitting over or into the LOCKET of the sheath. The reader anxious for information concerning the development of the sword and dagger will find abundant material in most of the general works quoted in the Bibliography. Lances bearing small pennons, banners, or bannerets occur throughout the century, but lose their vogue in the next epoch. The lance is steadily becoming lengthier and more massive. From the mid-fourteenth century the shaft thickens on either side of the grip. Simultaneously we find the first hint of the LANCE-REST or FEWTER. Curiously enough, this is rarely shown on brasses or effigies.[1]

There is no essential change in the arms and armour of the rank and file.

Pre-Gothic " Alwite " Harness

(1400–1455)

Instances of " alwite " armours, freed from the hitherto almost universal GIPON that conceals them, may be found as early as the last part of the fourteenth century ; from *c.* 1400 they rapidly become general, the armorial surcoat becoming rare and little worn between *c.* 1410 and 1460. A new form of outer covering—the TABARD—replaced the gipon as early as 1424,[2] and is not infrequent between 1460 and the end of the century, but the majority of effigies and brasses of the period show the armour uncovered. The character of this armour is clearly defined on Plate XXIX. Back and breast are each forged of a single shell, and from the waist down the trunk is protected by a series of lames called collectively a FAULD, hinged on one hip and buckled on the other. The front or abdominal portion of this would seem presently to have been known as the PAUNCE, that guarding the loins as the HOGUINE or CULET. The bascinet up to *c.* 1410 retains its pendent AVENTAIL, but is then generally completed by a GORGET or BEAVER of plates guarding the throat and chin, and as yet of rather primitive make [Fig. 39, C] ; a feature indeed incorporated from *c.* 1400 (or perhaps a year or two earlier) in the so-called " GREAT " BASCINET, in which, while the " pig-faced " outline is preserved, the lower portion (corresponding to the old

[1] Early continental examples in the reredos figure of St. George (Dijon) and the brass of Poincenet de Juvigny, 1419, Chalons-s/M.

[2] The gamboised armorial surcoat of the Black Prince († 1376) preserved at Canterbury has short, wide sleeves, and is rather of the tabard family.

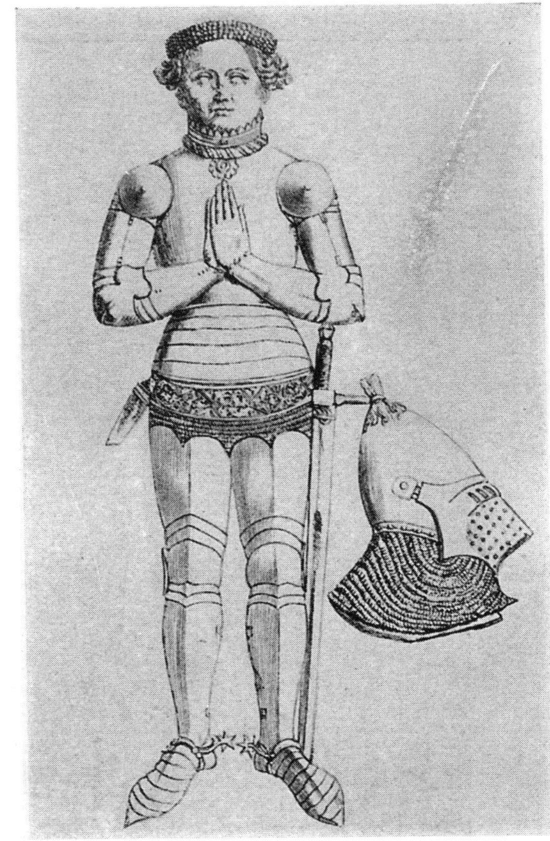

i. BRASS OF JOHN RUGGEWYN, 1412

hounskull.

ii. EFFIGY OF ROBERT DE BOUBERCH, *c.* 1410

Amiens Museum.

[In (i.) note mail collar of haubergeon, independent of aventail; in (ii.) the ornamental plume-socket on apex of hounskull.]

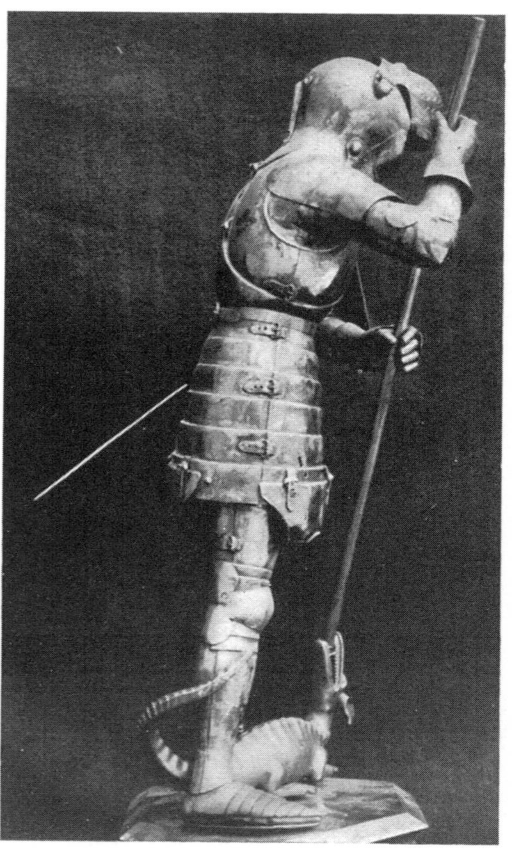

i. ii.

ST. GEORGE (SILVER STATUETTE), *c.* 1435–1445

[Armour for a dismounted man-at-arms.]

Barcelona, Capilla de San Jorge.

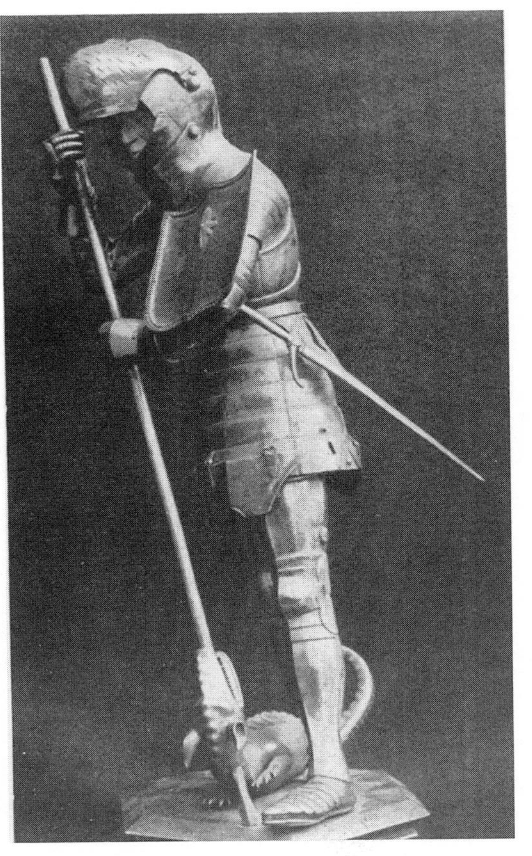

i.

ii.

ST. GEORGE (SILVER STATUETTE), *c.* 1435–1445

Barcelona, Capilla de San Jorge.

i. EFFIGY OF A MARTYN, *c.* 1480

Puddletworth, Dorset.

ii. BRASS OF SIR WM. DE TYRINGHAM, 1484

Tyringham, Bucks

[In the Tyringham brass, the absence of beaver, spurs, and sabatons suggests an infantry leader. The tabard is well shown; but of special interest is the broad-buckled chin-strap of the salet.]

aventail) is of solid metal, wide enough to admit the wearer's head and rest on the shoulders—in fact, it fulfils the functions abdicated by the helm, now reserved for use in the lists. Otherwise the only appearance of mail is at the exposed joints of the harness and in the form of a narrow fringe below the fauld. In all likelihood this latter represents no more than a skirt or kilt of mail attached to the padded leathern undervest (*arming doublet*). The bascinet between 1410–1420 loses its high-peaked apex, becoming more obtuse and rounded—in fact, reminiscent of its forbear of *c.* 1325–1350. The gauntlet is now accurately jointed throughout, and reaches its zenith of perfection by *c.* 1460–1470.[1] Although the hip-belt appears on effigies till *c.* 1455 at least, from the very outset there is a tendency to discard it in favour of a diagonal sword-belt. The defence of the limbs remains as before, the SABATONS often pointed, but not unduly "piked." Mostly the armpit is protected by BESAGEWS, round (or rectangular, or other-shaped) plates attached between breastplate and rerebrace. A novelty about 1410 is the PAULDRON, an independent shoulder-guard overlapping the CUIRASS front and back. With the general adoption *c.* 1430 of this piece, the word rerebrace tends to lapse, the whole arm-guard (including the COUTERE and excluding the PAULDRON) being henceforth dubbed VAMBRACE. By 1430–1440 it is not infrequent to find the breastplate and back-plate of two or more overlapping plates for mobility's sake (these overlap upwards on breast, downwards on back), the edges of the plates at their junction being cut more or less in chevron form. By 1408 one or two small rectangular plates are added at the centre-base of the paunce. These, however, soon proved of little value, and were replaced almost immediately by TASSES, which at first are small rectangular plates [Plates XXX., XXXI.], appended by straps and buckles over either thigh. As early as the 'forties the TASSES become enlarged and assume a vaguely shield-like outline, fluted on the surface and "engrailed" at the edges. About the 'thirties or earlier begin to appear armours having the left-hand pauldrons and couteres more massive than the right, which are less exposed and require more freedom of action in the use of sword, lance, etc. The right pauldron in particular was generally cut away under the arm to allow of the lance being couched in arrest.

The HAUTE-PIECE, that upright ridge to the pauldron so marked a characteristic of "Maximilian" armour,[2] begins to appear towards the middle of the century, but till *c.* 1490 is a simple "rebate" at the pauldron's upper edge, or sometimes a mere ridge embossed out of the plate; later it is a separate plate riveted to the pauldron.

The exaggerated Gothic forms have not yet developed. In the second quarter of the century the "grand" bascinet assumes a globose crown and visor [Plates XXX., XXXI.]. It would seem that by the last years of the period in question "double pieces" (*i.e.* additional reinforcing plates attached by "points" or spring-pins) were in use, and the extra-large

[1] For the evolution of the gauntlet see COSSON: *Gauntlets*.

[2] Meyrick's "passguard."

(left-hand) pauldron and *coutere* appear at times to be of this nature. We also find smaller *tasses* on the flanks and occasionally a broader one strapped to the HOGUINE behind (well shown on the famous Warwick effigy and in Plate XXXI. ii). As alternatives to the bascinet, the CHAPEL is still worn sometimes with a BEAVER or chin-piece of varying height (now covering the chin only, again reaching to below the eyes) ; and now first appears the SALET (see next section), *the* distinctive Gothic head-piece. The couteres and poleyns from *c.* 1440 onward begin to develop flanges of larger size, curving round to afford a measure of protection to the bend of arm and knee. And here a word of warning may be in place regarding the brasses of the second half of the fifteenth century, notably in the 'seventies and 'eighties. These often show PAULDRONS and COUTERES of vast size, such as do *not* appear in paintings, MS. miniatures, or sculptures of the period ; nor are they confirmed by such fragments of actual armour as have survived. The fact is that brasses of this period show a marked falling off in drawing and balance. The whole figure is often entirely out of proportion : puny figures with enormous heads occur, natural proportions are ignored, and the details are rendered with little heed to the constructive essentials of armour. On the other hand, the effigies and other church-carvings of the fifteenth century are wholly free from such freak-forms as a rule.

We meet with the BRIGANDINE by name from *c.* 1420. In principle it had been known from early in the fourteenth century ; it is essentially one with the " plates " covered with velvet, silk, leather, etc., so common in texts of that era.[1] It was a very general form of armour for the rank and file, but the knights also used it extensively on account of its superior flexibility. In their case, as also with certain picked troops attached to particular leaders, the covering materials were velvet, silk, and the like, and the " nails " (rivet-heads) gilt or silvered ; the rank and file wore brigandines covered with leather, fustian, or cloth. They were not infrequently reinforced in the lower part by a PLACARD of " white harness." The knights and heavy-armed cavalry completed them more or less with " alwite " and mail for head, throat, hips, and limbs. On the whole, however, it would seem that the English gentry preferred the cap-à-pie armour of solid steel, as this is universal in brasses and effigies. The Latins—Italy in particular—were more partial to the easy and showy brigandine, reinforced as above mentioned. In the fifteenth century it was sleeveless or with GARBRACES (a variant of the pauldrons) to match, attached by points.

The highly developed cap-à-pie armour of the day made the shield superfluous. It was little used henceforth except on foot. Dismounted knights were commonly armed with POLE-AXES, the knightly lance—though sometimes cut down to half its length for such emergency—being ill-adapted to pedestrian encounters.

[1] Its evolution is worked out to demonstration in BUTTIN : *Guet*, but I am personally disposed to believe the term " plates " also applies to similar defences of *un*covered metal.

The arming of the rank and file consisted of various open head-pieces with tippets (*standards*) of mail, brigandines (sometimes reinforced on either breast with a circular plate of metal), or else quilted jackets (JACKS), generally supplemented in one form or other by mail. Excepting the archers and cross-bowmen, who added a sword to their distinctive weapon, the foot-soldiery wielded one form or another of HAFTED WEAPONS, with a short sword, CURTLE-AXE, or dagger as a last resource, and often a BUCKLER.

" *Gothic* " *Armour*

(1455–1485)

" Gothic " was originally applied in the eighteenth century, as a term of reproach, in the sense of " barbarous," " uncouth," to the master-pieces of the Middle Ages. Why in modern parlance the adjective, now admitted as an honourable name for a well-defined period, should come to be limited to armour of the later fifteenth century is hardly evident. This is undoubtedly the golden age of armour. It combined the utmost practical freedom of action with the minimum of exposure, toughness of material with lightness. The lines, both from the æsthetic and practical standpoint, are perfect of their kind. The graceful flutings and curves are craftily adapted to deflect a hostile thrust ; the ridges prevent such blows glancing off to a vulnerable spot.

The breast of the CUIRASS, commonly of two or more overlapping plates (the lower rising in a point over the upper), now often has the edges of the lower plates " engrailed " or cut out in a decorative pattern, which is repeated *en suite* in the (downward lapping) plates of the back-plate and the principal lames of the harness. It has a faint keel-like ridge down the centre. The finest armours,[1] generally speaking, are of German (Nürnberg) or Milanese origin, and no evidence, so far as I know, remains that our native armourers could equal them. Indeed, we know that as early as the end of the fourteenth century our greater nobles had placed orders for armour abroad. The famous latten effigy of Richard Beauchamp, Earl of Warwick (Beauchamp Chapel, Warwick), is one of the finest plastic renderings of armour in existence (he died in 1439, and the figure was completed in 1454) ; and we cannot doubt that the model is *Italian* (Milanese) from the far-famed Missaglia workshops. The harness of Roberto di Sanseverino (*c.* 1470) at Vienna by Antonio da Missaglia, and Mantegna's (1492) " St. George," in the Accademia, are virtually identical in construction. Effigies showing admirable Gothic armours are common in Germany, the head being generally protected by SALET and BEAVER. A splendid example *c.* 1490 is the upright effigy of Ct. Otto von Henneberg (cast at V. & A. Museum ; woodcut in article, " Arms and Armour," *Ency. Brit.*, 11th ed.). In English monuments the salet is relatively rare (but see Plate XXXII.) ;

[1] The term " *suit* of armour " seems a modernism. The old name in inventories, chronicles, etc., is " *an* armour," or " a harness."

a new form of helmet is about this period introduced from Italy, the ARMET, gradually adopted in the West. It was a round, visored helmet, lighter and more ingenious than the helm or great bascinet, of which latter (in its ultimate form, *c.* 1430–1450) it may be regarded as a development. In its later evolution it is generally described as a CLOSE HELMET. In fact, while the French retained the term ARMET for the visored headpiece of the heavy cavalry in general (to which they also ultimately

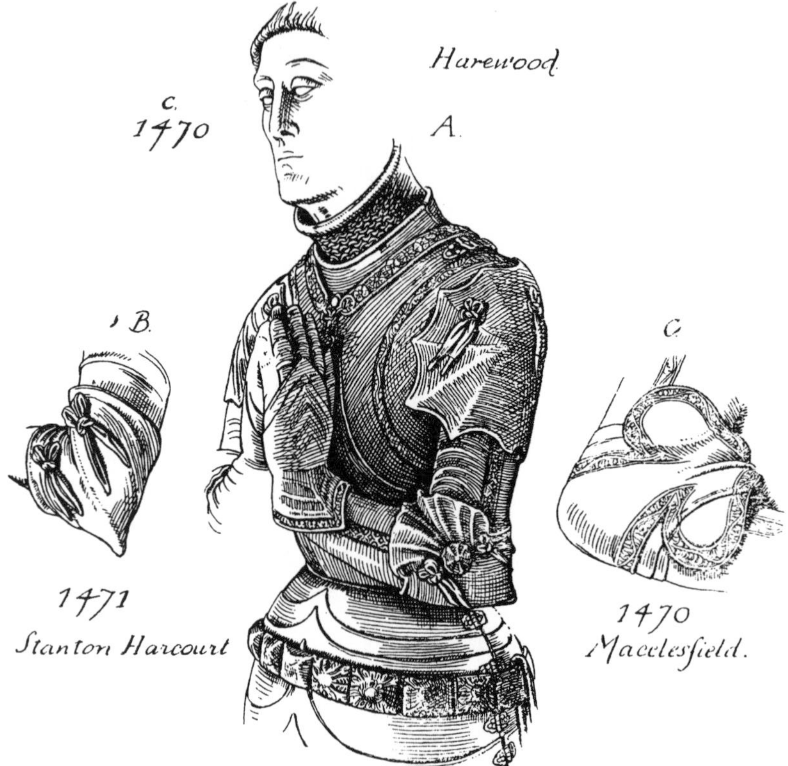

FIG. 42.—Note attachment of (A) pauldrons and (B) couteres by means of knotted *points.*

transferred the name of SALADE), in England the term seems never to have greatly "caught on." [1]

The cuirass of this period was fairly long, and tapered to a narrow waist. In the best German models the BACK-PLATE in particular is often of peculiarly graceful make. Despite the presence of Italian armourers or their handiwork in England and France, the forms mostly favoured by these nations are more akin to the German type. Even at this date it would seem that the English, at least, eschewed the very long

[1] The word "armet" does not seem derived from Italy (unless, perhaps, from *elmetto*). There seems no particular reason for restricting its use to the special form of fifteenth-century close-helmet with which late English writers have identified it.

piked SABATONS common in France and Germany, and in our own *civil* fashions. The TASSES develop in bulk, and are, generally speaking, of elongated, pointed shield-shape, with " engrailed " (*i.e.* forming indented arcs) edges, and radiating flutings. Their individual forms vary considerably. As the tasses develop, the laminated apron or FAULD shrinks upwards. The loin-guard or HOGUINE, at first co-terminous and similar in outline with the fauld, is now independent in construction (see pp. 46, 47). English monuments show individual peculiarities in the form and number of the tasses. Thus in some cases these are buckled, not to the lowest lame of the fauld, but nearly half-way up [Plate XXXII. i ; Fig. 44]. Again, in the effigy of the great Talbot, Earl of Shrewsbury, a series of very large *contiguous* tasses is seen, hanging in front and on the hips.

The use in battle of the armorial TABARD seems to have been optional. In the Warwick Roll (1485–1490) Earl Richard wears it, as does King

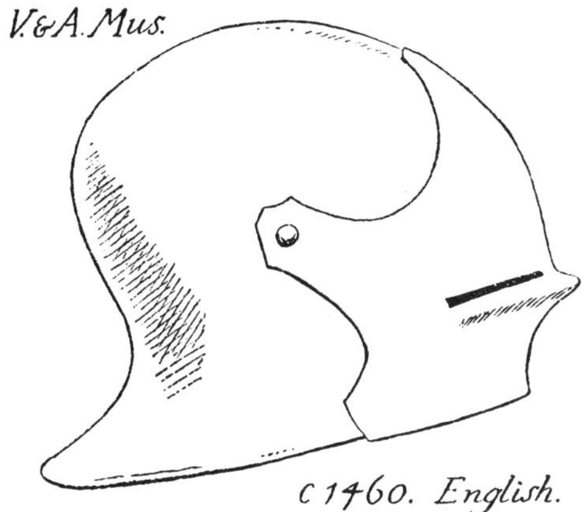

FIG. 43.—Visored salet.

Richard III. On the whole there seems a preference for fighting in one's bare armour, although *c.* 1480 tabards apparently recovered a degree of favour. A fashion, revived from the first thirty years of the fourteenth century, of wearing the sword slung diagonally in front, reappears at this time, but goes out before the end of the century.[1]

There is no particular change to notice in the equipment of the rank and file till towards 1530 (see Vol. II.). In the Gothic period the better-armed infantry had poleyns of metal, with plates added extending some way over thigh and shin. From this century dates the *man-at-arms*[2] or picked heavy cavalryman, armed *cap-à-pie*, as was the " knight " before him. He dates from the institution under Charles VII (1422–1461) of France of a standing (" skeleton ") army (the so-called " *Com-*

[1] Very possibly a mere artistic convention of the brass engraver,

[2] French *homme d'armes* (pl. *gens-d'armes*) ; later *gendarme* (pl. *gendarmes*). The modern *gendarme*, who takes his title hence, is a military policeman (on the cavalry reserve), distinct from the civil police (*agent de police, sergent de ville*), and corresponding to the R.I.C., N.W. Mounted Police, etc.

pagnies d'Ordonnance "). Apparent references to the use of two-handed swords by mounted knights in the fourteenth-fifteenth centuries really apply to BASTARD (or " hand-and-a-half ") SWORDS, which could be wielded *ad lib.* with one or both hands. " Hand-guns " of a primitive sort—a clumsy adaptation of a cannon—with a touch-hole, fired *by hand* with a slow match, were in use by 1446. Cumbrous and uncertain to a degree, they could not compete with the old English long-bow, and it was not till Elizabeth's later days, after a number of radical improvements, that they finally ousted it from popular favour as a military weapon. [*Note.*—The Emperor Maximilian I. (1477–1519) ranked our bowmen as peerless and was anxious to recruit them for his armies.] The HALBERD had by now taken its place in the ranks side by side with the BILL, used by the English infantry from the thirteenth century, and essentially a national and democratic weapon. " Bows and bills ! " was long the cry when riots were afoot. The halberd combined in one long-hafted weapon a short pike, cleaver, and pick-axe ; the bill was a hafted military edition of the hedger's bill-hook.

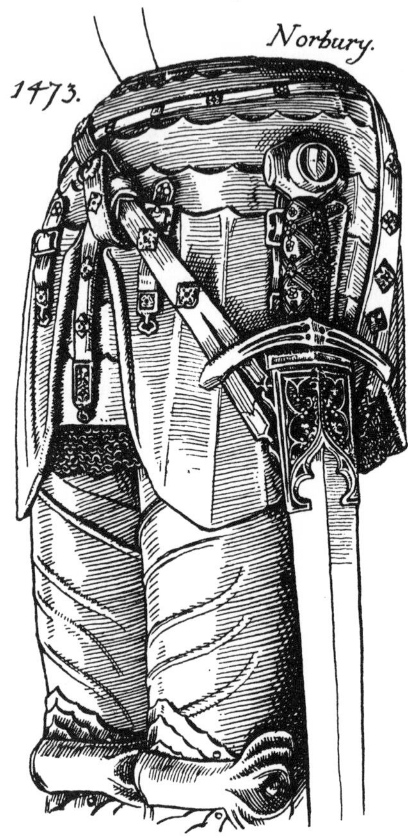

FIG. 44.—Tasses buckled at *mid*-fauld. Note Gothic flutings.

The terminology of so-called " hafted " weapons generally has so far eluded final classification. They are practically all of plebeian origin, adapted from agricultural or other implements of civil life.

Postscript.—For a well-digested account of Italian pre-Gothic and Gothic "white harness," see MANN : *Sanctuary*, etc.

BIBLIOGRAPHY

THE following list nowise aims at completeness ; indeed, many of the works included contain far fuller bibliographies. They are selected as dealing primarily, though by no means exclusively, with the subject-matter of the present volume. Under the sub-headings the books arranged are : (1) English ; (2) French ; (3) German. The square brackets in the right-hand column contain the abbreviated form in which, for convenience, the particular work is referred to in the *main text.* Where only one work of an author is referred to, it will be found cited merely under his name ; where several works by the same writer are quoted, the *title* also will be given in the abbreviated form indicated. Thus Stothard's *Monumental Effigies,* etc., figures simply as Stothard ; while Buttin's *Notes sur les Armures à l'Épreuve* and *Le Guet de Genève et l'Armement de ses Gardes,* etc., are quoted respectively as BUTTIN : *Épreuve* and BUTTIN : *Guet.*

In conjunction with the present work, we would specially commend to the reader :

For English costume in general—
FAIRHOLT, F. W. : *Costume in England* (Dillon's edition, 1896).

For armour—
HEWITT, JOHN : *Ancient Armour and Weapons,* 1859–1861.

Taken all round, these are still by far the best *general* text-books. The illustrations, however, are too often crude and inaccurate, and need supplementing from other sources. (Quoted respectively as FAIRHOLT and HEWITT.)

COSTUME AND GENERAL WORKS

CALTHROP, D. C. : *English Costume.*

LONSDALE AND TARVER : *Illustrations of Mediæval Costume;* 1874. [LONSDALE]

NORRIS, HERBERT : *Costume and Fashion,* ii. "Senlac to Bosworth, 1066–1485." * [NORRIS]

PLANCHÉ, J. R. : *British Costume ;* 1874 [PLANCHÉ]

„ „ *Cyclopædia of Costume ;* 1879.

STRUTT, JOSEPH : *Dress and Habits,* etc. ; 1842.

ENLART, CAMILLE : *Manuel d'Archéologie française,* iii. "Le Costume." [ENLART]

GAY, VICTOR : *Glossaire archéologique,* etc. [GAY]

HARMAND, ADRIEN : *Jeanne d'Arc.** [HARMAND]

JACQUEMIN, RAPHAEL : *Iconographie du Costume* (plates only).

PARMENTIER, A. : *Album historique.*

---

* Includes patterns and suggestions for making up.

PITON, CAMILLE : *Le Costume civil en France.*
QUICHERAT, J. : *Le Costume en France.* (*The* standard history). [QUICHERAT]
RACINET, A. : *Le Costume.**
VIOLLET-LE-DUC, E. : *Dictionnaire raisonné du Mobilier français,** vols. iii., iv. [VIOLLET]

BOEHN, MAX VON : *Die Mode . . . in Mittelalter.*
FALKE, J. VON : *Kostümgeschichte der Kulturvölker.*
HEFNER-ALTENECK, J. VON : *Trachten des christlichen Mittelalters.*
HOTTENROTH, F. : *Handbuch der deutschen Tracht.*
„ „ *Trachten,* etc.
KÖHLER, BRUNO : *Allegemeine Trachtenkunde.*
„ KARL : *Die Trachten der Völker in Bild und Schnitt.**
MASNER, KARL : *Kostümausstellung.**
MÜTZEL, HANS : *Vom Lendenschurz zur Modetracht.* [MÜTZEL]
POST, PAUL : *Studien über die französisch-niederländische Männertracht . . . der Spatgotik.* [POST]
QUINCKE, W. : *Handbuch der Kostümkunde.*
ROSENBERG, C. A. : *Geschichte des Kostüms.*
SCHULTZ, A. : *Das höfische Leben zur Zeit der Minnesinger.*
THIENEN, F. VAN : *Das Kostüm der Blütezeit Hollands, 1600–1660.* [THIENEN]
WEISS, HERMANN : *Kostümkunde.*
Zeitschrift fur historische Waffen-[*und Kostüm-*]*kunde :* Leipzig and Dresden. (*In progress.*) [*Z.H.W.K.*]
Zur Geschichte des Kostüms (in Series "Münchner Bilderbogen").

ARMOUR

CAMP, S. J. : *Catalogue of Arms and Armour in the Wallace Collection.* [CAMP]
COSSON, C. A. DE : "On Gauntlets" (in *Archæol. Journ.,* xli., 1884). [*Gauntlets*]
„ „ and W. BURGES : "Catalogue of Helmets and Mail" (*ibid.,* vol. xxxvii., 1880). [*Helmets*]
DEMMIN, A. : *Arms and Armour* (transl. by C. C. Black).
DILLON, H. A. (Viscount) : "Armour Notes" (in *Archæol. Journ.,*).
FFOULKES, C. C. : *The Armourer and his Craft.* [FFOULKES]
LAKING, G. F. : *Record of European Armour;* 1920–1922. Mainly a sumptuous *catalogue raisonné* of extant "show"-pieces. [LAKING]
MANN, J. G. : "Notes on Armour . . . of the Italian Wars" (*Archæologia,* lxxix. 1929). [MANN]
„ „ *The Sanctuary of the Madonna delle Grazie, with notes . . .* etc. (*ibid.,* lxxx., 1930). [*Sanctuary*]
TRAPP, OSWALD : *Armoury of the Castle of Churburg* (transl., with a Preface, by J. G. Mann). [*Churburg*]
WALLER, J. G. : "The Hauberk of Chain Mail," etc. (*Archæologia,* lxx., 1904). [*Hauberk*]

---

* Includes patterns or suggestions for making up.

BIBLIOGRAPHY

Buttin, Charles : *La Collection Stibbert.* [*Stibbert*]

" " *Le Gisant d'Ulrich de Werdt.* [*Gisant*]

" " *Le Guet de Genève*, etc. [*Guet*]

" " *Notes sur les Armures à l'Épreuve.* [*Epreuve*]

Cosson, C. A. : *Le Cabinet d'Armes . . . de Dino.* [*Cabinet*]

Demay, G. : *Le Costume . . . d'après les Sceaux.* [Demay]

Duyse, Hermann van : *Catalogue de . . . la Porte de Hal* (Introduction).

Viollet-le-Duc : *Dictionnaire raisonné du Mobilier français* (vols. v.–vi.). [Viollet]

Böheim, W. : *Handbuch der Waffenkunde.* [Böheim]

Hefner-Altenck, R. J. von : *Die Waffen.* [Hefner]

Zeitschrift . . . etc. (*vide supra*), p. 76. [*Z.H.W.K.*]

An unusually full bibliography of Armour has been appended by Mr. F. H. Cripps Day to Volume V. of Laking : *Record of European Armour.*

ICONOGRAPHY

UNDER this heading are comprised works, not *primarily* concerned with costume or armour, whose illustrations are none the less invaluable to the student for the wealth of information they afford on these subjects: books on monumental effigies, brasses, illuminated MSS., and the like.

SCULPTURE

CROSSLEY, FRED H.: *English Church Monuments.*

CHANCELLOR, FREDERIC: *Ancient Sepulchral Monuments of Essex.*

GARDNER, ARTHUR: *Alabaster Tombs of Gothic Period* (*Arch. Journ.*, lxxx., 1923).

HARTSHORNE, A.: *Recumbent Monumental Effigies of Northamptonshire.*

HOLLIS, T. and G.: *Monumental Effigies.*

PRIOR, E. S., and ARTHUR GARDINER: *An Account of Mediæval Figure-Sculpture in England.*

STOTHARD, C. A.: *Monumental Effigies of Great Britain.* [STOTHARD]

BRASSES AND ENGRAVED SLABS

BOUTELL, C.: *Monumental Brasses.*

COTMAN, J. S.: *Brasses of Norfolk and Suffolk.*

CREENY, Rev. W. F.: *Incised Slabs on the Continent of Europe.* [*Slabs*]

" " *Monumental Brasses on the Continent of Europe.* [*Brasses*]

HAINES, Rev. H.: *Manual of Brasses.* [HAINES]

WALLER, J. G.: *Monumental Brasses.*

In the matter of illuminated MS. illustrations, sumptuously illustrated volumes of reproductions nowadays appear in profusion every year. We may refer here to:

MILLAR, ERIC: *La miniature anglaise du Xe au XIIIe siècle.* [*Min. angl.*]

" *English Illuminated MSS. of the XIVth and XVth Centuries.* [*English MSS.*]

The Roxburghe Club notably has reproduced a splendid series of mediæval MSS., mostly under the masterly editorship of Dr. M. R. James and Mr. S. J. Cockerell, of which we name in particular *The Treatise of Walter de Millemete; La Estoire de S. Aedward li rei; The Trinity College Apocalypse; The Apocalypse of St. John the Divine; Illustrations to the Book of Genesis; An Old Testament Picture Book; The Pageants of Richard Beauchamp; The Apocalypse in Latin and French.* Dr. James has also contributed valuable papers to the Walpole Society's annuals.

A number of MSS. in the Bibliothèque Nationale, Paris, have been reproduced (H. Omont, editor), also not a few in the Bibliothèque de l'Arsenal, under the direction of M. Henry Martin, who has also produced very ably *inter alia*: *Le Boccace de Jean sans Peur* and *Le Térence des Ducs*. M. le comte P. Durrieu is responsible for sumptuous monographs on the *Très riches Heures du duc de Berri*; the *Grimani Breviary*; the *Quarante Fouquets*; and the *Boccace de Munich*. Of the treasures of the Royal Libraries at Brussels and Munich not a few have been published under the editorship respectively of Father J. van den Gheyn and Dr. E. Leidinger. Of especial value in this department are the publications of the *Société française de réproductions de MSS. à peintures.*

INDEX AND GLOSSARY

Reference to the page is made in ordinary Arabic numerals, to the inset line illustrations in italicized Arabic figures, and to plates in Roman numerals.*

Items of such general character as boots, stockings, cloaks, hairdressing, etc., being duly discussed under their appropriate headings in the text, have been ignored here.

In the interests of the general reader we have endeavoured throughout the book to avoid too lavish a use of technical terminology.

* Where followed by an asterisk (*) the reference is to a *footnote*.

† I have to thank the researches of my erudite friend, Mr. C. R. Beard, for this excellent word (Germ. ***hundsgugel***).

P.S.—A number of omissions may be noted. In the case of armour terms these are generally of *words* to which *modern* writers—notably Meyrick—have lent a spurious currency.

To attempt in every case rigidly to limit the *application* of mediæval terms for costume or armour is apt at times to lead to rather arbitrary decisions, in view of the number and variety of transitional and hybrid forms in use at most periods. Cf. p. x.

A Short History of Costume & Armour

VOLUME II

1485–1800

A GENTLEMAN IN RED

By gracious permission of His Majesty the King. *Hampton Court.*

PREFACE

AT the outset it may not be out of place to refer to certain particularities which the reader may notice in the *letterpress* of this volume :

(*a*) Since all but ten years of the period covered by Part I. (Civilian) coincides with that already treated in our *Historic Costume*, during which our English " Society " borrowed its modes in the main from the Continent—generally from (or *via*) France—the features common to Western civilization at large must perforce be restated here. So far as possible, however, stress has been laid on the distinctly English traits.

(*b*) More obtrusive is the occasional reiteration of statements or definitions, often within a short space. On reflection, it has been decided to let these stand as partly obviating cross-reference in the text.

On the other hand, the great majority of the *illustrations* offer material wholly fresh in reference to costume or armour. For further illustration of civilian modes we may be pardoned for referring readers to the above-mentioned work, which includes a fine selection of typical *English* costume-pictures of the sixteenth to eighteenth centuries.

In Part II. we have repeatedly been indebted for valuable assistance to Messrs. F. H. Cripps-Day, J. G. Mann of the Wallace Collection, and C. R. Beard, whose researches into arms and armour have notably enriched the literature of the subject. It is hoped that our own summary, slight though it be, may prove a useful introduction to a fascinating topic. Our present limits do not allow of controversial matter ; but where—notably in questions of terminology—we appear to be at variance with the accepted text-books, we have rarely committed ourselves without mature consideration of contemporary evidence. On the whole, however, it has been our aim not to confuse the ordinary reader by a plethora of technical terms, often requiring fuller justification than our present limits admit of ; also we have given preference to old English terms and forms wherever possible, e.g. *monnion, sabaton, salet, tasse,* instead of the *espalière, soleret, salade, tasset* of modern " armour jargon," and definitely condemned the Meyrickian *tuiles* and *tuilettes*.[1] The substitution of *Spanish morion* for the more familiar " Cabasset " appears quite justified.

Except as a pastime for leisured pedants, the study (?) of costume has hitherto subserved no more serious end than that of an excuse for fancy dress, or an embellishment of " historic " pageants, stage and film

[1] The current differentiation between " taces " and " tasses " is quite arbitrary : *taces, taches, taisses, tasses* (and Scotch *tasletis*) are synonymous. The form *tasse* is late seventeenth century, Frenchified and rare. On armour-terms, *see* article by C. R. Beard in *The Connoisseur*, Aug. 1928, p. 235, and letter from J. G. Mann, *ibid.*, October 1928, p. 121.

productions, book-illustration, etc. It is gradually being realized that, logically pursued, it forms one of the most valuable criteria we have in dating examples of the art of the past; and even determining their attribution. Many a hoary impostor, long enthroned in general esteem by a succession of " popular " picture-books, would long ago have been relegated to its proper place, had it been confronted with this test.

The subjects on frontispiece and Plate II. are from the Collection of H.M. the King, by whose gracious permission they are reproduced.

For other subjects from private collections we must express our grateful thanks to His Grace The Duke of Buccleuch, Plate XXVIII.; His Grace The Duke of Beaufort, Plate XXX.ii; His Grace The Duke of Devonshire, Plate XI.iii; His Grace The Duke of Sutherland, Plate XXXI.ii; His Grace The Duke of Leeds, Plate XXVIII.ii; The Most Noble The Marquess of Salisbury, Plate IV.; The Right Hon. The Earl of Scarbrough, Plate XXXI.i; The Right Hon. The Earl of Verulam, Plate XII.; The Lord Leconfield, Plates III.ii and XI.ii; The Lady Margaret Douglas, Plate XXII.; Lady Vansittart Neale, Plate VII.; Sir Stephen Lennard, Bart., Plate IX.i; Sir Joseph Tichborne, Bart., Plate XVI.; Daniel H. Farr, Esq., of New York, Plate XXIV.; Harold Hill, Esq., of Newcastle-upon-Tyne, Plate XXX.i; A. J. Nesbitt, Esq., Plate XIII.; C. D. Rotch, Esq., Plate XX.; Archibald G. Russell, Esq., Plate VI.ii; and Lt.-Col. F. T. B. Wingfield Digby, D.S.O., Plate IX.ii.

A number of subjects are also included from the British Museum, the Victoria and Albert Museum, The National Portrait Gallery, Cambridge University Library, Plate Xii; Kunstgewerbemuseum, Berlin, Plate XV.; and Kunsthistorisches Museum, Vienna, Plates VIII. and XXIX.iii. We should like to record our indebtedness to the authorities of these institutions.

We must acknowledge the helpful co-operation of Messrs. Christie, Manson & Woods, Plate XXXII.; Messrs. P. D. Colnaghi & Co., Plate V.i; The Editor of *The Connoisseur*, Plates VII. and XX.; Edward Hudson, Esq., of *Country Life*, Plates VI.i and XI.i; The King's Galleries, Chelsea, Plate XVII.; Messrs. Spink & Sons Ltd., Plates X.i and XIII.; Sir Emery Walker, Plates III.i and X.iii; G. D. Hobson, Esq., M.V.O., of Messrs. Sotheby, Wilkinson & Hodge, Plate XXXV.; and to the Rev. F. Sumner and F. H. Crossley, Esq., for permission to include subjects from their valuable collections of photographs.

The remainder of the illustrations are reproduced from the authors' and publishers' collections.

To B. T. Batsford, Ltd. (in particular to Mr. Harry Batsford and to Mr. Lucarotti), it is a pleasant duty for their loyal aid once more to record the thanks of

F. M. K.
R. S.

Note.—Though in the main the illustrations have been selected from native sources, we have not scrupled here and there, where the result seemed to justify it, to include foreign material.

CONTENTS

ERRATA

Vol. II. page v (footnote)—

Line 1. "... between 'taces' and 'tasses' ..." *should read* "... between 'taces' and 'tassets' ..."

Lines 2–3. "The form *tasse* is late seventeenth century, ..." *should read* "The form *tasset* is late (seventeenth century), ..."

Plate XXXI.ii. The original of this picture is now in the possession of Messrs. Thos. Agnew & Sons, to whom thanks are due for its reproduction in this volume.

Page 80, line 27. "*separate* plate riveted to ..." *should read* "*separate* (detachable) plate to ..."

GENERAL NOTE

WHEN, with the fall of Richard III. at Bosworth Field, in 1485, the Feudal System in England got its death-stroke, the ground was sown for a new development in the minor arts of life. Only the death-grapple of York and Lancaster forbade our nation earlier leisure to assimilate "Humanism" and its concomitant Italian culture. France under Louis XI., Burgundy under Charles the Bold, had already, despite their intestinal quarrels, apprehended this tendency, and with the inception (1494–1495) of the Franco-Imperial struggles in Italy, the influence began rapidly to percolate westward. The civilian dress of the male section of the *grand monde* towards 1500 began to reflect the modes of Northern Italy. In essentials the great Italian nobles, as depicted in the works of Marco Marziale, Carpaccio, etc., might pass for English courtiers of the dawn of the sixteenth century.[1] Our ladies, by the way, remained largely unaffected by the example of the Italians. They but develop the old Franco-Burgundian tradition, shorn of some of its Gothic eccentricities. A certain austerity of outline (especially as regards the head) has earned their costume the generic term of "conventual." Soon the increasing importance of the Hansa merchants in England, the political importance of the Empire, and (finally) the Reformation upheaval tend to propagate in the West the German-Swiss modes (*c.* 1510–1545). As in the preceding era, squareness and fullness characterize this age; but puffs and *slashes*, applied rather wholesale, are peculiarly identified with the period. The Italianate tradition lingers on, however, into the 'twenties, and towards the 'forties we can see the approaching influence of Spain. The latter develops unmistakably between 1545–1555. Spain, mistress of the gold of the New World, the avowed champion everywhere of the Catholic Church, allied through her rulers with the Empire, loomed huge in the world's imagination. Like the French and *via* France, throughout this "Spanish" cycle, we borrowed fashions from the most diverse sources; not a civilized nation but we plagiarized. None the less, down from *c.* 1550 to 1620 the pervading Iberic element is plain to read in costume. By that date it was evident that Spain had shot her bolt. Between 1620 and 1633 gradually develops perhaps the most graceful costume, male and female, evolved since the Middle Ages. The Thirty Years War was responsible for many of its features, seen in embryo (in the early seventeenth century)

[1] In fact, in Carpaccio's great "St. Ursula" series (Venice), *c.* 1495, the "King of Britain," whether by accident or design, might in person and attire pass for Henry VII. himself.

in the Low Countries. The Germans have tried to claim these most elegant modes as of native invention, forgetting that the typical German beau of 1625–1635 was universally derided by his own countrymen as a " Mosje alla modo " (*Monsieur à la mode*). The fact is that the French adapted and embellished this type of dress for civilian wear, and their patterns were accepted very promptly both in the Low Countries and in England. This " Cavalier " style is popularly associated with Van Dyck. During his highly successful career in England (1632–1641) he had the good fortune to be contemporary with it, and to die at the moment when the first signs of deterioration in taste were creeping in. Between 1640–1655, the " Cavalier " style loses nearly all its careless grace, but France still leads the way as *arbiter elegantiarum*, so far as the stress of warfare and the dominance of the Puritan " bourgeois " element allows the English any leisure for fashion. With the Restoration (we might find hints between 1655–1660) the modes of Versailles come crowding in more ostentatiously than ever. A momentary attempt is made at Court to create a standard of national attire, nominally based on Russo-Persian models, in 1666 ; but (probably within a few months) it was discredited, and thenceforth, to the voluble indignation of native satirists, the only " elegant " wear was French. Paris to this day is still on the whole the Mecca of the would-be *élégante*. Over here in the second quarter of the eighteenth century an aping of rustic attire (doubtless in a strong " fancy dress " strain) was much in favour for all but State occasions. In the 'seventies the Englishman's inborn reverence for sport acquired a perceptible voice in fashionable everyday wear of both sexes ; indeed, by the 'eighties, elements of English origin penetrated—in a rather emasculated version—into France. It should not be forgotten that though, officially and by a majority, England during the Revolution backed the Bourbons, there was an undercurrent of Republicanism amongst us, and that in dress, as otherwise, reflections of this are discernible quite apart from politics.

A SHORT HISTORY *of* COSTUME & ARMOUR

VOL. II

PART I—CIVILIAN

I—*TRANSITIONAL*

(1485–1515)

MEN

[*N.B.*—To establish finally clear-cut lines of demarcation between the various body garments hereafter referred to is beyond our present scope. The reader will find most of them duly defined in the *Glossary* under the appropriate heading. To avoid repetition, the authors venture also to refer readers to their earlier book, *Historic Costume*, pp. 1–3, where the difficulties are briefly summarized.]

BODY GARMENTS.—The chief body garment from now till its disappearance after *c.* 1670 is the *doublet.* Between it and the *shirt* was worn the *waistcoat* ; above it frequently appears the jacket or *jerkin* ; the whole among people of rank or gravity being surmounted by either a *gown* or a *cloak.* The last named, however, save for travelling or the like, is rarely in evidence ; till *c.* 1550 the preference in England was for the gown.[1] As in other details of equipment the fashions in vogue at the close of the preceding age (see Vol. I. pp. 39, 41) remained with little or no change till *c.* 1500. No new eccentricities of outline or cut were introduced. The *waistcoat,* where intended to show at the openings of the *doublet,* was of rich material ; it was made with or without sleeves. Till nearly the close of the period the *slashing,* mainly confined to the sleeves, the breast, and of the doublet, revealed the full body-linen in great puffs, a characteristically Italian trait [Plate I. D]. The *doublet* itself, always more or less internally quilted (hence its name and Fr. *pourpoint*), was made with or without skirts of varying length. The upstanding open collar vanished from courtly

[1] We take no account here of such mantles as form part of coronation and peers' robes, or the habit of knightly orders, etc.

circles soon after 1490; in its place appears a rather deep, square *décolletage*—a dominant note of the period. Sleeves, unless slashed, are often close fitting except towards the shoulder, in any case close at the wrist. The *jerkin* may be sleeveless, or it may have wide long sleeves or hanging sleeves. Independent under-sleeves and decorated stomachers render identification of particular garments hazardous. The jerkin (more rarely the doublet) often has wrap-over fronts (is, in fact, "double breasted") and deep lapels, or opens to the waist in a deep V or U. The skirts are generally full and long in contrast to the close-fitting body; they often cover two-thirds of the thigh. A feature that comes in *c.* 1490 and reappears with some frequency up to 1540 is a skirt of formal tubular pleats, of which the numerous variants of Holbein's "Henry VIII." are familiar examples. These were apparently known as *bases*, are often mentioned as independent articles of attire, and (as such) much worn as a species of kilt over the knightly armour. A notable feature from *c.* 1490 is the increasingly high waist. [*N.B.*—The waist-line or *girdle-stead* is an essential landmark in every stage of costume.] The *gown* throughout this period is made very full and square with remarkably broad shoulders. The folds are full and massive; the sleeves are long and ample, generally with deep slits in front lengthwise or across to allow of their being worn as hanging sleeves [Plate I. D]. It had broad lapels widening towards the shoulders and continuing at the back into a deep square-cut *collar* (not unlike that of our bluejackets). Gowns could be left quite open in front, or gathered into the waist by a girdle or a narrow knotted *sash*; their length varied: some hanging to the feet, others (for men of more jaunty taste) ending about the knee.[1] Linings and edgings of various *furs* were in prime favour throughout this and the ensuing period.

HOSE.—In essentials these throughout the period in question show no change (cf. Vol. I. p. 41). They are still what we should now term "tights"; *i.e.* a single garment moulded to the figure and covering it from waist to toe. *Knitted* hose were as yet unknown: they were still of cloth, silk, or even velvet *cut on the cross* (this is essential).[2] The *cod-piece* is still in universal use (Plate I. D). The only point to notice is that some men of fashion wore hose striped or variegated, sometimes each leg independent in colour: a revival of past modes. Another and more novel touch is that the portion covering the hips (and now alluded to as the *breech*) is often itself different in colour, pattern, or material from the legs. This *breech* is not infrequently adorned with small *slashes* and tiny *puffs*, or again by a reticulated pattern of broad bands of material variously embroidered. The *hose* at this date were attached to the *waist-coat* or to the doublet by points passing through eyelet-holes set along its lower edge. *C.* 1495–1505, a kind of loose overstocking turned down in a broad fold at the knee (apparently an early form of BOOT-HOSE—*vide infra*, p. 20) is often met with (Plate I. D).

[1] The short gown is almost always worn open (ungirt).

[2] For a proper understanding for the evolution and construction of the mediæval hose, see HARMAND, pp. 123–145.

A B C D

ROYAL MS. 16 F. ii. POEMS OF CHARLES OF ORLEANS, FO. 188

British Museum.

Note (in A) the fur-lined train pinned up behind, the typical hoods of the three ladies, and (in D) the loose overstockings and hose trussed *at waist* like "tights."]

A B C D

HENRY VII., HENRY VIII., ELIZABETH OF YORK AND JANE SEYMOUR

R. van Leemput. *After* Holbein.
By gracious permission of His Majesty the King.

Hampton Court.

HEAD-GEAR.—Of the various hats, hoods, etc., worn at the close of the previous era (cf. Vol. I. p. 41), practically the only one to survive for courtly wear, or indeed (except for hunting, travelling, and the like) among fashionable folk, was the square *bonnet* [Plate I. D] with turned-up brim often cut away above the forehead (though the gap may be bridged by gold laces); indeed, with slight modifications, it is the dominant mode till *c.* 1510. The soft crown is often moulded or pinched to a four-lobed form, the prototype of the priestly biretta, or may be almost like the small *béret* popularized at Wimbledon by M. Borotra. After *c.* 1505 the brim, hitherto turned up vertically in "pork pie" form, frequently expands outwards like a broad platter, the crown becoming more of a tam-o'-shanter. The edges of the brim might be, towards 1510, slittered into tabs or small loops, and the brim itself decorated by a broad ribbon threaded through vertical slits, or else by ornamental points. These platter-like brims are often very broad, and not infrequently surmounted by a great *plume* of dyed ostrich feathers. Just over one temple (in all these hats) it was usual to wear a jewel or medallion. Another variant of the "platter" brim was cut in two portions, the hinder overlapping the foremost. While the close linen *coif* of the Middle Ages was confined to lawyers and professional men, a similar cap, tied under the chin, of black cloth, velvet, or silk, was affected by elderly men and worn under the broad hat. More fashionable was a small *béret*-like cap, or a close caul of network or embroidery, also worn under the hat, and covering the back of the scalp. These broad hats often had strings for tying them below the chin, and by these they were frequently slung between the shoulders at will.

FOOT-GEAR.—The pointed toes of the fifteenth century did not long survive Bosworth. They are supplanted rather suddenly by the splayed or "duck-bill" variety. (*N.B.* these very full *round* toes must not be confounded with the wide *square* or "bear's paw" form introduced about 1510 to their exclusion [Plate II. A].) Boots were little worn except by huntsmen, soldiers, and travellers. Sometimes they are made close-fitting after the Italian model, laced or buckled on the outer side, more commonly rather loose, and reached to the knee or above it. The tops were slit behind to facilitate their being turned down to display a lining of bright material. The *shoes* (except at the toes) fitted closely, covering the whole foot to the ankle in velvet, silk, cloth, and leather of various hues; or were low in front and strapped over the instep. The term "high-heeled," as found at this date, merely implies a shoe reaching well up *over the heel*; heels *in the modern sense* are rare till after 1600, and even under Elizabeth quite exceptional. *Slashing* of shoes belongs rather to the ensuing age.

BODY-LINEN.—Linen from now on is to assume an importance hitherto unknown. In the earlier Middle Ages, by which I mean the period of the Crusades, the *shirt* at most peeped forth at the throat and wrist in an embroidered border. With the low-cut square *décolletage* and the wide slashing of the doublet fineness of *lingerie* became imperative.

The shirt was neatly gathered into an embroidered neck-band at the top, but not at first revealed at the wrist. It becomes itself distinctly low-necked, *c.* 1505–1520 sometimes barely surmounting the doublet and/or stomacher and even baring the collar-bone. As is the case from the Middle Ages, it does not seek to cover the neck—a development re-introduced in the following period.

Hair.—At this period a bearded face was still uncommon; at least, among the upper classes, young and old went clean shaven. Men wore their hair fairly close-cut, or (in present-day parlance) "bobbed" with a fringe across the brow, or again flowing freely to the shoulders. This last mode, approved of the King, and carried to extremes by young bloods, became rare from *c.* 1515, while the "bobbed" fashion lasted well into the 'thirties.

Accessories.—Girdles, as in the previous age, are in general use, and from them hung the *pouch* and *dagger* (the latter as hitherto is commonly worn threaded through loops at the back of the former). It is not unusual at this time for the girdle to take the form of a narrow *sash,* knotted in front. Towards 1500 we here and there find a short *sword* worn with civilian attire. The nobility continued to wear rich chains of goldsmith's work about the neck. Rings on the finger, and even on the thumb, are in evidence. Plain *walking-sticks* of fancy wood were carried, sometimes rather tall, and about now begin to have ornamental metal knobs. Scholars appended to the girdle an *inkhorn* and *penner.* Apart from costly furs, the commonest trimmings of garments in this and the ensuing periods are *guards* or broad bands of velvet, braid, etc., along, or parallel with, the edges and seams. *Points* with elaborate *aglets* are used wholesale *as pure ornament.* The jewellery of this age is varied and elaborate, the metal-work throughout being massive. *Gloves* are mostly carried in the hand or thrust through the girdle; rarely worn. Soft gauntlet-gloves appear, the knuckles not infrequently slashed to show the rings.

WOMEN

Gowns.—Till well into the 'nineties the late Burgundian-Yorkist modes remain in favour. We then meet with fashions distinctive of early Tudor tendencies. The ladies' gowns grew low-necked with square, U- or V-shaped *décolletage.* Alternatively we find V-shaped openings to the high waist in front or—more rarely—behind, laced over a vest-piece or, perhaps, an under-robe. The front of the gown often turns back in a broad shoulder-collar. The body may be close and spread into a long, full train, or the whole garment may be full and hang in folds from shoulder to ground; or the second type may be worn over the first. Both are found laced up the back from the waist [Plate I. A], and, in the absence of a girdle, the fuller variety generally had a *brooch* or *points* behind the waist whereby the train might be looped up out of the dust, displaying a fur or silken lining [*ibid.*]. When not so looped the train was lifted by hand or tucked under the elbow. Very wide borders of fur, velvet, and embroidery are general. The sleeves of the upper gown were of ample, monkish form, or else swelling funnel-like to vast compass at the mouth. The rich lining might be displayed by turning the sleeve back over the wrist. Full sleeves confined at the wrist also appear, while earlier modes are recalled by long, close sleeves turned up in a broad cuff. From the wide upper-sleeves emerge under-sleeves (whether independent articles of attire or part of the under-dress) either close or full, but in all cases close-fitting at the wrist. Under-sleeves of close fit, but slashed or slit across or lengthwise, and caught together at intervals by *points*, occur amongst us more rarely than in Germany and Italy, the fine linen of the chemise bulging through the openings. Women of rank on ceremonial occasions often wore long *cloaks* tied across the breast with tasselled cords that passed through brooch-like clasps set on the cloak's edge; such mantles figure in mourning habits. The curious "sideless" gown of the fourteenth and fifteenth centuries, with its fur-lining, also occurs on effigies as late as *c.* 1526 as state-apparel.

HEAD-DRESS.—Nothing in female attire is more notable at this date than the disappearance, except in remote provincial centres, of the huge, fantastic fifteenth-century ladies' head-gear — "horned," "heart-shaped," "steeple" hennins, "butterfly" veils, etc.—and the general adoption of various *hoods* in their place. (The "butterfly" head-dress was the latest of the old styles to give up the ghost, probably *c.* 1495.) Of these we may distinguish three main types, all distinguished by full draperies behind:

(i) The Franco-Flemish—whose brightly lined front was turned back in a broad fold from the forehead [Fig. 1, A–C]; or alternately had the front edge scooped out above the brow, revealing the front hair and under-cap. It hung in ample folds, generally of dark material, about the shoulders, and soon after 1500 was slit up from the hem on either side, the resulting lappets being brought in front of the shoulders like the sides of our Lord Chancellor's wig. A *point* or brooch set level with either ear apparently allowed these lappets to be looped up, though this is rather a feature of the "*gable*"*-hood* from *c.* 1526. For the most part this type, like the next to be described, was set on an under-cap of linen, velvet, or gold tissue, which showed from under it in front and was evidently stiffened to the shape of the head. Such under-caps often had an embroidered or jewelled border, the hood of this period being often highly ornate.

(ii) *Peculiarly English* was the "*gable*"*-hood* or *kennel*, which, with modifications, held its own from *c.* 1500 into the 'forties. Indeed, old ladies clung to it till well into the reign of Elizabeth [Fig. 5]. It was wired at the top into its curious angular shape or had a stiffened foundation. Specially distinctive is the jewelled fore-edge of the frontlet, and the broad band of ornament running across the top and down the side-lappets. This, like the previous type of hood, sometimes shows a projecting linen or gauze under-cap.

(iii) A plain arched hood, usually of linen, hanging in full folds behind stiffened fronts closely framing the face and turning outward towards the shoulders. It was made with a faint dip in the centre of the forehead, which *c.* 1550 developed into the familiar " Mary Queen of Scots " form. The hinder part could be folded and pinned up in a variety of ways. This form was much favoured by widows and elderly

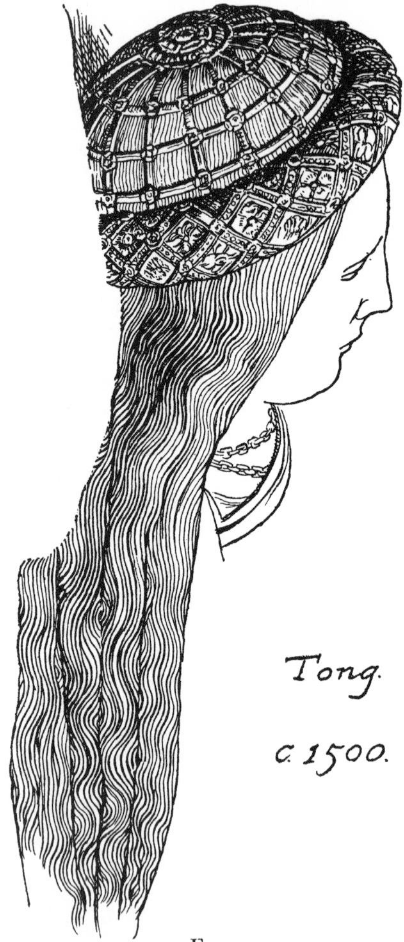

FIG. 1.

ladies, in conjunction with the *wimple* or *barbe*.[1] In process of time the tendency was to curtail the sides of this hood. There is evidence of the use of *cauls*, hair-nets, and turban-like rolls of stuff [Fig. 1], but such were more popular abroad than here. All the under-caps worn with the hoods, as also hoods of type iii, were held by a narrow tape or chin-strap under the jaw.

[1] A familiar example of the later widows' *barbe* is F. Clouet's well-known portrait of Mary Stuart in mourning for Francis II. (*le deuil blanc*).

c. 1550

i. LORD DE LA WARR
By H. Euwouts.
Late Holford Collection, Westonbirt.

1551

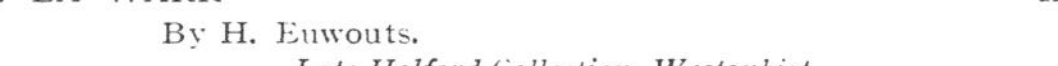

ii. MARY DUDLEY, LADY SIDNEY
By H. Euwouts, 1551.
Petworth.

Lawyer. Merchant.

A HORSLEYDOWN WEDDING, 1568–'69 (DETAIL)

By Joris Hoefnagel.

Hatfield House.

A comprehensive view of the dress of the English gentry, bourgeoisie and countryfolk.

HAIR.—So far as the pre-Bosworth Gothic modes endured, the hairless appearance of the ladies' forehead persisted, but with the adoption of the newer head-dresses we find the hair restored to view in the form of flat bandeaux dressed over the ears from a centre-parting ; less frequently dressed off the forehead. Brides wore their hair flowing loose over their shoulders with a wreath or diadem above it—a fashion that lasted into the seventeenth century. The *rolls* so typical of the later gable-hood (*vide infra*, p. 13) appear to date from about 1520.

HOSE were long tailored stockings, gartered by a tie or strap and buckle above the knees. The *shoes*, rarely visible below the full skirts, were fashioned like the men's. Thick-soled clogs or *pattens* were strapped to them at times.

LINEN.—This, where visible, is like that of the men, the *chemise* commonly rises towards the neck to offset the *décolleté* bodice.

ACCESSORIES.—Generally speaking, most of these are such as the men used. The *girdle* might be of the narrow sash kind or had a long hanging end, richly mounted, and depending from the buckle in front. The tendency up to 1525 is for a high-waisted effect. From the girdle often was slung the rosary or a Book of Hours—sometimes, even, a dagger.

II—*THE ERA OF PUFFS AND SLASHES*

(*c.* 1515–1545)

MEN

ALTHOUGH the English never seem to have carried the principle of slashing to such lengths as did the Germans or the Swiss, we have evidence sufficient that it was in general use at this date. Further, it may be, and doubtless is, true that the gowns and long-skirted jerkins of the period often hide slashed thighs and hips. Squareness and breadth become still more marked.

FIG. 2.

BODY GARMENTS.—The *jerkin* of this date in so many cases closely follows the *doublet* in fit and even in brevity as to render differentiation still difficult. The latter is, for the most part, low-necked, with a deep square *décolletage* found up to the 'thirties, when it begins to ascend, till about 1540 we have an actual collar or neck-band, which thenceforward grows steadily more high-necked. Up to the same period, too, we find skirtless doublets, but the general tendency is towards short shirts not infrequently tabbed or escalloped (" wrought in PICKADILS "). The puffing and slashing centres on the breast, sleeves, and upper legs. Both *doublet* and *jerkin* are found with double-breasted fronts. The *sleeves* are generally full, puffed, and slashed, but tight at the wrist. *Jerkins* remain much as before with such modifications as above suggested ; they may be sleeveless or with hanging sleeves. Quite usual are sleeves puffed to above the elbow, whence they continue close to the wrist or as hanging sleeves. Even before this period it is common to have the sleeves slit across in a T or + shape, whereby the nether half could be allowed to hang free [Plate II. A]. Not only do we find broad lapels and deep square collars, but the latter are sometimes marked off from the former by a V-shaped " step." *Bases* (see p. 2) continue in favour; but, whereas hitherto they had often been quite long, they now always fall short of the knees, and become obsolete in ordinary attire *c.* 1540, about which date we may note a tendency to lower the waist-line. While the short *gown* maintains its square outline, the male contour otherwise tends after 1540 to lose this quality in anticipation of the Spanish modes that followed. *Cloaks* are even rarer than before.

HOSE.—From now on we constantly find the *hose* described as consisting of *upper-stocks* (=breeches) and *nether-stocks* (stockings) although

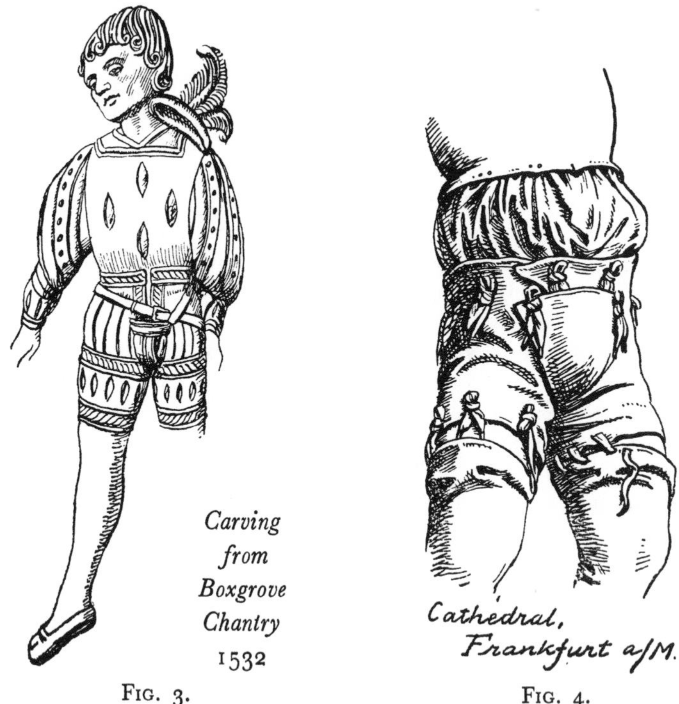

Carving from Boxgrove Chantry 1532

FIG. 3.

Cathedral, Frankfurt a/M.

FIG. 4.

still sewn together to form a single garment (*stock*, without qualifying adjective=stocking).[1] The breeches are now cut in a series of slashed puffs, and mostly of different material (sometimes of different colour) from the stockings: but whereas, on the Continent (especially in German-Swiss semi-military dress), it was quite usual to get the utmost variety of pattern, material, and colour between the legs, this does not seem to have obtained in England to any marked extent. Nor at this date does striping of the stockings appear ever to have "caught on" very much among us. Slashed stockings appear at all times to have been exceedingly rare outside of Germany and Switzerland. *Codpieces* [Fig. 4] become obtrusive.

[1] The fashion of connecting breeches and stockings by laces or points [Fig. 4] is almost exclusively a German *landsknecht* mode.

Garters are worn; more for ornament than necessity, including *cross-garters* (*re* which see next section), being mere ties of knotted ribbon about the knee.

HEAD-GEAR.—The first type of cap or hat described in the last section [Plate II. B] was relegated from *c.* 1520 to professionals (scholars, lawyers, clerics, etc.), elderly men, and the unfashionable [Fig. 2]. It tends to become quadrangular in crown, and to have the brim (often rather wide) cut away in front and maintained (when not lowered over the ears) by a ribbon tie over the crown. From *c.* 1520 a flat *béret*, with a slightly turned up platter-like brim of moderate compass, becomes *the* courtly wear. About the same period the profusion of plumes is discarded in favour of a couple of ostrich-tips [Fig. 3, A], or a single plume laid along the brim, which it overhangs on the right side [Plate 2, A]. From *c.* 1530 the slashed and looped brims lose favour, and in the late 'thirties the tendency is to have the brim quite flat or slightly drooping, so as to expose the crown to view, and gradually shrinking in compass.

HAIR.—" Bobbed " hair continues in vogue up to *c.* 1530 (and a trifle later in professional circles), but from the late 'twenties the tendency is towards a fairly close crop, which, from the mid-'thirties, becomes general in conjunction with a short, full *beard* (cut round or square). By the 'forties we find long, full beards worn even by young men. With the reintroduction of the beard comes the *moustache*, grown on its natural lines.

FOOT-GEAR.—The toes now are of exaggerated breadth and cut very square, the uppers being often little more than toe-caps, and the shoe secured over the instep by a ribbon-tie or strap and buckle. Towards 1540 the width is reduced, the uppers cover the instep, and there is a tendency to a round toe. Throughout the period we find the uppers variously slashed, and even on occasion studded with gems. Except by hunters, travellers, etc., *boots* are exceptional at this date. In general they are as described in the last section, the toes following the general fashion, and often slashed about the knees or on the lower leg.

LINEN.—Up to *c.* 1525 the shirt, low-necked, is gathered in fine pleats into a band about the throat and wrists. After that date it rises and encircles the throat with a broad neck-band, tied in front by strings. At the top of the neck-band often appears a small tuckered edge (the first hint of the *ruff*). Similar embroidered bands with gathered frills adorn the wrists, becoming quite notable in the 'thirties. Embroidery in black, red, and/or gold adorns the collar, wrist-bands, and breast [*Frontispiece*]. From the 'forties occurs a small down-turned collar or *band*.

ACCESSORIES.—*Swords* become rather more in evidence among the highest ranks of society, and by the 'forties are appended to the *girdle* by a simple form of *hangers*. At the same time the guards, hitherto little more than a cross-bar, become more complicated [*Frontispiece*]. The dagger now, among the great, is often slung from the girdle by a rich cord with a large hanging tassel [*ibid.*]. Instead of girdle and hangers, it is not unusual to find two narrow sashes knotted in front, the one encircling the waist, the other attached to it on the right, and hanging

i. HERCULE FRANÇOIS DE FRANCE, DUC D'ALENCON, 1572
F. Pourbus, Jun.
By courtesy of Messrs. P. & D. Colnaghi.

ii. MARY, LADY STRANGE(?), 1565
By Hans Euwouts.
Nat. Port. Exh., 1866.

iii. JAMES I. (AND VI.), AGED 8, 1574
National Portrait Gallery.

i. SIR JOHN PAKINGTON, *c.* 1580

Peasecod-belly and "Long-stocked" Trunk-hose.

[NOTE.—The artist has left the great ruff unfinished.]

ii. DRAWING BY NIC. HILLIARD, *c.* 1580

An ultra-wide "Spanish Verdingale.

Penes Archibald G. Russell, Esq.

SIR EDWARD HOBY, 1578

Penes Lady Vansittart Neale.

thence diagonally. Of gloves, rings, points, pouches, and walking-canes there is practically nothing new to report.

WOMEN

Gowns.—Up to *c.* 1525 there is little novelty to report. About 1530 the square *décolletage* tends to assume an arched form. The *décolleté* bodice fits closely, while trains shrink away till the full skirt just reaches

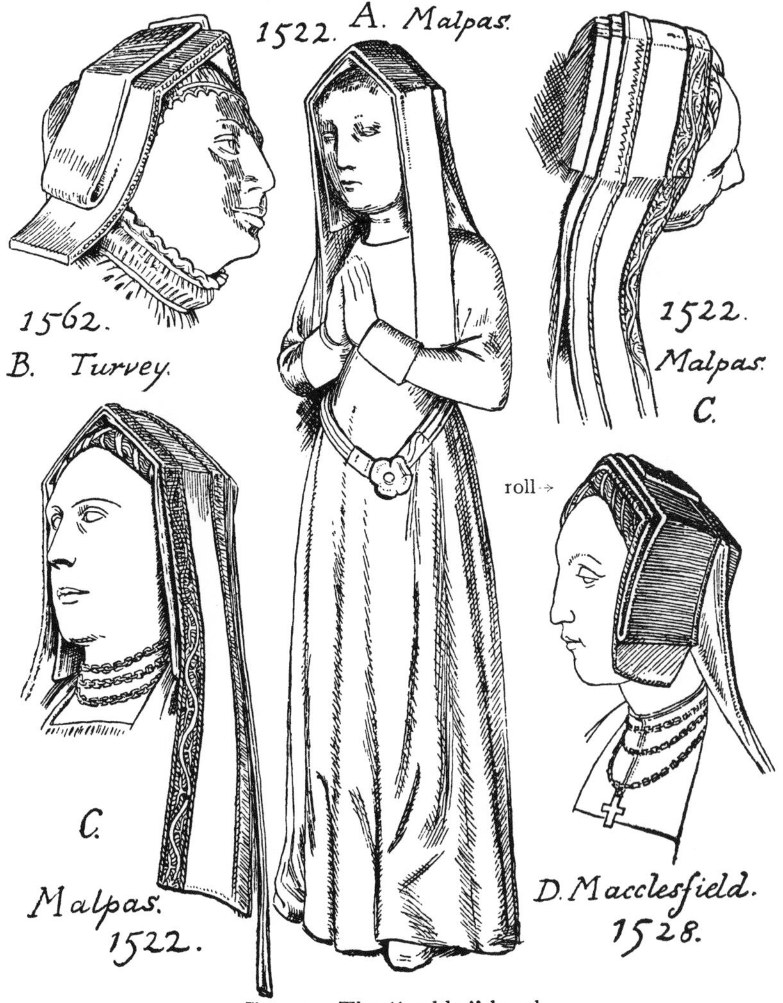

Fig. 5.—The "gable"-hood.

the ground all round. Between 1535–1540 we find a predilection for a funnel-shaped creaseless skirt, in fact, an embryo *verdingale* [Plate ii. d]. (The bodice commonly has its *décolletage* cut in a V behind.) The sleeve swells from the shoulder to a vast bell-mouth, whence it turns back in a huge cuff (often fur-lined) about the elbow. The under-sleeve (which frequently is an independent, tied-on *fore-sleeve*), made to be close-fitting or made in a series of slashed puffs with tight wrist-band, or cut flat and wide (often pleated and quilted lengthwise), the convex back-seam left open and tied at intervals by *points*, between which puffs out the *chemise*. In the latter part of the period the skirt often opens in a Λ over the petticoat in front. The vogue of the laced-across bodice dies out from *c.* 1520. A novelty in the last years of this era is a small shoulder-cape of dark material (a German-Flemish mode) or a close-fitting yoke-like shoulder-piece, with a standing " Medici " collar open at the throat [Fig. 6, B].

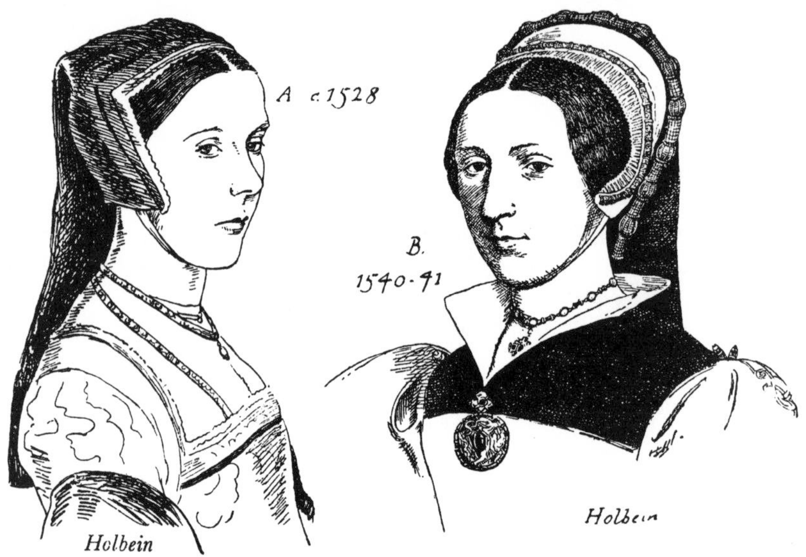

FIG. 6.—A, Anne Cresacre ; B, Catherine Howard.

The gown itself, towards 1540, is often high-necked with open, upright collar (cf. other portraits of Queen Catherine Howard).

HEAD-DRESS.—The three main types described (pp. 5 and 6) last, with modifications, far into this period ; the tendency being to curtail the sides. The ornamental front lappets of the " gable "-hood from *c.* 1525 are turned up level with the ear-lobes and folded over the crown [Plate II. D ; Fig. 5, D]. The fall of drapery behind is often split in two tails and pinned up over the crown, according to taste. The points of the stiffened under-cap of linen are bent out at right angles level with the jaw. [*N.B.—All* these head-dresses appear to have been secured by a white, tape-like band under the chin.] About 1540 the " gable " began to lose favour, being supplanted by the *French hood* seen in portraits of Catherine Howard, who possibly was responsible for its vogue [Fig. 6, B]. Like the " gable " it had a train or mass of black stuff hanging down the back in folds which could be pinned up over the crown, and by which henceforth the "French hood" was to be known in all its variants. Another form of hood, apparently as English as the gable, *c.* 1525–1545, shows an intermediary form between these two [Fig. 6, A].

HAIR.—Except with the "gable" the front hair, where visible, is mostly parted smoothly from the centre in flat bandeaux [Fig. 6], which by the 'forties begin to be waved. With the gable, however, went the so-called *rolls*, two long tresses (either braided spirally with ribbon or enclosed in cases of striped silk) brought forward from the back and crossing each other over the brow, they filled up the space between the angles of the hood and the forehead. They had gone out of fashion before 1548.[1]

BODY LINEN.—The chemise, often richly embroidered, grows higher-necked between 1535–1545. It may have an upstanding open collar, or else a gathered frill at the neck, repeated at the wrists. Sometimes it is left open up the breast and at the throat. Embroidery in black and red silk and gold thread often adorns the neck, wrists, and breast.

SHOES.—As under MEN.

ACCESSORIES.—The remarks on p. 7 *ante* hold good for this period; jewels, and especially pearls, being lavished over the apparel of the great. The skin of a sable or marten, lined with silk, the head and claws mounted in gold and jewels, was often cast about the neck in chilly weather, or hung from the girdle by a chain—a mode found through the next period.

[1] Elyot, *Dictionarie*, 1538 (*s.v. Antiæ*), has ". . . *nowe* gentylwomen *do* call them their rolles," while the 1548 edition reads—" . . . *did late* call them," etc The ends, unconfined, streamed freely down the back underneath the hood.

III—*THE SPANISH TREND*

(1545–1620)

MEN

BODY GARMENTS.—The waist-line, high-set till the mid-'thirties, from then till the 'forties resumes its natural position, and by the beginning of our present period tends to a long-bodied type of dress. The *doublet* fits closely and reaches high in the neck, by 1560 uncomfortably so. It has close sleeves to the wrist,[1] and these, like the body, are often made in a series of slight puffs, with vertical slashing [Plate v. i]. PICKADILS [2] are common to the body garments of both sexes and are specially characteristic of the dress of *c.* 1548–1570. The doublet has short skirts. These (*c.* 1550–1560) are sometimes double (a shorter one *over* a longer), and *c.* 1555–1565 the skirts sometimes end in front in an oblique overlap. The body of the *jerkin* now is closely fitted over the doublet [Plate IX. i ; Fig. 7], hence must conform in due season to the *Peasecod* mode (*vide infra*, p. 15).

From the late 'forties to *c.* 1575 occurs a jerkin borrowed from the military arming-doublet : made of buff or " spruce " (= Prussia) leather, practically sleeveless, and cut in narrow *panes* from breast to waist, the shoulders being quilted and pruked. Jerkins may or may not have sleeves, but these are commonly arranged to be worn at will as hanging sleeves. (These by the last quarter of the century—as in the case of cloaks—are mainly " dummies.") The shoulders of all body garments throughout the period are apt to be adorned by *wings* or overhanging projections at the armhole. In the 'fifties and 'sixties these are mostly *pickadils.* Note the variety of fastening of the doublet and jerkin alike. Normally they button, hook, lace, or tie up the front ; but some open at the sides. Certain very close jerkins open only at the breast and some way up the sides, being slipped over the head unfastened. Jerkins with long flaring skirts almost hiding the trunks also appear. Note up to *c.* 1575 the increased padding of the doublet in front and the droop of

[1] Close-fitting sleeves appear commonly, side by side with all other forms, from now up to *c.* 1650. They are characteristically Spanish.

[2] We use the term here in its original (Dutch) sense of a border cut out in scallops or tabs. It appears in *English* texts early in the seventeenth century ; mostly to describe a stiffened support for the ruff and whisk, but also in its wider acceptation.

A B C D E F

L. VAN VALCKENBORCH : "SPRING SCENE" (*detail*), 1587

Kunsthistorisches Museum, Vienna.

A—"À la mode de Fraunce."
D—Note single hoop at hem.

1602

1600

A B

i. SIR WALTER RALEIGH AND SON, 1602

By Marcus Gheeraedts.
Penes Sir Stephen Lennard, Bart.

A B C D

ii. FROM QUEEN ELIZABETH'S VISIT TO BLACKFRIARS, 1600
(*detail*)

By Marcus Gheeraedts.
Penes Lieut.-Col. F. T. B. Wingfield Digby, D.S.O.

i. FEMALE PORTRAIT, *c.* 1615–'20

Penes Messrs. Spink & Sons, Ltd.

ii. CHARLES I. AS DUKE OF YORK, 1613

By Robt. Peake.

iii. MALE PORTRAIT, 1611

Late Holford Collection.

the waist-line to a deep point in front [Plate v. i, iii; Fig. 7]. This develops 1575 to 1600—notably in the 'eighties—into the *peasecod-belly*, stuffed out into a hump overhanging the girdle (sometimes almost to the fork) [Plates vi. i; viii. A, E; Fig. 8]; the skirts, too, shrink to a mere

Fig. 7.

strip. The sleeves at the same time often assume a "bishop" or "leg-o' mutton" cut, often slashed and puffed and "borne out" by whalebone or wire hoops, from the 'eighties sometimes arranged to tie or button down the front. In the course of the 'nineties the peasecod dwindles,

FIG. 8.—From tomb of Mildred Coke, Lady Burleigh.

Fig. 9.—A, B, and E, Mandilion (B, from portrait of Sir Philip Sidney); C, trunk-hose with *canions*; D, short cassock.

and the skirts, following the droop of the waist-line, develop into a series of tabs overlapping backwards (*tassets*) [1] and sloping to a deep point in front. The *wings* which *c.* 1565–1590 were mostly slashed rolls towards 1600 tend to form a deep projecting welt at the armhole. *C.* 1600–1610 some doublets are short-skirted with horizontal waist-line and base [Plate IX. ii A]. In any case the doublet from 1600 becomes a veritable corset, busked and wasp-waisted. At the same time the wings grow in size and the *tassets* deepen. Sleeves are mostly close-fitting, but towards 1620 begin to be close-buttoned up the forearm, but full and cut in panes to the elbow. (Between the panes puffs out the linen of the shirt or—rarely—a coloured lining. The *points* trussing up the hose are visible, tied in bows along the waist-line of the doublet, after *c.* 1595 (as they had at times been down to *c.* 1560).) In the 'nineties appear not seldom doublets almost devoid of collar, therefore allowing ruff or band to lie flat on the shoulders.

Overcoats include besides the close jerkin, loose-bodied jackets: *cassocks*, *mandilions*. The latter is cut on the lines of a short dalmatic or herald's coat with hanging sleeves [Fig. 9, A, E]. It was often worn "collie-westonward" like a pursuivant's tabard: back and front overhanging the arms, and the sleeves dangling fore and aft [Fig. 9, B]. There is no essential change in gowns, now generally on the long side. They are worn either open or confined at the waist by a girdle or a narrow knotted sash.

CLOAKS.—These are in high favour, and vary considerably in shape, dimensions, and adjustment: short and long. The short Spanish cape is known by the deep hanging cowl at the back, the French *reître* reaches to the ankle or the calf [Plate VIII. A], often with a deep shoulder-cape, others barely reach the buttocks. Standing and falling collars, lapels [Fig. 8] (some with a "step"), shoulder-puffs, and hanging sleeves are all found throughout this period. The cloak was worn *ad lib.* on both shoulders, on one alone [Plate V. i], or draped about the bust after the manner of a Spanish *torero* [Plate X. iii]. After 1600, cloaks are either collarless or with a square "sailor" collar falling flat at back.

BREECHES.—"Whole hose" (*i.e.* breeches and stockings permanently united by sewing) continue in use and, in fact, last up to 1600, or later [Fig. 10]. But the term *hose* from now on (*c.* 1570 onward) tends to apply to the breeches as opposed to the stockings.

The most characteristic *breeches c.* 1550–1560 are the *trunk-hose* (*trunk-breeches*, *trunk-slops*, *trunks*, also *French hose*, *round hose*), short and wide, often out of all proportion to their length [Plates V. i; IX. i, A; Fig. 9 C]. Unless extended by the adjunction of *canions* (*vide infra*) they always have long tailored stockings of the old cut permanently sewn to them. Normally they reach to mid-thigh, and, besides having several linings, are commonly upholstered with flocks, horsehair, bran, etc. They are either very round like pumpkins, or swell out to a full, square base whence they are

[1] I venture to borrow this late *Frenchified* form exclusively of this detail of dress, as against the more English *tasses* to describe the thigh-flaps of an armour.

tucked under and gathered inward to the thigh. Usually they are *paned* (*i.e.* cut into vertical bands, showing the lining in the interstices; *panes* are peculiar to the trunk-hose genus). Often they are grotesquely bulky, especially *c.* 1565–1575 and 1595–1620. Fops about 1575–1595 were apt to curtail them to a mere roll of padding barely covering the

FIG. 10.—Whole hose.

hips [Plates VI. i; XXXII.]; *c.* 1610–1620 they often reach within a few inches of the knee.

VENETIANS (introduced 1570–1575) are merely "knee-breeches": buttoned or tied *below the knee*. Their width varied: sometimes tapering pearwise to the knee, sometimes skin-tight, sometimes like wide knickers.

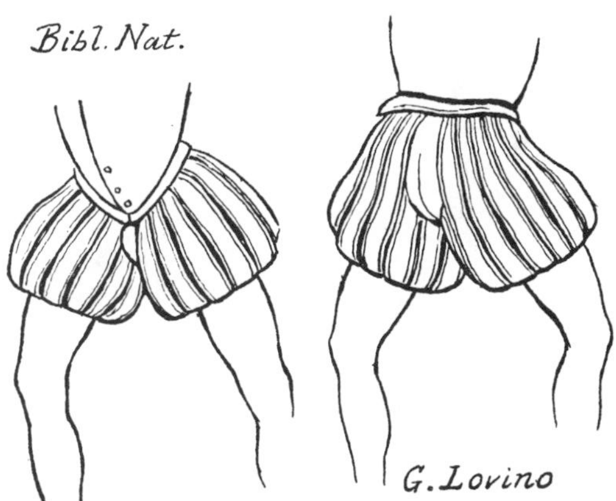

FIG. 11.—Trunk-hose *c.* 1575.

They were in great vogue in the 'eighties. They, too, might be padded [Plates V. ii; VIII. A, E; X. iii; XXXIV.; Figs. 7, 8, 9 D].

OPEN BREECHES were wide, tubular, and unconfined at the knee; in fact much like our "running shorts." In vogue *c.* 1585–1610 [Fig. 12].

The full breeches just to the knee on the lines of modern Dutch "knickerbockers" *may* be what were known as galligaskins.

CANIONS.—These from *c.* 1570 accompany the wide breeches, when divorced from the long sewn stockings. They form a kind of tubular extension to below the knee [Plate IX. i, A; Fig. 9, C]; according as they are close or open at the knee, the stockings are drawn up and gartered inside or over them. The *codpiece* began to be discarded from the 'seventies, practically vanishing with the century.

STOCKINGS.—Independent knitted stockings appeared early in this era, but the old tailored stockings sewn to the breeches held their own, especially in union with *trunk-hose* till after 1600. *Clocks* adorned with gold, silver, or coloured silk appear from the 'eighties. *Boot-hose* were thick overstockings intended primarily for use with boots as a protection

FIG. 12.—Open breeches.

for the finer stockings beneath (*c.* 1570 onward). Soon, however, they became ornate and were worn with shoes. *Garters* become important. In the seventeenth century they were very ornate, tied in a bow with fringed ends below the knee. *Cross-garters* (*vide* "Twelfth Night") occur as early as *c.* 1525. They were laid below the knee and the ends, *twisted* crosswise behind, were brought forward and tied, in front or at the side, *above* the knee. When the stockings are drawn over the breeches, the garter is usually concealed in the rolled top; [1] only the ends are visible beneath the "open" breeches.

HEAD-GEAR.—The small flat bonnet [*Frontispiece* and Plate III. i]

[1] In the picture at Hatfield, of "Queen Elizabeth's great horse" (1594), one of the groom's stockings, partly unrolled, shows a green garter and gold buckle.

remains unchanged into the 'sixties; in the course of which the brim shrinks and the crown rises, till by the 'seventies it assumes a high, gathered bag-shape probably stiffened inside [Plate v. i, iii]; it practically vanishes by 1600. It was an essentially Spanish type. The *copotain* with sugar-loaf crown and brim of varying width occurs from the 'sixties to the close of the century, and from the late 'seventies broad-leaved sombreros are increasingly favoured [Plate VIII. A]. Crowns are high and low, round and square. In modish circles the hat-band was often highly ornate (jewelled or wrought with gold) [Plate VII.], and pearls often sprinkle the sides of the tall bonnet. Very popular was the twisted *cypress* (crape) hat-band tied in a rosette or bow in front. Ostrich-tips, too, frequently surmounted by an osprey or three heron's plumes, were worn in full-dress, usually set at the side. Set in front, they also decked the low bonnets with gathered crown and rolled edge, that were in vogue at Court (worn at the back of the head), *c.* 1575–1595 [Plate VI. i]. After 1600 all hats were high-crowned with broad brims, flat or variously "cocked" (=looped up).

FOOT-GEAR.—Toes are faintly pointed or round throughout this period. They cover the whole foot up to ankle. Up to the 'seventies they are slashed in a stereotyped pattern. From *c.* 1575 we meet with an embryo tongue in front, across which the side-leathers are united by a small ribbon bow over the instep, presently leaving a small opening between them and the front on either side. These openings increase in size, till by the second decade of the seventeenth century the side-leathers become a mere ankle strap and the ribbon-tie grows larger and develops towards 1610 into a large formal *rose* (without quite ousting the tie). Heels in the modern sense are exceptional before 1600; once adopted they are tall and square, and for full-dress are coloured red, as is the edge of the soles. *Boots* till 1605 are rare, except for travelling,[1] sport, etc. In the sixteenth century the fashionable boot reaches to mid-thigh (though the tops, often indented or escalloped, could at will be turned down or folded below the knees) and cut to mould the limb by the aid of slashing, lacing, buckling, etc. From *c.* 1610 it was stylish to *walk* in boots and spurs; the boots now usually depend for their fit wholly on their cut. *Pantoffles*, or slippers covering the front of the foot only, with cork soles thickening from toe to heel, are worn—outdoors especially—over the fine shoes and boots from *c.* 1570–1575.

BODY-LINEN.—Coloured embroidery keeps its vogue. For neck-wear we have (*a*) the band (or *falling band* or *fall*) simply turned down over the high collar of the doublet (between *c.* 1590–1605 more akin to an "Eton" collar) [Plate IX. i, B]. Embellished with silk or metallic embroideries, lace, etc., this to some extent held its own, notably in the 'eighties, throughout this period, though not till *c.* 1630 did it finally oust ruffs from fashionable favour; (*b*) the *ruff* (or *ruff-band*), originally a mere frill or tucker, edging the band, evolves by the 'sixties into a collar of radiating tubular pleats (*sets*) at first worn open at the throat, but

[1] For *short* rides shoes are often worn even in the saddle.

after 1570 generally closed all round. In the ensuing decade it gradually increases its compass till by the 'eighties the huge "cartwheel" ruff [Plates VI. i; VIII. A; Fig. 8] requires to be starched and underpropped with wire. The pleats from thence onward are ordered (and *dis*ordered) in an infinity of ways by means of *setting sticks* (or *pokers*) of steel or wood. It may be of one or more ruffled layers of linen or lace. From the 'nineties, while still fairly wide, it is somewhat reduced; ruffs of moderate compass are found throughout. Towards 1620 appears the *falling ruff*, consisting of several layers of linen and lace, informally puckered into close, small pleats drooping to the shoulders. (*c*) The *whisk* (or *standing band*), a stiffly projecting, semicircular, wired-out collar on which the head rests as on a plate [Plate X. ii, iii] was introduced *c.* 1605 and goes out shortly after 1630. All this varied neck-wear was closed at the throat by *band-strings*, sometimes visible in front, oftener tucked out of sight. As the *handruff* or *ruffle* (though never of excessive size) corresponds with the ruff, so the turned-up *cuff* goes with the *falling band* (though at times worn with the ruff). (*N.B.*—Throughout this period all neck-wear was conspicuously lofty, the collar of the doublet being exaggeratedly tall between *c.* 1557 and 1574. An exception is the period 1590–1605, when the throat is often bare.)

HAIR.—Close crops last throughout this period, though less common after 1600. In the 'seventies the hair, close cut behind, is full at front and sides and trained to stand on end round the face. In the 'eighties dandies often sport a thick crop of curls over the pate [Plate VI. i], and the *lovelock* (a long lock of hair trailing on one side of the face, mostly plaited or tied with ribbon) comes in and lasts till the middle of the seventeenth century. In the 'nineties longer and fuller hair comes in (to below the ears, *very* occasionally to the shoulders) and remains usual up to *c.* 1630. In the 'fifties beard and moustache are short and full, grown on natural lines. From *c.* 1560 the "Vandyke" beard is most general. From the 'seventies the moustache either grows naturally or is brushed up from the lips. Very varied beards distinguish the last quarter of the century: the *pickdevant* (narrow and pointed), forked, *spade* (like a very full, square "goatee"), and *marquisotto* (cut close to the face) beards all enjoyed popularity. In the 'nineties the Earl of Essex set the fashion of rather long, square beards, otherwise reserved for elder men. From about 1600 the cheeks tend increasingly to be shaven. The flowing "Cavalier" locks are exceptional much before 1628.

ACCESSORIES.—Jewellery is increasingly lavished on the person from the 'eighties. Seed-pearls in particular were freely sprinkled over the attire of courtiers. Finger-rings were worn in profusion (even the thumb is often ringed). Rings were also worn in the ears (though a pearl-drop, often in one ear only, is commoner) and, after *c.* 1610, at the band-string. About this latter date, too, a narrow black string may be threaded through the ear-lobe. Rich neck-chains and pendants are in vogue. A rose tucked behind one ear is a rarity. Hair-dye, paint, and patches come into fashion. The sword became a *rapier* (long, narrow, and used chiefly for thrusting, with a hilt that grew ever more complicated), which was suspended by *hangers* to the girdle, and as often as not companioned by a dagger set almost horizontally behind the right hip. The dagger ceases to be *worn c.* 1605. Towards 1595 the gloves assume the familiar "gauntlet" form familiar through the better part of the seventeenth century. Masks of silk were worn by both sexes when they wished to go abroad incognito: they covered the whole face, and were often held by a button affixed inside and clenched between the teeth. *Very* occasionally a *scarf* is cast about the shoulders [Plate VII. i].

[*Note.*—Military men were licensed to display considerable "bravery" in their apparel, and hence with impunity made a more colourful and ostentatious show than was considered seemly in civilians. For this and other motives many affected a military cast in their attire: *e.g.* a buff-coat, "arming points" (*vide* p. 78) at their shoulders, and even a steel collar or gorget.]

WOMEN

Gown, Bodice, and Petticoat.—Though one-piece gowns are found in the higher ranks of society throughout this period it will in most cases be convenient to treat of the bodice as apart from the skirt. There is one form of loose upper gown which cannot be so treated. It has a standing collar, buttoned or tied at the throat, and beyond this the robe gradually widens extinguisher-wise to the hem: it stands open in a wide V from breast to foot over the inner robe, the sleeves from *c.* 1560–1590 have enormous shoulder puffs, and frequently end above the elbow. Similar sleeves also in the 'sixties and 'seventies accompany the bodice.

The *bodice* forms a long-waisted corset, drooping to a sharp peak in front. The arched *décolletage* of the Holbein type, surmounted by the high-necked, pleated chemisette, survives well into the 'seventies; at the same time the bodice itself is as often high-necked with a tall collar. The habit of baring the bosom, at first properly suggestive of maidenhood (and hence adopted by the Virgin Queen in her old days), comes in in the 'eighties, and becomes more and more general from 1600. From the 'eighties wide sleeves "borne out" with whalebone or wire hoops are common. Most of the male fashions in sleeves are followed by women; long hanging sleeves to the upper-gown are much worn [1] [Fig. 14]. The upper gown often has two pairs of sleeves, namely: (1) long full hanging sleeves matching the gown, and (2) close under-sleeves differing in stuff or colour (often matching the petticoat). Loose outer jackets, chiefly furred for winter, are occasionally seen.

The *skirt* and *petticoat* retain their rigid funnel shape, emphasized by the introduction *c.* 1550 of the *Spanish verdingale* (or *farthingale*) or stiff

[1] Note that the original hanging sleeves were designed to be worn *as sleeves* at will; they eventually become "dummies" pure and simple.

under-petticoat hooped from waist to hem with graduated bands of cane or wire or whalebone [Plates III. ii ; VI. ii]. Sometimes a single hoop at the hem sufficed. The *French verdingale* does not appear to have been general in England till close on 1590 [Plate IX. C]. It was a great hip-bolster like a motor-tyre whereby the overlying petticoat was borne out horizontally *at the top*, thence dropping vertically to the ground. With the Spanish type the silhouette below the waist forms a cone or bell, with the French a drum [Fig. 16]. There are also intermediate

FIG. 13. FIG. 14.

forms between the two. Towards 1600 the wheel-like effect of the French verdingale is heightened by a circular flounce of the same material as the skirt : lying flat, in radiating pleats, upon the padded hips, it resembles a second ruff placed immediately below the waist [Fig. 20, B, C]. There were also intermediate types of the verdingale, of beehive or cupola outline. Short skirts (ankle-length) are sometimes worn by the upper classes *c.* 1605–1620 [Fig. 17]. From about 1590 the overskirt is not seldom drawn up and tucked under at the sides to show the petticoat. The V-opening in front of the skirt continues throughout this period. *Pickadils* are favoured by ladies also [Fig. 19].

i. MARQUIS OF HAMILTON, 1624

ii. JAMES HAY, AFTERWARDS EARL OF CARLISLE, 1626

Petworth.

iii. DAUGHTER OF LADY CAVENDISH, 1628

By permission of His Grace the Duke of Devonshire

PORTRAIT OF SIR THOS. MEAUTYS, *c.* 1627

By Sir Nathaniel Bacon (?). *Gorhambury.*

HEAD-DRESS.—The *French hood*, modified, continues in favour well into the 'eighties.[1] The square outline associated with Queen Mary seems practically confined to the 'fifties [Plate III. ii]. About the same date the arched linen hood evolves into the cap romantically coupled with the name of Mary Queen of Scots. Unchanged in essentials, this mode, with or without pendant veil behind, outlasted the first quarter

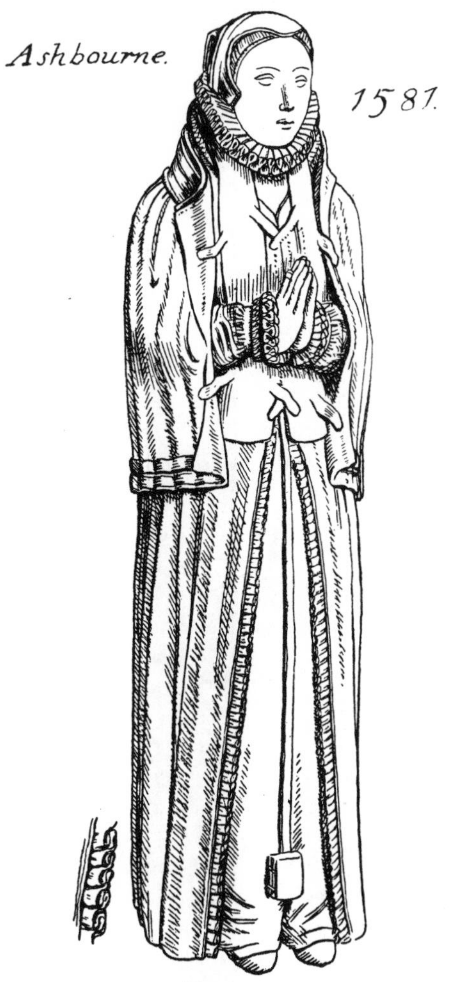

FIG. 15.

of the ensuing century. Towards 1590 the veil is frequently wired into arches at the back of the shoulders—a mode that lasts till *c.* 1615. Similar arches also grace gauze veils independently pinned to the head-dress.

[1] The term comes to be applied to any caul-like covering for the back of the head, having a broad, folded tail behind [Fig. 19], capable of being folded up and brought forward over the crown [Fig. 20, A].

From the 'sixties, even out of doors (except when travelling), there is a widespread tendency to uncover the hair, confined at most in a close caul or cap at the back [Fig. 18]. On the other hand, there arises a certain vogue for bonnets and hats based on contemporary men's fashions, especially for riding, hunting, and so forth [Plate IV. v, ii ; Fig. 20, B].

HAIR.—Down to the 'seventies the hair is waved or curled and puffed out over the temples on either side of a central parting. From *c.* 1575 the parting tends to vanish, and the front hair is trained off the forehead in a roll, or over a wire frame into twin arches above the brow, which grow taller till the 'nineties when they evolve into a high front trained

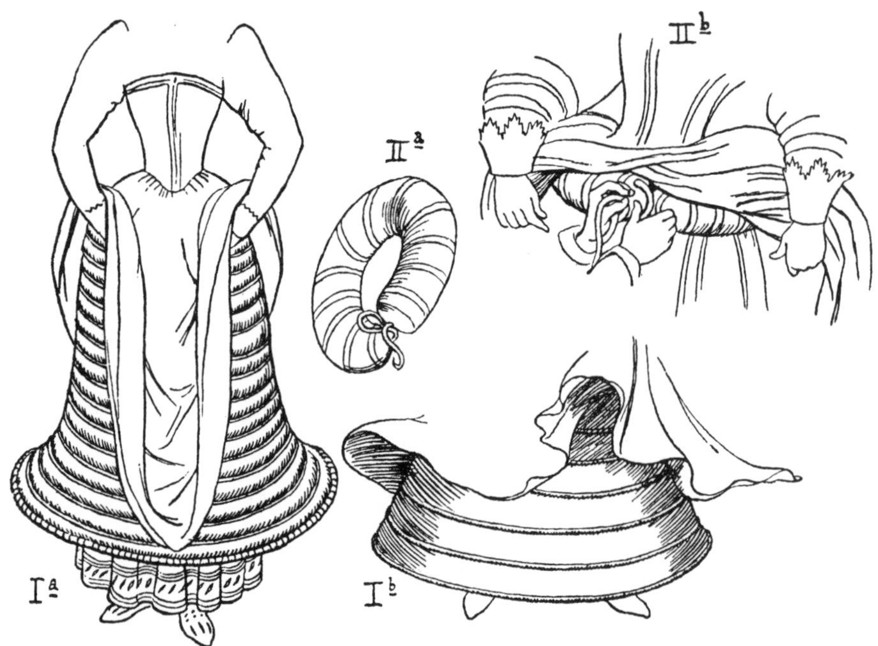

FIG. 16.—French and Dutch. I, *c.* 1570–1580 ; II, *c.* 1600.

over a pad [1] [Fig. 20, C ; Fig. 17] ; this lasted till after 1615 ; but already towards 1620 we find the hair dressed off the forehead and close to the head, hanging over the ears in a frizzled bush [Plate X. i]. The back hair *throughout this period and far into the next* is coiled in a flat " bun," which till *c.* 1610 was generally confined in a close cap or net. From the 'seventies on the hair at Court was liberally decked with jewels (especially pearls) to which from *c.* 1605 were added bows, scraps of lace, and occasionally a plume [Plate X. i].

FOOT-GEAR.—Only in evidence *c.* 1605–1620 these are fashioned like the men's in all respects [Plate X. i ; Fig. 17]. By women *pantoffles* were

[1] Almost the identical coiffure, popularized about 1907 by the American actress, Camille Clifford (" the Gibson girl ").

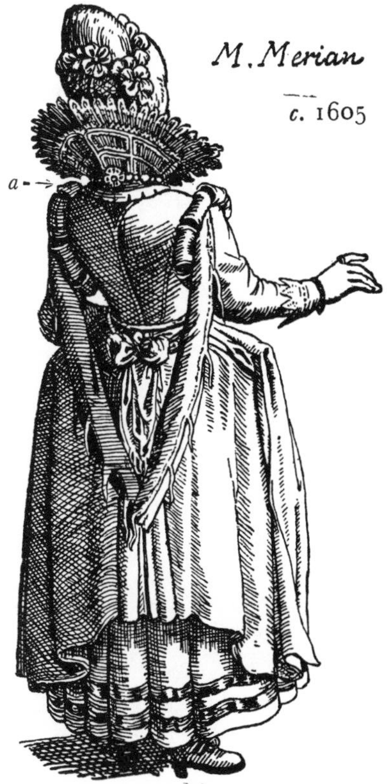
M. Merian
c. 1605
a

FIG. 17.—(*a.* wired *supportasse*).

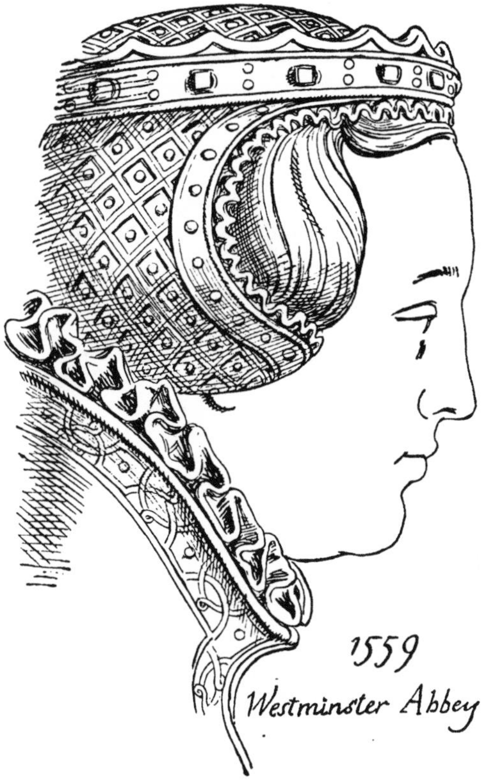
1559
Westminster Abbey

FIG. 18.

1587
Westminster Abbey
a

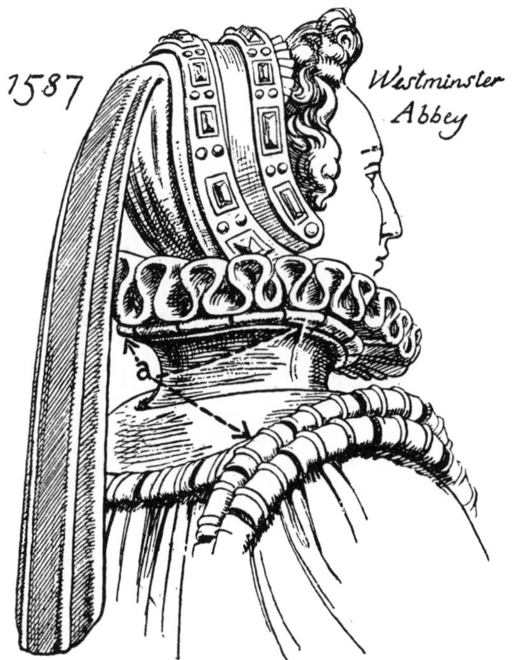

FIG. 19.—(*a.* pickadil).

Fig. 20.

FIG. 21.

largely worn to add to their stature. I can find no evidence that the pedestal-like *chopines* ever " caught on " here.

LINEN.—All the masculine fashions of neck and wrist-wear were common to the fair sex also ; but these had a few varieties of their own. Thus, till the 'seventies, the chemisette (filling the square *décolletage* in front) and ruff are left open in front. From the late 'eighties both chemisette and bodice begin again to expose the bosom, and the great ruff, instead of encircling the neck, in State apparel frames the sides and back of the *décolletage* like a peacock's tail displayed. Shortly after comes in a wired-out lace or linen collar, of like dimensions and fan-like contour rising behind the head. Even with the closed " cartwheel " and falling ruffs (and the whisk) a deep *décolletage* is frequently seen ; cut square throughout the sixteenth century, between *c.* 1605 and 1625 this sinks down in a deep U, not infrequently leaving the breasts quite bare.

ACCESSORIES.—Hair dye, paint, powder, masks, silken scarves, and jewellery of every description were freely patronized. *Fans* (often slung by a cord from the waist) are at first of the stiff, feather-edged type (often carrying a small mirror) ; the modern folding type appears in the 'nineties. Gloves are fashioned like the men's. We meet, too, with small *muffs* for cold weather. Tiny hand-mirrors often dangled from the girdle.

JOHN MORDAUNT, FIRST EARL OF PETERBOROUGH, *c.* 1635

By A. van Dyck.

[Note "turn-up" of sleeve and "clog" sole of boot.]

Penes A. J. Nesbitt, Esq.

IV—" *CAVALIER* " *MODES*

(1620–1660)

THIS might be succinctly described as the age of leather, lace, and lovelocks. Or, again, it might be called the " Van Dyck " era, since its most perfect expression practically coincides with that painter's life and work in England (1632–1641). From *c.* 1620 fashion is by degrees shedding the last traces of Spanish rigidity, till by 1633 it has evolved a more graceful and picturesque style than any recorded in modern times. Unfortunately even by 1641, when Van Dyck died, the first faint traces of degeneration are perceptible, and, in men's dress at least the fine taste of the 'thirties becomes utterly debased before 1650. It is a military age, reflected to some extent in the (male) modes of the day. The origins of certain features may be traced back to *c.* 1600 in the Dutch Wars ; and the Thirty Years War had its repercussions in our own country, quite apart from the armed struggle at home between Crown and Parliament. Note that Paris fashions were instantly copied in London.

MEN

BODY GARMENTS.—Up to 1632 the corset-like, busked doublet, with its pointed waist, *tassets*, and deep wings, holds its own [Plate XI. i, ii], though a tendency to an easier fit is perceptible from *c.* 1628. Four to six vertical slits are apt to adorn breast and back. Plain close-fitting sleeves are in vogue throughout the period, but with the slashed body the typical sleeve of the 'twenties is close buttoned from wrist to elbow, above which it forms a wide puff, paned to show the linen of the shirt (or, very rarely, a coloured lining) beneath [Plate XI. ii]. The *points* attaching the breeches form a row of bows along the waist-line.[1] From 1628 the waist grows easier, less acutely pointed, the *tassets* become deeper, ampler, and fewer, reaching down over the hips. By 1633 the cut of the doublet is most becoming. There is no undue rigidity of line : the waist-line is but slightly emphasized with a slight dip in front, the deep full skirts flare but moderately and end squarely ; the wings shrink

[1] Note that here and there the sleeve is unbuttoned at the wrist and turned back to show a coloured line [Plate XIII.]. This is the origin of the formal turn-up cuff presently introduced.

and disappear [Plate XIII.]. The slashing of the breast tends to vanish, and the sleeves are full from elbow to wrist and open in one long slit down the front, revealing the ample shirt sleeve. Sometimes they have a funnel-shaped turn-up at the wrist to support the spreading shirt-cuff. The points at the waist, so far as they are retained, are mere ornament in the shape of bows or rosettes ; for the breeches are no longer tied to the doublet, but united to it, inside, by hooks and eyes. The latter is often buttoned only the length of the breastbone, from which down it gapes open, revealing a triangular area of shirting above the breeches. In this shape the doublet retains a certain vogue up to *c.* 1645, but as early as 1640 fashion adopts a debased form that becomes general after 1645. This latest version is a skimpy jacket reaching barely to the hips,

FIG. 22.

with little or no " waist " or skirts (these latter survive only in the shape of a narow, tabbed border), the sleeves of a wide " bishop " type, still—mostly—slit to reveal the shirt below.

The *jerkin*, as a supplementary garment, tends to lose ground : generally sleeveless or with mere hanging sleeves (mostly dummies). At first cut on the lines of the doublet, with rather deeper skirts, it is also at times modelled on the *mandilion* (*vide* p. 18, *supra*) and fastens at the breast and up the sides. Very common from *c.* 1620 is the military *buff-coat* (or leathern jerkin), laced or tied with points in front. Sometimes it had loose sleeves to match, often arranged to hang at the back ; more often it was sleeveless or had close stuff sleeves attached, whereby the doublet might be dispensed with [Plate XII.]. It was the fashion to have these sleeves closely striped lengthwise or across with braid or lace. Loose coats of the cassock type to mid-thigh with wide sleeves turned up

i. FROM HOLLAR'S "ORNATUS MULIEBRIS ANGLICANUS," 1640

British Museum.

ii. "AN ENGLISH ANTICKE"; BROADSIDE OF 1648

iii. FROM HOLLAR'S "ORNATUS MULIEBRIS ANGLICANUS," 1640

"DANCERS" (*detail*)

By Hieronymus Jannsens, *c.* 1660

From lid of a spinet in the Kunstgewerbemuseum, Berlin

in a broad cuff at the wrist appear as winter wear, and grow in favour especially from the late 'forties (cut something like our " covert coats " or " British warm "). (*Note* that while all doublets have upright collars, the jerkins and coats are collarless or have a small flat turn-down at the neck.)

Cloaks and Gowns.—From the traditional dignity of the " long robe " and its age-old connection with authority and learning, elderly men still clung to the *gown* (in the form that still distinguishes " Mr. Speaker," chancellors, and mayors) as their State habit. *Cloaks*, except by a fop here and there, are no longer worn in abbreviated form : they reach to the knee or lower, and are still often draped as indicated on p. 18 *ante* [Plates xi. i, ii ; xiii. ; xiv. ii]. For *full-dress* the ruff or band is commonly worn *overlapping the cloak*.

Breeches.—Trunk-hose become unfashionable from *c.* 1620, but are retained till the end of the century by pages in full-dress livery ;[1] also in conjunction with peer's robes, at coronations and as part of the full habits of the Garter. Full knickers ending just above the knee with a row of points are the characteristic wear of the 'twenties [Plates xi. i ; xii.] ; by 1628 they begin to reach below the knees and to be accompanied there by garters tied in a large bow or by rosettes of ribbon ; they are commonly buttoned down the side, a few buttons being often left undone above the knee to show a puffed lining, generally of linen. In the 'thirties the breeches, full at the waistband, narrow to the knee where they are gartered as above, or (alternatively) they fit fairly close and are unconfined at the knee where they are finished off with a fringe of looped ribbons. From the 'forties the fashionable trend is ever more towards these tubular breeches (the old " open " type). From 1645 onward these grow wider and wider, and are garnished with ribbon loops at the knees and along the waistband [Plate xiv. ii ; Fig. 22, a] (often with a bunch of the same, narrowing downward in front and further bunches at the outside of the thigh). Now the breeches button in front, the fastening being mostly hidden in a vertical pleat. At the beginning of our period breeches are cut very high-waisted and remain so through the 'thirties. Between 1645 and 1650 the waistband drops right over the hips, the full shirt bulging out between the breeches and the short, open doublet.

Stockings.—Silk stockings are *the* fashionable wear. In cold weather several pairs are superposed. Between them and the boots are commonly worn *boot-hose* (or over-stockings) often edged with lace whose spreading tops often line the tops of the boots [Plates xiii. ; xiv. ii ; Fig. 22, a]. In the 'fifties boot-hose are often worn with shoes. Pierced with eyelets at the edge, they can be pulled up over the knee and attached to points fixed outside the breeches. *Boot-hose tops* are a trifle later and only differ in lacking the parts beneath the calf. Garters are tied in a great bow below the knee [Plate xi. ii ; Fig. 22, b].

Head-dress.—The universal covering is the broad-brimmed *sombrero*

[1] The paned variety at least would seem from about 1600 to be reserved for formal occasions.

with moderately high crown. The brim is variously *cocked* (=looped up) and garnished with one or two trailing ostrich plumes, or a fringe of ostrich-fronds by way of hat-band [Plate xi. i, ii; Fig. 22, a]. After 1640 high conical crowns and flat, often narrow, brims are the smart wear, and the plumes are partly discarded in favour of ribbon loops [Plate xiv. ii]. For informal wear and sport a cap with a brim capable of being turned down or up, and often split in front (the *montero*), is much used after 1645.

Foot-wear.—Spurred boots are now all the rage. The long, close boot (though commonly turned down or folded into a cup below the knee [Plates xi. i; xiii.]) recurs throughout; but the tendency is for the tops to expand more and more. From *c.* 1628 we also find shorter boots (*i.e.* not above the knee) with "bucket" tops. From the late 'forties the boots, short or long, have excessively wide-spreading tops [Plate xiv. ii; Fig. 22, a]. The spur-leathers from *c.* 1630 assume a butterfly shape at the instep, later growing so large as almost to cover the foot. From the 'forties the toes taper to a square tip. The shoes are very open at the side, the side latchets often being a mere ankle-strap. The roses over the ankle are huge, but from *c.* 1655 tend to be supplanted by large, limp bows of ribbon. Heels are high and square and for dress-wear continue, like the edges of the soles, to be dyed red. Spurs have shanks that bend sharply up at the heel and then downward at an angle, the rowels being star-shaped.

Hair.—The hair up to 1628 is dressed off the brow to one side and hangs level with the jaw [Plate xi. i, ii] (lovelocks continue to be fashionable) [Plates xii.; xiv. ii]; then it lengthens, generally hanging on the shoulders, and sometimes is dressed in a fringe over the brow; though hair dressed in the earlier fashion occurs in the upper classes till 1650 or after. While the cheeks are generally shaven, the "Vandyke" beard continues into the 'forties; but from the 'thirties the tendency is to a mere tuft below the lip, the moustache being brushed upward or allowed to grow naturally. From 1645 the chin-tuft tends to vanish. The moustache alone is not rare after 1640, and in the 'fifties the face is often clean-shaven.

Linen.—The *whisk* lasts up to the 'thirties, but *the* characteristic wear of the 'twenties is the *falling ruff* [Plate xi. i, ii]. The *falling band* also appears in the 'twenties, but generally is of modest dimensions, stiff, and droops a little from the angle of the jaw [Plate xii.]. In the 'thirties it spreads limply, in linen or lace, over the shoulders [Plate xiii.], which it tends completely to mask. From the 'forties it shrinks again, and is cut more square [Plate xiv. ii]. The cuffs turn up in a deep funnel, which in the 'fifties becomes a limply projecting ruffle. The body-linen now tends to bulge out in the openings of the doublet, and over the low waistband of the breeches.

Accessories.—Very broad sashes tied in a great bow behind often confine the waist over the buff-coat—a fashion borrowed from military wear. They are not otherwise adopted by civilians. The girdle with

B A C D E F G H

THE TICHBORNE DOLE (*detail*)
By Gillis van Tilborch, 1671.

Tichborne House.

A B

FAMILY GROUP, 1688

The King's Galleries, Chelsea.

hangers lasts well into the 'thirties [Plate XI. i, ii], but from *c.* 1628 it is supplanted increasingly by the *shoulder-belt* or *baldrick* [Plate XIII.], with which the hangers are incorporated. This gradually grows wider and more ornate. The *sword* up to *c.* 1650 is of the *rapier* type with elaborate hilt; it then suddenly approximates to the modern court-sword (*small sword*) with knucklebow, short quillons, and small shell-guard. The deep-gauntleted gloves are often fringed and embroidered [Plates XI.; XIII.].

In this, as in the preceding age, it was by the better classes considered ill-bred to appear in public in *cuerpo*—*i.e.* without a cloak or gown—although up to the 'eighties the head, at least by the host and principal guests, was very generally covered indoors. In dancing, the cloak was discarded and the hat retained.

[*Note.*—The Puritan in general differed from his neighbours *only* by a certain sobriety of attire and avoidance of modish excesses—love-locks, ribbons, lace, etc. Most of the Parliamentarian leaders wore more or less long hair. Many old-fashioned or provincial Royalist squires were as plainly habited as the average Puritan. The popular conception of a "Roundhead," based on Royalist satires, was always an exceptional type, chiefly restricted to fanatics of the lower middle classes. Under the Protectorate, Cromwell's "Court" was not free from foppery: as when that grim Puritan, Major-General Harrison, appeared at an official reception in scarlet smothered with silver lace and ribands (!).]

WOMEN

Bodice.—The deep-pointed wasp-waist and stomacher hold their own well into the 'thirties, though generally in part hidden by the gown (*vide infra*), but by 1630, or a trifle earlier, a low-necked bodice, with a high waist and skirt-tabs like a male doublet, comes into favour, generally opening over a long round-pointed stomacher to match. It, too, has wings, and sometimes close sleeves to the wrist; though the more typical form is puffed out and paned above and below the elbow up to the mid-'thirties. Another shape restricted to the 'twenties is of the old leg-o'-mutton type made in a series of slashed puffs. Nevertheless, the old sharp-pointed and closed bodice never quite went out, but reappears towards 1650. From the 'thirties on, the sleeves, usually forming a single gathered puff, tend to shorten and bare the forearm; by the 'forties they have shrunk back almost to the elbow and the mouth of the sleeve often opens fairly widely, revealing the sleeves of the chemise. These sleeves are for the most part unslashed, rarely open up the front. The chief difference in the bodices of the 'fifties is a return to the long, wasp-waisted type, pointed in front and laced behind. Less often they lace down the front, sometimes with jewelled clasps or ribbon bows.

Skirt and Petticoat.—In the course of the 'twenties the last traces of the verdingale in the form of padding at the hips vanish in the upper classes. The skirt, gathered at the top, hangs freely. The habit of tucking it under at the sides to uncover the petticoat dies soon after

1625. The Λ-shaped opening over the petticoat obtains throughout the period, but *c.* 1635–1650 the skirt is oftener closed all round.

GOWNS.—The old type of gown, closed at the throat and thence hanging open in spreading folds is mostly restricted to the graver dames. Another form of open gown regularly worn till the 'forties has a fitted body and full-gathered skirt. The full elbow sleeves (sometimes continuing as hanging-sleeves) open down the front are caught together by a bow or rosette at the bend of the arm, and a narrow ribbon tie with bows or rosettes confines the gown at the waist [Plate XI.].

HEAD-DRESS.—Even out of doors ladies now for the most part go bareheaded, though loose gauze veils [Fig. 23] and loose hoods tied in at the throat are not uncommon, especially from the 'forties. The broad-brimmed "cavalier" hat, plumed or not, is rarely worn except for riding. Modified survivals of the old "French hood" and "Mary Queen of Scots" cap, except for widows and elderly women, are rare outside the *bourgeoisie.* Under Puritan rule in the 'fifties, plain high-crowned, broad-leaved hats (over close lace caps) enjoy a transient phase of popularity.

FIG. 23.

FOOT-GEAR.—Seldom visible after *c.* 1625 the shoes were as described for men.

LINEN.—The fan-shaped, wired-up ruffs and collars hold sway till *c.* 1635 [Plate XI. iii], and older ladies long adhere to the great cart-wheel ruff; but before 1630 the broad falling collar of linen or lace begins to creep in and is general by 1635, sometimes high in the neck, sometimes low-cut. In its last phase (in the early 'thirties) the upstanding fan-collar is combined with the falling collar. Apart from this the square, low neck of the bodice is usually edged with lace. The *décolletage* is shaped like a V, or round, or square. A square kerchief of linen or lace, folded diagonally, is laid from *c.* 1635 over the low-cut falling collar and largely masks the exposed shoulders and bosom [Fig. 23]. From *c.* 1640 the tendency is to expose the shoulders more and more, and in the 'fifties the *décolletage* commonly runs horizontally round the bust and appears to be falling from the shoulders. From *c.* 1630 the hand-ruff is out of fashion, and replaced by spreading, turned-back cuff. The short, loose-fitting bodice-sleeve is often edged with lace, beneath which peep out the cuff and sleeve of the chemise [Plate XIV. i]. Laced aprons are seen at times.

HAIR.—The hair is strained off the face to a flat bun at the back and hangs in short full bunches over the ears. From *c.* 1620 the front hair is dressed in a fringe over the forehead, and this from *c.* 1633 is arranged in a series of separate " kiss curls " [Plates XI. iii ; XIV. i]. The side-locks in the 'thirties grow longer by degrees, and from the middle of the 'forties reach to the shoulders in formal " corkscrew " curls. About the same time the fringe in front is often omitted. The chignon, more compact and projecting, is carried a trifle forward and sometimes enclosed in a tiny caul. The hair is sometimes decked with pearls or (after 1650) bows of ribbon.

ACCESSORIES.—The indiscriminate profusion of jewels and embroidery that characterized the Jacobean age gradually abates between 1620–1630. Possibly the death of the magnificent Buckingham in 1628 contributed to give it its quietus. From *c.* 1633 jewellery is used sparingly : chiefly in the form of pearls—necklaces, bracelets, earrings, and miscellaneous pendants. About 1640 the shorter sleeves give rise to an exclusively feminine type of glove : long, close-fitting, and generally of plain white kid or doeskin [Plate XIV. i ; Fig. 23]. It reaches to the elbow where it is secured by a *glove-band* of plaited horsehair or by ribbon ties. Muffs are in general use in winter, and masks and fans continued as before. Patches seem to have come into general use in the 'forties ; despite contemporary satire by pen and pencil, they would seem generally to have taken the small circular form.

V—*FRENCH MODES: COAT, WAISTCOAT, AND CRAVAT*

(1660–1720)

WRITERS on English costume are fond of repeating that, in their main features, the origins of men's fashions, as we know them to-day, are retraceable to the "vest" introduced at Court by Charles II. in October 1666. That the reign of the Merry Monarch saw the birth of our modern "gent's wear" is at least arguable, but that this *particular* "Eastern fashion of vest" had any such far-reaching consequences is a suggestion flatly contradicted by the evidence. After, as before, Paris was the focus of fashion, and King Charles' half-hearted attempt at a counterblast was but a momentary interlude in the evolution of costume.[1] As a matter of fact, by the year 1666 the "vest" was no longer a novelty in England.[2] It derived from the *justaucorps à brevet*, instituted in 1662 by Louis XIV. of France, originally a quasi-military fashion. Throughout this age, and far into the following century, one sex derides the other, and both are a standing butt of contemporary satire for their incorrigible addiction to French fripperies.

MEN

Body Garments.—By 1660 the days of the *doublet* are numbered. Its modish form is a mere abridgment of the skimpy jacket in vogue for the preceding ten, or more, years, disclosing the bulging shirt in front and round the waist. The full sleeves, open down the front, end below the elbow in a deep fringe of looped ribbons [Plate xv. B, D; Fig. 24]. About 1665 the front-opening of the sleeve vanishes for good, and the sleeve, now merely easy-fitting, is turned up from the elbow in a close buttoned cuff. A longer form of doublet to the hips, with a close body and skirts slightly flaring, also occurs in the early 'sixties. The *beau-monde* gave up doublets soon after 1670.

[1] " . . . . vests were put on at first by the King to make Englishmen look unlike Frenchmen; but at the first laughing at it all ran back to the dress of French gentlemen." Anon. *Character of a Trimmer*, 1682. Cf. Evelyn: *Diary*, 18th and 30th October 1666, and Anon. *England's Vanitie*, 1683.

[2] An autograph note in the author's own copy (Bodleian) of Evelyn's *Tyrannus, or the Mode*, 1661, states "that this was publish'd 2 *years before* the Vest, Cravett, Garters, and Boucles came to be the fashion. . . ." Vests, therefore, were in vogue by 1663–1664.

i. QUEEN MARY II., WIFE OF WILLIAM III, 1694 (?)

ii. LOUIS XIV. OF FRANCE, 1694
After Bounard.

Plate XIX.

i. WALKING DRESS

ii. A BEAU

iii GALA DRESS

ENGLISH FASHIONS, 1744–'45

Engraved by Truchy. *After* F. H. Gravelot.

The soldierly *cassock* of the preceding period also occurs round about 1660, worn jerkin-wise over the short doublet. The *jerkin* proper survives only in the military buff-coat. But by 1664 at latest the fashionable world began to patronize the *vest*—a term at the outset ill-defined.[1] This fashion takes its name from the long *sleeved* waistcoat (*vest*) which formed its distinctive feature.[2] Over this was worn a long coat (*tunique*) akin to the *cassock*. At first the coat mostly reached a trifle below mid-thigh and

FIG. 24.—From a French print *c.* 1660.

the waistcoat about to the fork, though in the first decade of their adoption the relative lengths of the two garments varied greatly. In October 1666 the Court adopted a particular vest "after the Persian mode" (so Evelyn; Randle Holme says the *Russian* embassage provided the model)

[1] The term was then (as later) generically applied to the *caftan* of Orientals and Slavs. Evelyn uses it in referring to the long, open gown of the Venetian signory.

[2] The *term* "waistcoat" occurs as early as the fifteenth century to describe a short, close under-doublet, worn (after the manner of a modern "Cardigan") immediately over the shirt. Vests with backs of coarse material were known as "cheats" by the 'eighties (R. Holme).

which we have failed definitely to identify.[1] The terms *tunique* and *vest* were replaced ere long by *coat* and *waistcoat* respectively. By the 'seventies the coat reaches below the knee and has easy-fitting elbow-sleeves, turned up in broad cuffs ; it is slit up to the hip on either side and at the back, these openings being trimmed with a close row of (mostly dummy) buttons. It is arranged to fasten at will in front from throat to hem with similar close buttons, which also fasten the wide pocket-slits [Plate XVI. ; Fig. 25]. These, set *below* the hips, are at first either vertical or horizontal. The waistcoat is of equal length, cut on the lines of the coat; both are collarless, and hang straight down without a " waist." The sleeves (waistcoats, down to *c.* 1760, nearly always have sleeves) fit rather close and reach some inches beyond the coat sleeves, over which they are mostly turned up at the elbow. Some dispensed with the vest, when a double turn-up to the *coat*-sleeve (the second made of a contrasting material) might camouflage its absence. Towards 1680 coat and vest

FIG. 25.

begin to be cut on " frock-coat " lines and the sleeves to lengthen towards the wrist [Plate XVII. B ; Fig. 26]. By the 'nineties the waist is strongly marked—a feature emphasized by the expansion of the coat-skirts, now gathered at the side-openings into two bunches of fan-like pleats radiating from a single button at the hip [Plates XVIII. B ; XX. C]. The coat-sleeves by 1690 have lengthened, and gradually widen from the shoulder to the wrist where they turn up. The small turn-up (or cuff) of the 'sixties rapidly widens, growing to huge expanse by 1700. The coat is now mostly worn unbuttoned, the waistcoat fastened only at the waist (three or four buttons, the rest dummies), the better to show the shirt. The turn-up cuff of the waistcoat shrinks from *c.* 1700 and vanishes after 1710 ; its skirts from *c.* 1695 fall short of the knee (the coat still reaches over the knee-cap).

[1] See *K. and S.*, 2nd edition, pp. ix. and 296; also *The Connoisseur*, August 1931: " A Comely Vest after the Persian Mode." *Diaries* of Evelyn and Pepys; Rugge's *Diurnal*.

A B C

A CONVERSATION PIECE, *c.* 1715–20, BY QUINCKHARDT(?)

[Note the ladies' oddly "Victorian" caps.]

Penes C. D. Rotch, Esq.

CLOAKS.—Though the old "cavalier" type of cloak worn on both shoulders to some extent survives into the 'seventies, cloaks in general after that are used only as wraps for travelling and foul weather. We meet with *roquelaures*, *wraprascals*, etc., right through the eighteenth century, though they are increasingly replaced by a variety of loose overcoats.

BREECHES.—The kilt-like *rhinegrave-* (or *petticoat-*) breeches[1] are the favourite Court-wear of the 'sixties, laden with ribbon-loops at the waist, hem, and sides [Plate xv. ; Fig. 24]. With the adoption of coat and

FIG. 26.

vest, their vogue declines, though they occur, curtailed to mid-thigh, throughout the 'seventies [Plate XVI. c]. The very full lining, gathered into the leg, is often visible below the breeches at the knee. From *c.* 1670, however, full breeches, gartered at the knee, are the usual wear [Fig. 25] ; they grow narrower during the 'eighties, till from the 'nineties plain close-fitting breeches fastened below the knee with a strap and buckle and/or some half-dozen buttons oust all other modes. They are cut full in the seat and fulled on to a waistband, void of ornament, and, where not uniform with coat or waistcoat, mostly of black velvet. A

[1] Also known here as *pantaloons* : a sense of the term peculiar to seventeenth-century England.

type prevalent round about 1680 is fairly full, and caught in above the knee where it is turned up in an inverted flounce.

Stockings, etc.—To the earlier forms of stocking we now have to add "long stirrup hose," widening above the knee, and attached by points to the inside of the petticoat breeches ; over them was often worn a second pair whose wide tops droop over the garters below the knee [Plate xv. c ; Fig. 24]. *Boot-hose* and *boot-hose tops* are still found up to *c.* 1680. A kind of drooping vallance of lace, linen, etc. (*cannon* or *port-cannon*) [1] was in great favour, 1660–1670. Garters are below the knee as before ; often, up to *c.* 1680, trimmed on the outer or both sides with ribbon-loops or scraps of lace.[2] After 1680 all these knee trimmings vanish, and the stockings begin to be rolled over the breeches, and the garter, a plain buckled strap, is commonly concealed by the rolled tops of the stockings, which from the 'nineties are drawn up above the knee over the close breeches.

Head-gear.—In the 'sixties we still find the steeple-crowned hat with the flat brim wider [Plate xv. e]. Between 1665–1675 the crown is low and flat—in fact, the hat resembles a broad-leaved "boater" or the Spanish *cordoves,* as still worn by bull-fighters in mufti. Both plumes and ribbons adorn it till after 1680. In the course of the 'seventies low round crowns and very wide brims, variously *cocked* (=looped up), are in favour. After a number of experiments in cocking, about 1690 the formal three-cornered hat (*i.e.* symmetrically cocked, one corner projecting directly in front) gains the day, and from 1700 reigns supreme. By the same date the sweeping plumes are discarded in favour of a fringe of ostrich-fronds along the brim, which for some time had been edged with metal lace or braid. For travelling, sport, or indoor *négligé* a round cap variously turned up with fur or stuff (*montero*) was in common undress use throughout the period [Fig. 26, a].

Footwear.—Boots immediately after 1660 lost vogue except for riding. The tall, close-fitting boots with tops spreading above the knee appear far into the 'seventies, but from 1665 the rigid, tubular *jack-boot,* with square cuff-like top above the knee, square toe, and large spur-leather predominates. From the late 'seventies a lighter form of jack-boot caught in by buckles, buttons, or lacing to the small of the leg appears ; also, from the 'nineties, high leather *spatter-dashes* (leggings) of similar cut are worn, the large spur-leathers masking their junction with the shoe, so that we cannot distinguish in contemporary illustrations between leggings and actual boots.[3] These now are generally black, and the red heels, etc., are reserved to the dress-*shoes.* Up to

[1] Not to be confused with the earlier *canion.* Cf. *Notes and Queries,* 2nd series, vol. i. p. 164, 1916.

[2] The term "hose" now finally reverts to its original sense of "stockings" as prefigured by the terms "boot-hose," "stirrup-hose," etc. In Germany "hose" still=breeches, trousers.

[3] "Buskins," mentioned by Evelyn and Rugge, are probably the close-fitting boots, clasped down the front, with a fanciful turn-over at the knee, adopted from the pseudo-Romans of the tragic stage.

c. 1680 these still have round upstanding tongues in front. Shoe-roses have vanished; large "butterfly" ribbon-ties, stiffened out or drooping limply, being in vogue till the late 'seventies [Plate XV.; Fig. 24]. From *c.* 1680 ornamental shoe-buckles (worn since the late 'sixties) become universal [Plate XVII. B; Fig. 26]. In the 'sixties small ribbon-bows appear also at the toe. In the 'nineties the tall fronts are cut out in a "Cupid's bow" and turned over to show a red lining. The buckle at the instep, at first small and oval, from the 'eighties to *c.* 1710 is often large and square—a form which predominated eventually from *c.* 1750.

LINEN, ETC.—The shirt is very full in body and sleeves, the latter caught in at the wrist (and at times—till *c.* 1680—below the elbow), usually with ribbon-ties, which vanish *c.* 1680. The wrists are garnished with deep, falling ruffles. The breast-opening is often edged with a ruche or frill of linen or lace: this is the true *jabot* (therefore *not*, as in pre-war ladies' fashions, a kind of falling cravat). The *falling-band*, which disappears soon after 1670, now forms a deep oblong bib over the breast with rounded corners [Plates XV.; XVI. A]. It is gradually superseded from the middle 'sixties by the *cravat* or *neck-cloth*, a folded strip of linen tied at the throat in a bow with short falling ends,[1] or with a *cravat-string* (*i.e.* a bow of coloured ribbon) [Plate XVI. C, D, E, H; Fig. 27, B]. Early in the 'seventies various "made-up" cravats obtained and remained in vogue. In the 'eighties the cravat-string was discarded, and the ends of the cravat, often tasselled, hang longer and more freely [Plates XVII. B; XX. C; Fig. 27, A]. During the 'nineties the cravat-string makes a brief reappearance as a mere ornament, generally double or treble, projecting rigidly *behind* the falling ends of the cravat. In the early 'nineties also appears the *steenkirk* with long ends loosely twisted and tucked through a buttonhole or else caught down by a brooch [Plate XVII. B]. The *term* died out by the end of this period, but old-fashioned folk and provincials retained the *thing* far into the eighteenth century.[2]

COIFFURE.—Clean-shaven faces are common from the 'fifties. The moustache has dwindled to a narrow thread from the nostrils to the corners of the mouth [Fig. 27, B] and disappears *c.* 1685. *Very occasionally* a tiny tuft on the nether lip survives in the 'sixties. With the Restoration the great French *periwig* became universal, not, as before and since, to disguise a natural deficiency, but openly worn over the cropped or shaven poll. In the 'sixties it forms a great, irregularly curled mane over shoulders and back; by the late 'seventies becomes a huge mass of formal corkscrew curls [Fig. 27, B]. From *c.* 1695–1720 it towers high above the brow, often in twin peaks. This tall foretop then dwindles by degrees till after 1720. For Court wear it maintains its unwieldy bulk throughout this period, though not a few were normally content with a natural growth [Fig. 27, A]. For travelling, shorter but very full wigs were commonly used from *c.* 1675, and towards 1680 the flowing ends began to be tied back to the nape by soldiers and sportsmen. Thence, towards

[1] With military undress the cravat appears occasionally from the 'forties.

[2] Cf. Garrick, *Bon Ton*, 1775.

1710, developed the various queues (*bags*, *ramillies*, etc.), so typical of the following age, but till after 1720 worn as undress only.

ACCESSORIES.—The 'sixties is an age of looped ribbons lavishly distributed over the whole person. During the 'seventies these are discarded by degrees, till from the 'eighties they are practically reduced to the *shoulder-knot* (a bunch of loops at the right shoulder), which soon after 1700 was relegated to lackeys; sometimes it was of looped cord. The sword-baldrick or *shoulder-belt* becomes ever longer, broader, and

FIG. 27.

richer; it disappears towards 1700 [Plate XVI. E]. A broad, loosely knotted sash was often worn about the hips over the coat *c.* 1665–1680; sometimes, between 1670–1695, over the waistcoat, with short ends hanging level in front [Plate XVI. A]. When girt about the coat it often served to confine the shoulder-belt, which now carried a " small sword " of the type still worn at Court. After 1700 this hung from a sling or " frog " under the waistcoat, the hilt and scabbard-tip protruding from the coat-skirts. A broad, tasselled *sword-knot* commonly adorned the hilt. A huge, beribboned muff often hung from a waistbelt. Tall canes—malaccas for choice—were carried, beribboned or with a tasselled cord. The laced pocket-handkerchief often dangled from a pocket; handsome snuff-boxes and combs were freely used in public by dandies. Paint and patches were in vogue.

WOMEN

Bodice.—This resumes the form of a tight-laced corset, baring the shoulders—though the *décolletage* may be modified by the upper border of the chemise or by light filmy scarves variously draped about the opening—with full elbow-sleeves, sometimes slashed down the front, gathered in tight pleats at the armhole and below [Plates xv.; xvi.]. The body fastens up in front or (oftener) laces behind. The front opening may be garnished with large bows of ribbon or jewelled clasps. In the earlier part of the period the corset effect is often enhanced by the bodice being prolonged over the hips where it flares out in a skirt of petal-like tabs. From the 'seventies the sleeve ceases to be puffed and becomes tubular and easy-fitting, without gathers; often reaching but a short way below the shoulder, a mode which endured for Court-dress up to *c.* 1710. At the elbow it was commonly finished off in a fringe of ribbon loops (till the 'eighties), lace, or a buttoned-up cuff. Where the latter was worn it was increasingly the vogue to gather it across the armbend with loop and button, or a clasp.

Skirt and Petticoat.—Up to the mid-'seventies the skirt was closely pleated into the waist. More often than not it opens in front over the petticoat, the edges of the opening being caught back at intervals by bows or clasps, or they may be looped back in the centre and fastened behind to display the lining. The fulness behind becomes emphasized towards 1690 by the insertion of a bustle (*cul-de-Paris*), though by 1711 the old "Spanish" verdingale was revived under the name *hoop*. Especially *c.* 1680–1710 tended to be laden with ribbons, lace, furbelows, etc. The fashionable skirt, where not looped up, trails on the ground behind.

Gowns.—Gowns with close, shaped bodies modelled on the separate bodice, full, looped back-skirts, and trains occur *c.* 1680–1710. The sleeves follow the current modes. We hear also of informal loose gowns termed *manteaux*. The *sack* is referred to by Pepys, but is difficult to identify till the closing years of the period. Possibly the loose circular gowns, hanging straight from the shoulders, that occur in the second decade of the eighteenth century, may be of this class.

Head-gear.—Till well into the 'eighties no striking novelties appear in this class. Up to then, though loose kerchiefs and hoods are worn [Fig. 28], bare heads are the general rule. For riding, etc., not a few dashing ladies affected hats of the masculine pattern (to say nothing of coat and waistcoat—accommodated to the feminine figure—cravat and sash; some went so far as to wear riding-wigs and light dress-swords). From *c.* 1660 the hair was mostly adorned over the ears with bunches of ribbon [Plates xv. a; xvi. f, g]. These, developed by the 'eighties into loops of ribbon across the crown, often eked out with scraps of lace, and formed the origin of the *fontange* (alias *commode* or *tower*) so conspicuous a feature of the period, 1690–1710. This was a close linen cap worn at the back of the head, garnished in front with upright, graduated tiers of wired-out lace and ribbon nodding above the face, at the back with long lace lappets that could be pinned up [Plate XVIII. i]. Over it could be worn hoods and kerchiefs [Fig. 29]. In the 'nineties the fontange was often absurdly tall. From *c.* 1700 it shrinks, and by 1710 a small linen cap appears with narrow quilled border, but retaining the long lappets [Plate XX.]. By 1720 this had shrunk to the merest apology for a cap.

FIG. 28.

HAIR.—The typical *coiffure* of the 'sixties is puffed or bunched out above the ears, with clusters of corkscrew curls wired out to hang well clear of the cheeks [Plates XV. A ; XVI. F, G]. In the 'seventies the side-curls hang close to the face, but there is a growing tendency to adopt long curls brought from the nape forward over the shoulders. Another mode of the 'seventies was a close crop of curls all over the head (Fr. *hurluberlu*) ; yet another round about 1674 was the *taure* or bullhead, in which a mop of curls overhung the forehead. In the 'eighties the hair on top is dressed in a curly mass on either side of a centre parting [Plate XVII. B]. In all these *coiffures* it forms a small " bun " at the back, while long corkscrew ringlets fall down the back or are brought forward over the shoulder. During the 'nineties it is built up high in front [Plate XVIII. A], generally forming two towering peaks. Between 1700 and 1710 this dressing gradually sinks ; till, in the last decade of the period, the hair is dressed quite close to the head and curled back over the brow ; the long locks at the nape being more and more reserved for State occasions. About 1700, powder begins to be much in vogue, and from *c.* 1715 is general.

Shoes.—From now on ladies' shoes have a cut of their own. With the 'sixties begins the vogue of the ultra-high " Louis " heel, and the toes increasingly taper to a " needle " point. For full-dress, the satin, brocade, or needlework shoes are retained right through the next century ; they are adorned at the instep with buckles or bows (the latter occur till mid-eighteenth century). *Mules* now appear ; high-heeled slippers with uppers covering only toe and instep. From *c.* 1665–1690 instances occur of tall *buskins* of satin or fine leather, used for riding and hunting.

Fig. 29.

Linen.—Though deep, high-necked collars (*gorgets*) linger into the 'sixties they are early relegated to widows, old ladies, and the *bourgeoisie*. An overlapping border of lace often edges the low neck of the bodice. From the 'nineties till the second decade of the eighteenth century the masculine *steenkirk* was not rarely adopted, the ends secured by a brooch. [*Note.*—Where the male coat and waistcoat were likewise borrowed, the steenkirk was twisted through a buttonhole.]

The full-puffed elbow-sleeve visible below the embryonic bodice-sleeve was commonly caught in by bows. From the 'nineties it was largely replaced by a deep lace vallance hanging from the sleeve of the bodice ; and the old formal cuffs and ruffles are replaced by a variety of lace frills.

Accessories.—*Aprons*, as objects of display, were much worn from *c.* 1690 : often quite short, of rich material, garnished with lace and embroidery. Their vogue lasted through the eighteenth century, though from *c.* 1710 the tendency was to wear them longer and less elaborate. The long, close elbow-glove is now general for full dress: of silk and fine leather. The modern " kid " (*glacé*) glove dates at least from the early part of this period. Long lace or silk mittens often take their place for summer outdoor wear. Muffs, now generally large, are much used in cold weather. Long, broad scarves of rich stuff, lavishly decorated and worn about the shoulders stole-wise, were common, for outdoor use, from *c.* 1695 till *c.* 1775 [Fig. 29]. Tall canes were sometimes carried by ladies, and in summer stiff *umbrelloes* (parasols) richly fringed were used. At first these were long-handled and borne over their mistress's heads by pages. Hair-powder rendered paint more popular than ever, and patches were general. Ribbon-trimmings in the form of loops and bows, also embroideries, fringes, etc., were profusely employed up to *c.* 1700, after which their use was gradually restricted. From the accession of Queen Anne, costume, except for full Court-dress, was generally less ornate in detail.

VI—*THE HEYDAY AND DECLINE OF POWDER*

(1720–1800)

DESPITE the widely voiced distaste for "Frenchified" ways, the social influence of the French Court over the polite world at large had gained too firm a footing easily to be renounced. But English ways and culture were gradually becoming to a large extent emancipated. English wealth, comfort, and practical common sense combined with the all-prevalent cult of "Nature" to impress the growing continental reactionaries against the artificial culture of Versailles. England, too, was pre-eminently the home of sport. For all but the most formal of State occasions, English modes began to spread to the Continent including even Paris. Nor, on the other hand, was the Revolution without its echoes here.

MEN

COIFFURE.—For once, reversing the order hitherto adopted, let the barber's craft have pride of place. The old *full-bottomed* wig continued for Court-wear till the middle of the century, but the tendency was more and more to curtail it and carry the fullness towards the nape, the heavy front lappets being obsolete by the mid-'thirties. Even from *c.* 1730 modish men discarded it, and, variously modified, it characterized elderly folk and the professional classes. From now on the wig is rolled off the forehead in a low *toupee* (Fr. *toupet*) and usually dressed at the nape (mostly with a black bow tie) in a *queue.* Of outstanding fashions in queues we may note :

(1) The *tie*—a mere bunch of curls caught together by a black bow tie.

(2) The square black *bag*, trimmed with a bow at the top, in which the back hair is encased and held by a running string.

(3) The *ramillie*, or braid of plaited hair, with a bow at nape and often at end. From *c.* 1790 this queue may be looped up to the back of the wig by means of a comb.

(4) The *pig-tail* encased in a spiral black ribbon case (like a miniature umbrella-case).

We may mention further the *major* wig whose queue formed a single "corkscrew" curl, and the *brigadier*, often confused with it, but ending in two such curls [Fig. 30, D]. About 1770 appears the *catogan* or *club*, a broad figure-of-eight queue much affected by the *Macaronies* (Plates XXV. B; Fig. 32).

The toupee towards 1750 shows a tendency to grow higher, which in the early 'seventies especially was carried to excess by Macaronies [Plate XXIII.]. The side-locks formed *pigeons' wings*: a curly bush of hair hanging in front of either ear. From *c.* 1745 these are mostly replaced by one or more horizontal roll-curls at each side of the face. By the 'eighties a single broad roll often runs with an upward curve from ear to ear round the back of the head. About the same period the hair over the crown often forms a rough, dishevelled crop. Under the wig the head was close-cropped or shaven, except, at times, for small bunches at brow and nape, which were powdered and dressed into the toupee and queue. There were also those whose abundant hair was powdered and

FIG. 30.

arranged in imitation of a modish peruke. Powder was sometimes omitted; this for everyday wear grew increasingly common from the 'sixties and general by the 'nineties. The natural hair in everyday usage at that date was often worn long and dishevelled, or short behind and full in front. By the close of the century quite short hair occurs [Fig. 34].

COATS.—For full-dress the fashion of coats introduced with the eighteenth century remain virtually unaltered till the end of the 'fifties [Plates XIX. ii; XXI.; Fig. 30]. The close waist, low neck, spreading skirts, huge cuffs, and great pocket-flaps remain much the same. The skirts reaching well over the knee-caps are still buckramed out in front to rival the ladies' hoops. Individual taste might modify the length and spread of the skirts and the tight fit at the waist; occasionally a broad collar fell flat upon the shoulders. These modifications occur among the "quality" as early as 1731 in imitation of rustic styles—an affectation revived at intervals till the end of the century. The coat was left open or at most buttoned only at the waist. A general shrinkage

i. PORTRAIT OF A GENTLEMAN
British School, Eighteenth Century, *c.* 1750.
National Gallery.

ii. NIKITA DEMIDOFF, 1756
By L. Tocqué.
Penes Princess Abamalek-Lazareff, Pratolino.

[The dress of ii. exemplifies the late survival (in Russia) of the court modes of 1735–'40.]

A B

HORACE WALPOLE PRESENTING KITTY CLIVE WITH A PIECE OF HONEYSUCKLE, *c.* 1765(?)

By Arthur Devis. *Penes the Lady Margaret Douglas.*

sets in towards 1750: in the following decade the flaring skirts lose favour, and the fronts begin to be sloped backwards below the waist, the side-pleats to be shifted backwards [Plate XXII.]. In the course of the 'sixties the coat is cut rather on a "morning-coat" model [Plates XXIII.; XXIV.]; the sleeves grow reasonably close, and the cuffs, no longer open at the back, lose their bulk.[1] In the 'eighties appears, at first for ordinary smart wear, a high-waisted, double-breasted "cut-away" coat, often with large

FIG. 31.—Riding-coats (French prints).

pointed lapels and very long, square tails below which, when buttoned, peeps forth the short, skirtless waistcoat [Plate XXVI. C, F, G, H; Figs. 32, 34]: a mode carried to extremes in the *Directoire* style (*c.* 1796), occasionally adopted by Englishmen of republican sympathies. The coat till the 'sixties was mostly low-necked. From the late 'sixties it is

[1] Even from the late seventeenth century the "turn up" of the sleeve was often closed all round. The rounded corners of the open cuffs were termed "hounds' ears" from *c.* 1680.

cut closer to the neck and surmounted by a standing collar : single for gala-wear, double—*i.e.* like our modern " rise and fall " shirt-collars—for ordinary occasions. By the 'nineties the coat collar rises almost to the ears. The coat-cuff is not only increasingly smaller and tighter, but reaches down to the wrist, revealing henceforth only the ruffle of the shirt. In its earlier wider form it fell just short of the wrist, affording a glimpse of the full shirt-sleeve. From the late 'fifties the pocket-flaps also lose volume.

For travelling and country wear a variety of overcoats were worn, generally of loose fit (though some are based on the fashion in ordinary coats) [Fig. 31]. They have large cuffs and wide, flat collars—often double—which might be turned up and buttoned. These, from the middle of the century, developed into capes, double or treble.

FIG. 32.

The *waistcoat* (originally *vest*). Till the 'sixties sleeved and with full skirts fore *and aft*. The hind skirts and the sleeves below the elbow match the fronts. At the back the waistcoat is closely laced up or tied in with tapes. The skirts reach within an inch or two of the knee, less frequently (at first) to mid-thigh, and are, till the 'fifties, buckramed in front. From then on the stiffening vanishes likewise from hinder skirts and sleeves, and they shrink steadily upwards. From the 'eighties appear double-breasted, skirtless waistcoats, with large, pointed lapels often overlying those of the coat. Down to the 'seventies the waistcoat is usually buttoned at the waist only, the opening above freely displaying the shirt with its puckered jabot, now forming a projecting double frill [Plate XXI. ii]. Full-dress waistcoats throughout the first half of the century often have a heavy fringe to the deep skirts [*ibid.*]. The shorter waistcoats button from breast to waist. Down to 1750 the waistcoat sleeve just peeps out under the coat sleeve.

BREECHES.—Where long waistcoats and tall, rolled stockings are worn these are at times almost hidden. The cut varies little before the last third of the century, when the fashion is to shape them to give a wrinkleless fit to the thigh. Skin-tight buckskins for riding are common from the 'eighties. A buckle and several buttons secure the breeches at the knee, though for the smoother set of the rolled stockings they may depend wholly on cut without such fastenings. Bunches of strings or ribbons at the knee were often worn instead in the last quarter of the century. Tight pantaloons (=trousers), buttoned below the calf, were at times worn *as undress* in the 'nineties [Fig. 34, A].[1]

FIG. 33.

STOCKINGS.—For State occasions still " clocked " with gold and silver.

[1] Not to be confused with the "pantaloons" (p. 41, note 1, *ante*) of Charles II.'s day.

Till after 1745 the " dressy " type were *rollers* : long stockings drawn *over* the knee of the breeches in a broad, flat roll, which usually hid the garter ; afterwards the breeches are gartered over them.

HEAD-GEAR.—The three-cornered hat holds its own throughout the

FIG. 34.

century, varying mainly in its proportions and the relative elevation of its corners. The edges continue to be commonly bound with braid or lace, and (till the 'sixties) fringed with feather [Plates XIX. ii ; XXI. ii]. At intervals the cocking prefigures the *bicorne* of the Revolution and

A B C D E F

INTERIOR OF THE PANTHEON, 1772 (*detail*)

A and D approach the *macaroni* type.

Engraved by Robt. Earlom. *After* Brandoin.

A B C D

THE DUTTON FAMILY, 1775

By Zoffany.

Penes Daniel H. Farr, Esq.

Napoleon's familiar *petit chapeau*. This is especially the case, from before the 'fifties, with the *Khevenhuller* affected by military men, led captains and the like. From the 'seventies the front peak tends to point markedly upward, and by the 'eighties develops gradually into the aforesaid *bicorne* [Plate XXVI. C, F; Fig. 33, A], without, however, quite ousting the earlier form. The tiny *Nivernois* hat was much favoured by the "Macaronies." Wide Quakerish hats had been worn by the soberer sort from 1700 and became pretty usual for everyday wear after 1770 [Plate XXVI. G, H], especially for sport. Tall beaver hats, with tapering crowns, were favoured by bucks in the 'eighties, and in the late 'nineties approached the true "topper" form [Fig. 34, A].

The *night-cap* and the *montero* often replaced the wig for indoor undress in company with the *nightgown* (*i.e.* dressing-gown) worn over the *waistcoat.*[1]

FOOT-GEAR.—Throughout the 'twenties square toes are still worn with men's shoes and boots but then give place to a more normal cut. The high, square fronts shrink and become inconspicuous above the buckle, which from the 'thirties to the 'seventies is smallish and elliptical, then once more large and square. In the last quarter of the century the red heel vanishes except for Court-wear. From the 'eighties strings often replace the buckle.

The original *jack-boot* (cf. Chapter V.) vanishes about 1725. A more smartly cut boot, the top hollowed out behind the knee, and often secured beneath it by a strap and buckle, replaced it. The spur-leathers still have wide flaps over the instep. Tall, shaped *spatterdashes* of black leather, buttoned or buckled at the side, were also used for riding. *Top-boots* (still in use by jockeys and huntsmen) appear as early as 1735, but became fashionable with walking dress among bucks in the last quarter of the century, and *Hessians* towards 1800. Short *spatterdashes* (our modern "spats") were also worn in the 'nineties, especially for shooting and country sports, but were never "smart."

LINEN, ETC.—The *steenkirk* and cravat with falling ends, though they lingered among old-fashioned country gentlemen till the 'seventies, were from *c.* 1730 rapidly supplanted by the plain folded *stock* buckled at the nape. The fine shirt has lawn or lace ruffles at the wrist, and the *jabot* becomes increasingly prominent in the opening of the waistcoat [Fig. 33, B]. A broad, black ribbon (*solitaire*) attached to the tie of the wig often hangs loose about the shoulders, the ends being tucked into the breast of the shirt or caught into a brooch at the throat. *C.* 1725–1750 the solitaire is frequently drawn tight about the stock and tied in a bow at the throat (Fig. 30, B). The "Macaronies" in the 'seventies favoured a new form of cravat: a muslin neckerchief tied in a bow in front. The very tall cravat, knotted in front, of the 'nineties fully deserves the name of "choker."

CLOAKS.—See Chapter V.

[1] The waistcoat, made with back and sleeves to match—as in its original form—the fronts, served independently as an indoor lounge jacket.

Accessories.—The light dress-sword hung from a frog and belt under the vest, or from a cut-steel sling hooked into the waistband of the breeches, the hilt protruding between the skirts of the waistcoat, sometimes between the coat-skirts also [Fig. 30, D]. From the 'seventies it was rapidly discarded except in full Court-dress. Canes varied in length, malaccas being in special favour. Amber and ivory knobs, grotesque heads, and tasselled cords were much patronized. The vogue of muffs continues to be pretty wide ; likewise of highly ornate snuff-boxes.

WOMEN

Bodice.—This retains in essentials its corset shape ; the front either open and laced or otherwise fastened over a busked stomacher, or it might have false fronts (Fr. *compères*) sewn to it inside, which buttoned or hooked together, simulating a stomacher or corset ; or again the bodice was uniform, without suggestion of a stomacher. It might be fastened, visibly or invisibly, behind. The *échelle*, or series of graduated bows

A B C D E

Fig. 35.

down the front-opening, was a favourite trimming. Although the deep *décolletage* persisted through the century, there was an increasing tendency to modify the exposure with fichus and scarves.

With both independent bodice and gown, the elbow-sleeve retained ts hold on favour to the end of the period ; the small turn-up cuff lasting till the 'fifties, though bell-mouthed, flounced, and gathered trimmings gradually prevailed from the 'forties. For ordinary wear long close sleeves, often of mannish pattern, reappeared towards 1780.

Skirt and Petticoat.—In the 'thirties, and in varying degrees thenceforward till towards 1780, these, except for full-dress, were often of ankle-length in smart society.[1] The skirt, gathered full on the hips and to a minor degree behind, was generally open in front. In the 'seventies and 'eighties the revival of the bustle transferred the fullness to

[1] Round about 1730, in particular, pseudo-rustic fashions were the last word in *chic*.

the back. Skirt and petticoat were adorned in front or all round with ruches, flounces, appliqués, etc., in great variety. *Trains* were a feature of Court-dress and were to some extent reintroduced (they had been in favour *c.* 1680–1700) into ordinary fashionable attire together with the bustle. The petticoat worn over the hoop had, like the skirt, pocket-holes concealed in the side-gathers. Quilted petticoats were much worn in the third quarter of the century.

Gowns.—Down to the 'forties the loose *sack* was the typical fashionable gown. At first hanging loose all round, by the 'thirties it develops the

Fig. 36.—The "Watteau pleat."

so-called "Watteau pleat" (wholly foreign, by the way, to Watteau's art and age) at the back, and the body, sometimes loose, was increasingly shaped to mould the waist beneath these folds [Figs. 35, c; 36]. The sack may open in front to the ground or only to the waist. Generally the open fronts are edged by a broad revers-like pleat. Till the 'seventies the characteristic box-pleats behind hang free from the shoulders, dying away into the ample skirt. From then on, except for State functions, the tendency is to sew these pleats flat down as far as the waist; but by the latter part of the 'eighties it had become old-fashioned.

The *polonese*, beloved of the 'seventies, had the fronts curving away to the back [Fig. 39, A, B, D]. The body fitted tightly to the figure, while vertical running-strings looped the full skirt into three great festoons: behind and on either hip. Some poloneses are actually "made up" (*i.e. cut* into festoons), the tasselled cords being then mere ornament. The polonese might also be combined with the "Watteau pleat."

From the middle of the century full skirts, whether in one with the gown or separate, are often tucked under, and the edges pulled out through the pocket-holes [Fig. 39, D].

In the later 'seventies came into vogue gowns closely moulded to the figure from bosom to over the hips on the lines of what in our own times was known as a "princess" dress. [*N.B.*—These were adopted in France under the name of *robes à l'anglaise.*] In the last years of the

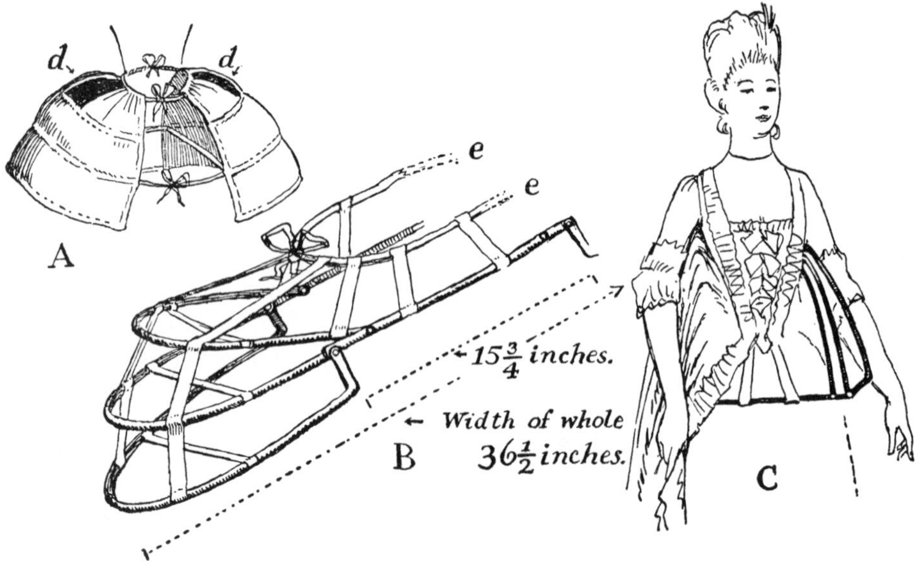

FIG. 37.—Side-hoops, after Leloir.

century loose diaphanous frocks in would-be imitation of the antique were worn. The so-called "Empire" fashions really begin at this point. It was in 1794 that the "waist" was carried up under the armpits, and the loose frocks of that date are compared to "the petticoat tied round the neck and the arms put through the pocket-holes."

HOOPS AND BUSTLES.—The hoop by the 'twenties assumes a domed outline. From the 'thirties it is flattened fore and aft and expanded at the sides, till by the 'forties it spreads almost wholly sideways, with a tendency to reach its maximum width at the hips. To pass through a narrow door thus clad, it was necessary to double the flexible hoop together in front or else to walk sideways [Plate XXII.]. Hence the invention, by the 'forties at least, of twin side-hoops tied about the waist, and a little later of a hinged metal frame capable of folding upwards from the hips [Fig. 37]. The hoops had pocket-holes at the hips and bag-like pockets

A B C

TIGHT LACING; OR, FASHION BEFORE EASE, 1775–'80

Engraved after John Collet.

[In A note *stays* and pockets *outside* the petticoat; in B the *catogan*; and in C the *dormeuse* cap.]

Plate XXVI.

A B C D E F G H

From Malton's "Dublin," June 1796 (*detail*)

suspended inside. In the last quarter of the century, except for Court functions, the bustle (Fr. *tournure*) ousted the hoop, to vanish itself by 1794.

COATS, JACKETS, ETC.—For riding, hunting, etc., adaptations of the current masculine coats and waistcoats to the fashionable female figure,

FIG. 38.

never wholly abandoned, enjoyed increased favour in the last quarter of the century, when riding coats with collar, lapels, capes, pocket-flaps, etc., were much worn [Fig. 40]. Loose undress jackets with short sleeves, chiefly for indoor wear, occur throughout the period ; in the 'seventies and 'eighties there are attempts to incorporate in them features from the gowns—sacks, poloneses, and whatnot—in vogue.

Cloaks, Pelisses, etc.—A variety of loose, cloak-like wraps with armholes occur throughout the period, also pelisses, scarves, and hooded capes (*cardinals*).

Head-gear.—For State functions no head coverings were worn except by widows or elderly dames. For ordinary wear small lace or linen caps, mostly with long lappets behind, were worn, barely covering the top of the crown [Fig. 41]. About the middle of the century the quilled edge often has a slight dip in front that recalls the " Mary Queen of Scots " cap. Elderly ladies and the middle-classes throughout wore them larger. From the 'sixties the caps increase in size, often notably,

Fig. 39.

with a tendency to follow the development of the coiffure. Some were enormous. Drooping, frilled edges grew in size and popularity. No form is more typical of the 'seventies than the *dormeuse* [Plates xxiv. d; xxv. c]. " Mobs " date also from this period.

As a consequence of the craze, about 1731, for the mock-pastoral, wide-brimmed " milkmaid " straw hats, gaily beribboned (often tied under the chin), rose into general favour, often worn above the lawn and lace caps. In the 'seventies and 'eighties the variety of hats, often preposterous in size and decoration, in every imaginable material or materials is very noticeable.

For riding and sport, beaver hats of the wide-awake and " topper " type were freely adapted from their male prototypes from *c.* 1770 onward [Fig. 40].

While the hair continued to be dressed fairly close to the head, the

Fig. 40.

small hood of Stuart days was retained without essential change ; but the vast capillary erections fashionable in the 'seventies and 'eighties demanded coverings to match.

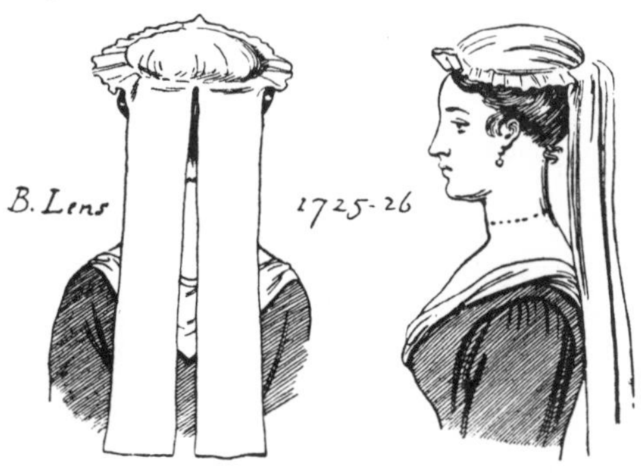

Fig. 41.

Most notable of these was the *calash* mounted on a hinged frame of hinged metal hoops, capable of being raised or lowered like the hood of a perambulator [Fig. 39, B, F]. A lighter covering was the *thérèse* of gauze or thin silk over wires or whalebone. In the last five years of the century came in small bonnets of a modest "poke" ("coalscuttle") or helmet shape, trimmed with ribbon, often on a straw foundation [Fig. 34, c]; also turbans.

HAIR.—Till the end of the 'fifties the hair is curled off the forehead and over the ears, close over the crown, and in a small " bun " behind. The long, curled neck-locks continue in vogue for full-dress—either hanging down the back or brought forward in front of the shoulder—and

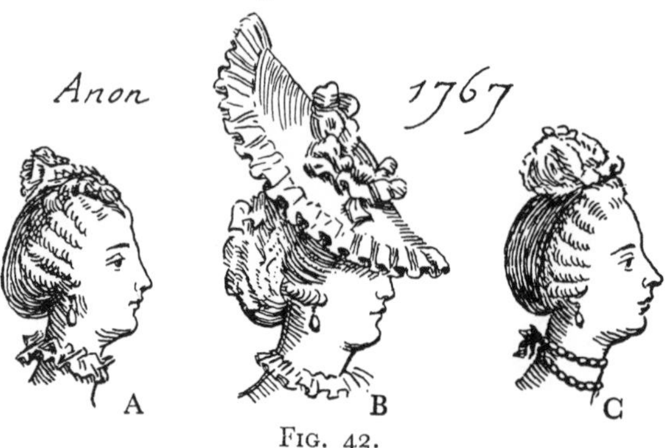

FIG. 42.

are rather uncommon for ordinary wear from the 'thirties to the end of the 'sixties ; but then enjoy wide popularity till the late 'nineties. Powder is always worn for State occasions and till the last quarter of the century in all but informal wear. There is a tendency for the hair to be dressed higher towards 1760, and in the ensuing decade the coiffure is a tall, egg-shaped erection with formally arranged roll-curls at the sides. As these increase from *c.* 1770, pads and masses of false hair help to

FIG. 43.

increase their volume to incredible bulk [Plates XXIII. E ; XXIV. A ; XXV. A ; Figs. 38, 39, 40, 43]. After 1775 the crown of the head becomes a crazy conglomeration of false hair, ribbons, feathers, scarves, and as if this were not enough it is surmounted by models, in blown glass, straw, etc., of windmills, ships, a coach-and-four, and the like. Towards 1780 this mass swells out broad and flat at the summit and thenceforth breadth is cultivated at the expense of height. The back hair from *c.* 1770 hangs down in a large chignon or a *catogan* after the male pattern, combined still pretty generally with the long ringlets from the nape. For ordinary

i. EFFIGY OF SIR JOHN PECHE (*d.* 1522)

Lullingstone, Kent.

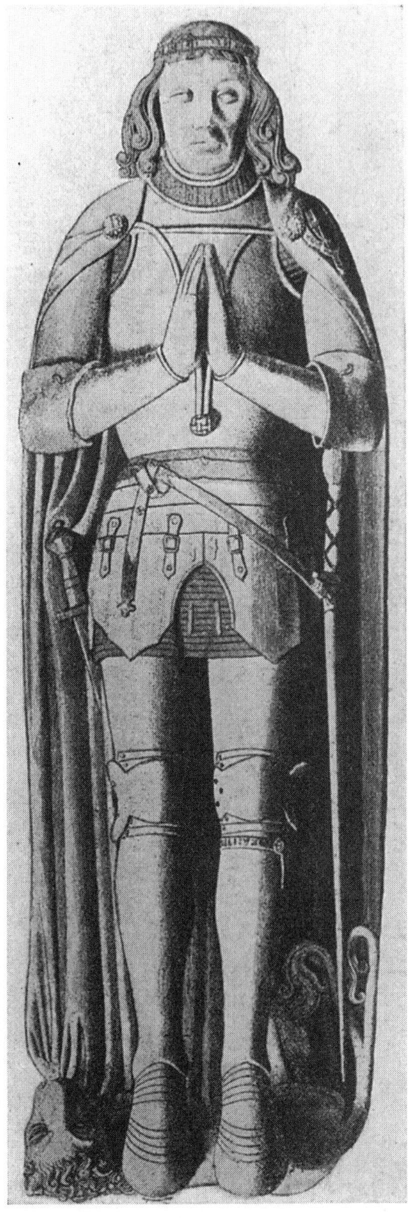

ii. EFFIGY OF JOHN DE LA POLE, 2ND DUKE OF SOMERSET (*d.* 1491)

Wingfield, Suffolk. *From Stothard.*

PLATE XXVIII.

i. SIR NICHOLAS CAREW
Painted 1536, by Holbein.
Bowhill, Selkirk.

ii. JOHN, FIRST LORD MORDAUNT OF TURVEY, *c.* 1540
Hornby Castle, Yorks.

[Both figures, owing to the absence of ruff or band, afford an unusually clear view of the *collar* of the armour, supporting cuirass and pauldrons.]

wear in the 'eighties a full crop of curls over the crown and very long hair behind were in vogue. Except at Court, powder in the last quarter of the century tended more and more to be discarded, or used very sparingly. It vanished in the course of the 'nineties, when a " natural " or pseudo-classical style became the rage.

LINEN.—Till the 'seventies little more than a narrow lace frill peeping

FIG. 44.

above the bodice is visible of the chemise. From under the short sleeves of the bodice hang deep lace ruffles. As already stated, the exposure of breast and shoulders is often more or less modified by scarves and kerchiefs whose ends are tucked into the bosom. Towards 1790 appears the *buffont*—an extra full fichu, bulging out, like the breast of a pouter-pigeon, above the bodice ; it lost favour about 1795. About the same date broad-frilled collars often cover the shoulders. From the 'thirties close bands of ribbon knotted in front were tied high under the chin, partly supplanted from the late 'forties by tiny lace ruffs. When masculine

FIG. 45.

coats, hats, etc., are affected, the appropriate cravat, stock, jabot, etc., usually goes with them.

Shoes.—Though very lofty " Louis " heels are worn till the 'nineties, especially for full-dress, one notes from *c.* 1760 a growing tendency towards lower, flatter heels for informal wear. Ribbon ties or rosettes are not rare in lieu of buckles. The pointed toes in the last decades of the century gradually give way to round toes. About 1790 came in a new form which gained steadily in favour : very flat and all but heelless : in fact, the heel is often little more than a thickening of the sole behind. They are often in the form of a low satin slipper with tiny ornamental bow in front, or else like a ballet-shoe with sandal ribbons.

Accessories.—The long gloves and mittens (these latter often of kid) last through the century, *umbrelloes* (parasols) and tall canes were often carried in the 'seventies and 'eighties. In the second half of the century the ornamental apron gradually ceased to have other than a strictly utilitarian rôle. Flowers, real and artificial, are worn in the hair and at the bosom.[1] Muffs outlive the century. Paint and patches are almost *de rigueur* at Court to the close of the century, since hair-powder was held to kill the brightest of natural complexions. Otherwise, with the return to " nature " in the last years of the century, all three fell into disrepute with the rising generation and the would-be " progressives."

[1] Flattened glass receptacles for water were sewn inside the top of the bodice or corset to receive the natural posies.

PART II—ARMOUR

(1485–1650)

THE art of the armourer reached its apogee during the short reign of the Yorkist dynasty. Not England, France, or Burgundy led the way, but Italy first, and then Germany. As early as 1398 the Duke of Hereford (Bolingbroke, after Henry IV.) was furnished by Gian Galeazzo Visconti, Duke of Milan, with Milanese armour (from the Missaglia workshops, no doubt) for his abortive duel with the Duke of Norfolk, who, on his part, sought his armour from Germany. At an early date the Milanese armourers' works were pouring through the mountain-passes into South Germany,[1] where presently were to arise schools of hammermen—at Innsbruck, Nürnberg, and Augsburg—capable of challenging Italy's best. We have already seen in Vol. I that the famous Beauchamp effigy (completed 1456) reproduces an unmistakably Milanese (Missaglia) armour. In France, Louis XI., in Burgundy, Charles the Bold had enlisted the services of Italian masters of the craft. The careful researches of my friend, Mr. C. R. Beard, into contemporary records go to show that in the fifteenth century most important armours were foreign imports, the London Armourers' chief work being mainly alterations and repairs: always excepting headpieces, at which the native craftsmen were of approved competence.

[*Note.*—To the Italian and German "hammermen" brought here by Henry VII., and to the "Almain armourers" presently established at Greenwich, I forbear to make more than passing reference. Both Mr. Beard and Mr. F. H. Cripps-Day, who have, in a measure, made this province their own, are, I believe, preparing to publish, independently, the results of their wide and searching study of the records. Meanwhile the reader may be referred to LAKING, Vol. IV, chap. xxix (this section has been edited and developed by the two experts just mentioned), for information on Greenwich armours, and also to FFOULKES. On the great continental schools—Milan, Innsbruck, Nürnberg, Augsburg, etc.—and masters—the Missaglias and Negrolis, Campi, Piccinino; the Colmans, the Seusenhofers, Lochner, Peffenhauser, etc.—he may consult BÖHEIM, DE COSSON, and VALENCIA DE DON JUAN.]

[1] See Mr. J. G. Mann's "Preface" to Trapp's *Churburg*.

i. *ANIMA*, OR (?) ALMAIN CORSLET, *c.* 1560

Musée de l'Armée, Paris.

ii. SEPULCHRAL SLAB TO GOTTFRIED ZU ZIMMERN, AT MESSKIRCH, 1551

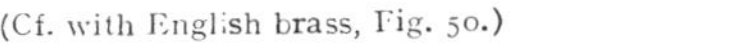

(Cf. with English brass, Fig. 50.)

iii. A "BRIGANDINE," WITH TASSES

(Mid-Sixteenth Century.)

Kunsthistorisches Museum, Vienna.

[The spotted pattern on the velvet is formed by the rivet-heads of the steel plates which line it.]

i. THE EARL OF ESSEX, 1572

ii. SIR GEORGE SOMERSET, *c.* 1576

Penes His Grace the Duke of Beaufort.

" Field armour " highly decorated

EARLY TUDOR ERA

(TO 1545)

Though the Gothic style lingered on here into the early sixteenth century, what is conventionally termed " Maximilian " armour evolved about the last decade of the fifteenth. It is characterized by roundness and breadth in marked contrast with the angular, tapering forms of Western " Gothic." Mr. Mann [1] has pointed out that it probably represents a fusion of Italian with German elements as a result of the Italian wars ; also that it is primarily a type presenting a certain well-defined outline and belonging to a definite age, and that the distinctive CRESTING (=fluted or ribbed surfaces) was by no means general outside of Germany, and *rare in England*. And here one may offer a word of warning touching the evidence of brasses. Apart from their generally debased and mechanical quality *c.* 1490–1550, it should be remembered that brasses are a much cheaper form of memorial than stone or bronze effigies in the round ; so that persons thus commemorated tended to belong to the lesser gentry and middle-classes, provincials, and people largely unaffected by the latest modes patronized by the *grand monde*, who then, as before and since, looked abroad for novelties. Hence we repeatedly find persons of, say, the reign of Mary attired and armed after the style of *c.* 1525–1535.

Armour was on the eve of being called upon to justify its existence, and though the sixteenth century is the age of sumptuous harnesses, engraved, gilt, and embossed, the hour of rapid decline is not far distant. Our object being to concentrate on English armour (*qua* armour, and not as a vehicle for display), we shall waste time neither on highly ornate " parade " pieces nor on tournament-gear. Still less shall we dwell on such eccentricities as the imitation in steel of human hair and features, vulture-headed or other grotesque casques, and metallic reproduction of civilian fopperies. Even on the Continent they were never common, being at best *tours de force* designed for individual patrons : princes and great nobles. *A fortiori*, so far as individual specimens found their way here, they are *aves rarissimæ*.

The " Maximilian " style, which remained fashionable up to *c.* 1545, while profoundly modifying the general outline of the harness, betrayed no decline in mere technical skill ; nor, except perhaps for some increase in weight, was it inferior to Gothic as a defence. Its distinctive features were a high-waisted cuirass with prominent, globose breast-plate, large *tasses* extending well round the hips, *pauldrons* of large size to which were riveted very marked, upstanding *hautes-pièces* [Plates XXVIII. ; XXIX. ii], improved defences for the elbow and knee and broad-toed *sabatons*. In England, in the first fifty years or so of the period, there seems to have

[1] MANN in *Archæologia*, lxxix.

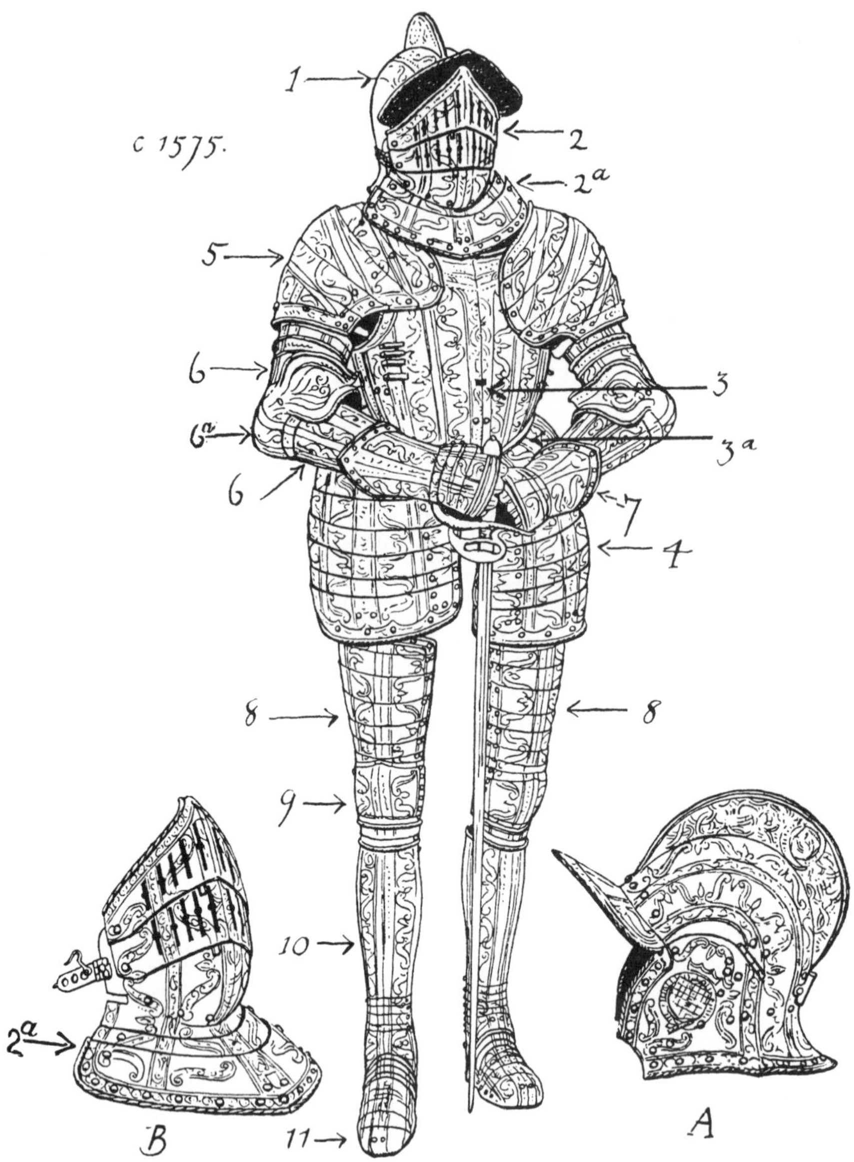

Greenwich Armour (late XVIth Century),

1, Headpiece (burgonet) ; 2, Buffe or falling beaver with 2*a*, Gorget-plates ; 3, 7, Gauntlet ; 8, Cuish ; 9, Kneecop ; 10, Greave ;

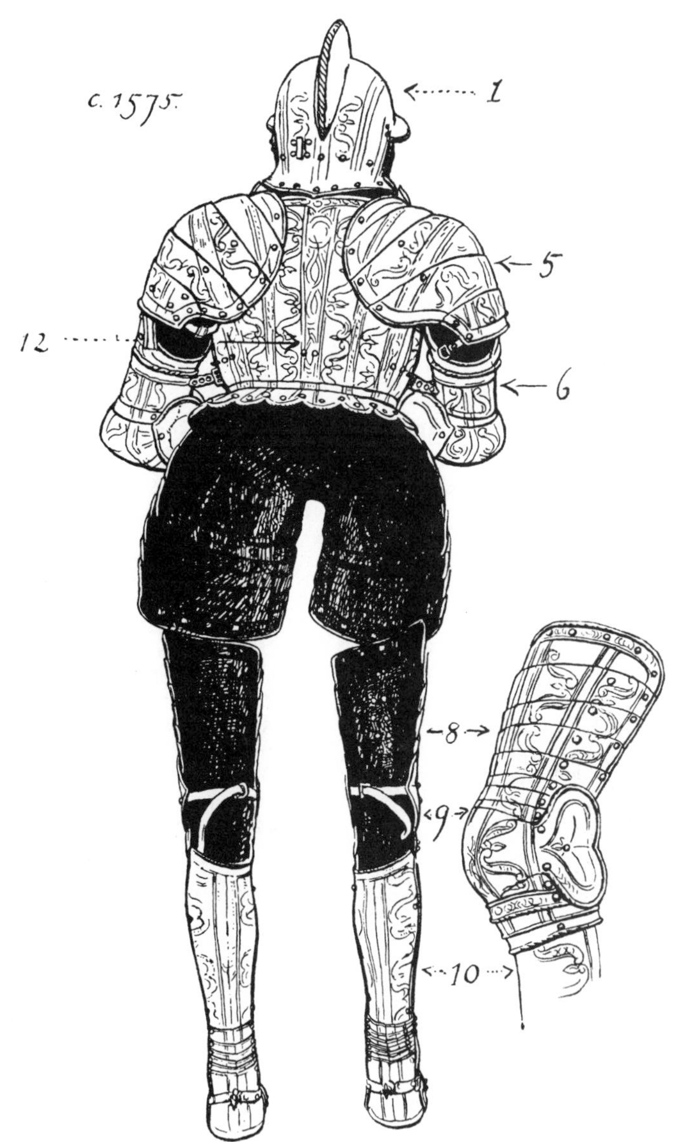

belonged to Henry Herbert, 2nd Earl of Pembroke.

Breast; 3*a*, Skirt; 4, Tasse; 5, Pauldron; 6, Vambrace (6*a*, Elbow-cop); 11, Sabaton. A. Burgonet; B. Buffe.

been a general tendency to wear a deep *breech of mail* under the cuirass, sometimes to within a few inches of the knee, and to retain the Gothic form of tasses. In discussing the development of these and later forms, one must take into account the periodical importation of armours, corslets, etc., from Germany in the sixteenth century, whereby details of form alien to the native traditions were introduced here. The problem, a very urgent one, that came increasingly to the fore from the first quarter of the sixteenth century, was to make armour capable of

FIG. 46.—Late Gothic armour.

resisting the increasing power of firearms. Hence were evolved armours musket-proof, caliver-proof, pistol-proof, etc. Armours not so " proved " (=tested by a point-blank shot) were commonly referred to as " light," or else " good and sufficient." [1]

The helmet used by the heavy cavalry or *men-at-arms* was at first a close helmet of the *armet* class, and in fact was pretty closely akin in outline to the Italianate headpiece to which modern antiquaries have seen fit to restrict the term : a close-fitting, round-topped casque with obtuse

[1] In France we find the same expressions : *à la légère* and *bonne et suffisante.*

i. JOHN, LORD LUMLEY, 1588

Lumley Castle.

ii. ROBERT DUDLEY, EARL OF LEICESTER, *c.* 1575

Penes His Grace the Duke of Sutherland.

MINIATURE BY ISAAC OLIVER, *c.* 1585

Greenwich Armour (Tasses missing).

"sparrow-beaked" visor or face-guard in one piece. This might have articulated gorget-plates fore and aft, or alternately it might end abruptly below the chin in a "bead" or hollow-rim fitting closely over a similar rim at the top of the *collar* (which from now on takes the main weight of body and arm-defences) whereby the head could be turned readily to right or left.[1] This latter variety had the compensating fault of not allowing forward or backward flexion, and by the middle of the sixteenth century was relegated to the tilt-yard where the defect was less important.[2] A mere ridge or keel along the skull-piece from brow to nape developed towards 1510 into an embossed comb. Generally the visor fitted over the chin-piece, more rarely inside. Some helmets of this class, described by Laking as English, have faintly pointed crowns. Over the forehead is riveted a cusped reinforcing-plate, and the *sight* is either cut in the visor itself or formed by the interval between the closed visor and the forehead-plate.

The *salet* no doubt lingered on in its old form among old-fashioned and provincial folk;[3] indeed the *term* is found in English texts till 1588 or later, but it doubtless applies to a "tin hat"-like headpiece of the *chapel* class. Meanwhile the *close helmet*, as I shall henceforth call it, went on quietly developing; the comb grows steadily higher, and soon after the first quarter of the sixteenth century the visor or face-guard is divided into two: the *visor* proper perforated for sight and, when lowered, fitting into a *beaver* (=in this case the plate covering the lower part of the face and perforated for breathing); the *visor* locked with the *beaver*, and the latter with the chin-piece generally by means of a spring-pin. At the same period the beaver sloped upward and outward, forming a more acute peak just below the eyes in front. All three pieces worked freely on the one pair of pivots set above the ears. Other forms of beaver, more akin to the original fifteenth-century variety, which covered *primarily* the chin, were the reinforcing beaver or *buffe*, occasionally strapped over the ordinary beaver and chin-piece for greater security, a survival from the early Italian armets; and the "falling" or "standing" buffe worn with the *burgonet*. This latter was a helmet built on pseudo-antique lines which first appears *c.* 1505, and, though less secure in itself than the *close helmet*, gave a fair amount of protection, and was far less "stuffy" [Figs. 47, 48, B]. Moreover, by the addition of a *buffe* (strapped on, or

FIG. 47.—Burgonet (early form).

[1] Such, at least, is the hitherto-received idea, and doubtless was (with the increased impenetrability of the neck-defences) the makers' object. In practice these helmets will *not* rotate, and hence proved well-nigh useless for serious fighting (communicated by Mr. C. R. Beard).

[2] Meyrick mistook this form for the "burgonet," and his error is still largely propagated in German handbooks.

[3] It is unmistakably shown on the monument to Sir Robert Shirley, 1549, Wiston, Sussex.

affixed by catches), the *burgonet* became at will little, if at all, inferior defensively to the *close helmet*, and might be worn by the men-at-arms, but it soon became the favourite wear for the various categories of light horse, for infantry officers and N.C.O.'s, pikemen and halberdiers. It lent

FIG. 48.—A, " Spanish " morion *c.* 1580 ; B, Burgonet *c.* 1570.

itself readily to elaborate decoration, and so won the regard of the highest in the land. The *buffe* worn with the earliest *burgonets* was often a mere chin-piece ; but presently the taller buffe, either perforated for vision or leaving a gap for the purpose beneath the forepeak or eyeshade (FALL), became the rule. The *morion* was known here by the 'forties at least.

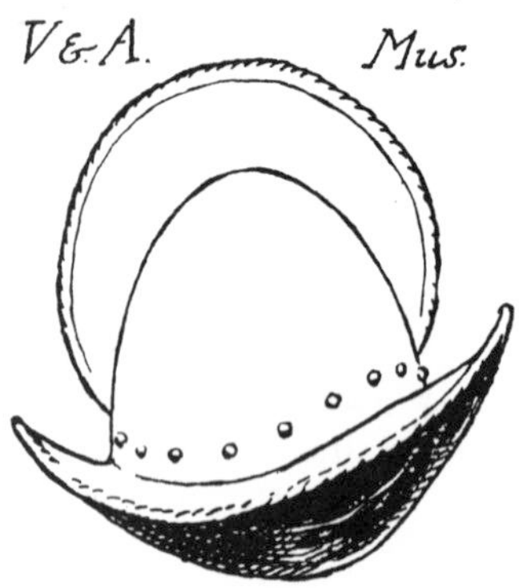

" FIG. 49.—Comb " morion *c.* 1565.

Coming now to the *cuirass*, the focus or nucleus of the whole armour, we may pause to revert to the question of *proof*. Even in the first quarter of the sixteenth century, *hand-guns*, as they were first termed, showed (relatively) striking improvements. The *arquebus* and *musket* did not long delay their appearance on the battlefield.[1] Whereas, at first, attempts seem to have been made to " prove " the entire harness, the consequent weight was prohibitive ; hence ere long the main strength of metal was concentrated on the most vital plates : the front of the headpiece, breastplate,

[1] The subject of proof, of the long struggle between the armourer and the gunsmith, is too extensive for treatment. It has been handled in masterly style in C. Buttin's classic, *Notes sur les armures à l'épreuve.*

and certain lames of the pauldrons and tasses. The armour was generally more or less lined throughout, and in the place of the gambesons, acketons, etc., of the earlier Middle Ages, we have the *arming-doublet* (a legacy from the fifteenth century) of leather or canvas, often quilted, also *arming partlets* and *arming bolsters*. Since foreign armour was periodically imported, it seems probable that not only the greater nobles but the better-equipped troops were armed after the German, Italian, or Franco-Flemish modes. Consequently we may assume that the characteristic continental profile to the breastplate was used by them : at first globose ; towards 1530 with a vertical central keel ; from *c.* 1535 the keel, two-thirds of the way down, shows an obtuse angle where it curves in toward the waist, which angle about the 'forties develops into a marked projection. The *fauld* or *paunce*, though still in wear, is rarely referred to (by the name of SKIRT) in old records. What novelty it had once had had long departed, and it was now taken for granted as an integral part of the breastplate, as the ELBOW-COP is of the VAMBRACE. The *tasses*, now very broad, are laminated.[1] The exposed armpits are defended by *gussets* either of mail attached to the arming doublets, or in the form of movable extra plates affixed to the breastplate by means of springs which allow the shoulder-joint to move freely without exposure of the vulnerable spot. The *elbow-cop* of the man-at-arms likewise continues to be ingeniously fashioned to encircle the joint bracelet-wise, without seriously hindering flexion.

The *average* Englishman, however, long retained certain national peculiarities : in addition to the deep skirt of mail we find a fluted and " engrailed " *placard* over the breastplate, very reminiscent of late Gothic, and the large fluted *tasses* of one plate (the miscalled " tuiles " of modern antiquaries) [2] are relics of the same period. These all are to be regularly found in brasses, etc., as late as Queen Mary's reign [Fig. 50]. The continental close helmet, with " bellows " and " pug-faced " visors, was probably exceptional here even among the upper classes ; the latest mounted suits of Henry VIII. in the Tower show close-fitting convex visors of one plate, imparting a distinctly globular outline to the whole head, and appear to be home-products (cf. Plate XXVIII., which recalls the fifteenth-century " basnets " for foot-combats).

A very important innovation contemporary with the transition from the Gothic to the " Maximilian " forms is the COLLAR or GORGET, not merely as a defence for the neck [Plate XXVIII.], but especially because it is designed to *take the weight* of the whole body-armour, pauldrons, and (often) vambraces; the secondary point of support was at the hips. Hence the necessity for padded under-collars (ARMING PARTLETS) and

[1] Where the laminated *skirt* is absent, the tasses are attached directly to the rim of the breastplate.

[2] *Pace* the *Oxford Dictionary*, and its entries under " Tuile " and " Tuilette," after many years' research I can find no evidence for this acceptation of the term in armour-terminology. It is one more of Meyrick's inventions that have apparently struck deep roots.

" bolsters " at the waist beneath the plates. In connection with the *partial* " proof " of armour (*vide infra*) the double thickness at the points where the plates overlapped should be borne in mind.

Before quitting the " knightly " panoply of this era a few more words should be added. The cuirass about the 'forties became longer waisted, the waist-line drooping to a faint point in front. The broad-toed *sabatons* of 1490–1510 grow more splayed out up to the 'forties when (though still square) they lose their exaggerated width, retained by the lesser gentry till the 'fifties. Perhaps the finest English mid-sixteenth-century armour-brass is of Christopher Lytkott, 1554 [Fig. 50], at Swallowfield, Berks, where the persistence of old-established fashions is notable. In the finest of English armours, strength and boldness of outline appear as the main distinction.

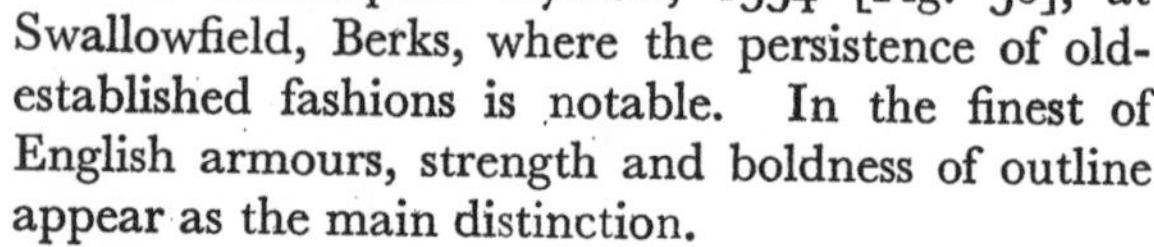

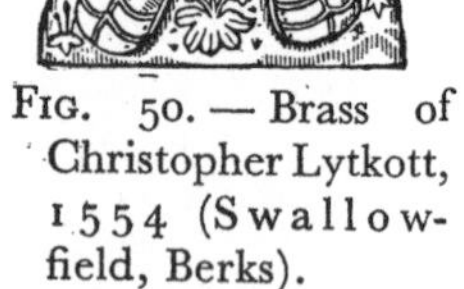

FIG. 50. — Brass of Christopher Lytkott, 1554 (Swallowfield, Berks).

The lance of the man-at-arms grew heavier and bulkier than ever in its last days. The lance-rest, horn-shaped in the fifteenth century, but now straight and made to fold up when not in use—a strong spring maintained it in either position—was ever the mark of the heavy cavalry ; its absence and the presence of symmetrical shoulder-guards denote the light-horseman or foot-soldier. Lances more akin to those of the modern lancer mark these other classes of riders. As late as 1590 the " stradiots " bore *lancegays* (=double-headed javelins) for use in the mêlée. The essential forms of the sword varied little before the middle of the sixteenth century, when *knuckle-bows*, *portes*, *pas d'armes*, etc., were added to the hilts. The true military sword-hilt, however, especially that of the heavy cavalry, was rarely as complicated as that used by civilian courtiers and duellists.

The other weapons, such as *battle-axe*, *mace*, etc., varied mainly in minor details of form.

Already three distinct categories of infantry, each with its own particular accoutrement, begin to appear. At first, as M. Buttin[1] points out, the general bewilderment over the destruction wrought by firearms (*c.* 1500–1525) resulted in uncertainty how best to fit out the ordinary troops ; but, he goes on, " the armourer was still master of his craft." The experience of the Italian wars modified the current tactics, and by the end of the 'thirties new ways of fighting led to a systematic re-arming of the light horse and infantry. The two main divisions of foot consisted at first of pikemen and arquebusiers, to which were soon added musketeers. Each company consisted of a definite

[1] BUTTIN, *Épreuve*, pp. 38–39.

[2] Note that *c.* 1525–'70 *codpieces* (cf. *supra*, pp. 2, 9, 20) of mail or plate are often adapted to the infantry-corslet.

PLATE XXXIII.

PEREGRINE BERTIE, LORD WILLOUGHBY, *c.* 1595

[Pauldrons missing.] *National Portrait Gallery.*

Plate XXXIV.

i. A PIKEMAN, 1587

ii. A MUSKETEER, *c.* 1585

iii. AN ARQUEBUSIER, 1587

proportion of all three classes. An admixture of bill-men and halberdiers was interspersed "for the slaughter" (*i.e.* to follow up and aid the arquebusiers in pursuing and disabling the flying foe). All bore the weapons whence they derived their names [*Pike*, *arquebuse*, *musket*, *bill*, *halberd*]. The pikemen had, in addition, a sword; most of the others either a sword or dagger for close grips. The pikemen wore a *corslet* or *almain rivet* with a *burgonet*, the halberdiers and bill-men the *almain rivet*, or a *corslet* with mail-sleeves, the "shot" *brigandines*, *coats of plate*, or *jacks* with tippets (and sometimes sleeves), of mail and either a *salet*, *morion*, or *skull*. Company officers (captains, lieutenants, and ensigns) wore *corslets* and, in addition to sword, dagger, and (presently) a pistol, and fought armed with *partisan* and round *target* of *proof*. Up to the moment of going into action the captain's *partisan*, *target*, and *burgonet* were carried by a "page" in attendance. The sergeant's distinctive arm was the *halberd*.

In the cavalry various divisions of light horsemen were evolving, to which we shall refer in the following section. In fact we are perhaps premature in already arming our infantry in so definitely standardized a manner. Except for certain corps of guards attached to the sovereign, there were as yet hardly any "regulars." The county-levies were armed in somewhat "scratch" style, and bows and bills were still the mainstay of the English foot. From documents of the period we find that for particular campaigns overseas or over the border, special equipment and kit was issued to the troops. Coats of various colours were prescribed, but, on the whole, the distinctive "uniform" of the national troops was blue, guarded with red, throughout the century.[1] Cavalry, other than the men-at-arms, wore *almain rivets* or *corslets*[2] and *burgonets*, though, as late as 1591, Sir John Smythe complains that the light horse of many of the shires were rudely armed with "red or pied caps" lined with steel skulls, and spears called "gads." We find on special occasions a body of troops armed throughout with black armour imported from Germany.

LATE TUDOR (1545–1600)

From now onward we have the advantage not only of numerous portraits of English gentlemen in armour (Holbein's English portraits, excepting that of Sir Nicholas Carew (Plate XXVIII. i), all show civilian dress), but for the last quarter of the century there is the famous "Almain armourer's album" of "Jacobe" (Jacob Halder?) by which many existing armours have been identified with historical personages.

The *cap-à-pie* harness between now and 1600 underwent considerable modifications. The *cuirass* gradually grew longer, and the waist-line

[1] The different "units" were differentiated by a distinctive badge or token on the sleeve.

[2] On the meaning of this term *in the sixteenth century, vide infra*, p. 77. The lighter *almain rivet* may possibly have been of the *anima* type, *i.e.* with a flexible cuirass of overlapping horizontal bands of steel [Plate XXIX. i].

of the *breastplate* dipped to an increasingly acute point in front. This in the late 'seventies developed into the *peasecod* form so characteristic of the last quarter of the century. The *tasses*, now consisting of many narrow *lames*, were made from the 'sixties in a spreading form with a marked "spring" at the waist, to accommodate the fashionable *trunk-hose* of civilian life. The *pauldrons* are "well-arming," *i.e.* provide a reasonable amount of protection for the shoulders and adjoining parts. The right-hand pauldron is still cut away at the arm-pit to allow the heavy lance of the man-at-arms to be laid in rest. In the armour of the light cavalry the pauldrons are symmetrical; alternatively we find MONNIONS,[1] a laminated variety, covering only the cap of the shoulder and the outer side of the upper arm—often supplemented at the arm-pits by BESAGEWS, or detachable metal discs. The loin-guard or *culet* goes temporarily out of vogue, the defence of the seat being committed to a skirt of mail. The collar, pauldrons, base of cuirass (sometimes), and tasses are lined round the edges with a border of leather, velvet, etc., cut out into an ornamental pattern of escallops, tabs, or the like (PICKADILS). The heavy cavalry still continued to wear the *close helmet* "with his beavers" [Fig. 51] (the term is now commonly transferred to the *ensemble* of the movable face-guards),[2] though many leaders seem to have preferred the burgonet, with or without *buffe*. About the last quarter of the century the *greaves* were made in a series of *lames* at the ankle, giving extra freedom of action, or they end at the ankle, the foot being protected by a mail shoe with toe-cap of plate. The broad "Maximilian" toes of the *sabatons* have from *c.* 1550–1555 quite gone out in favour of a more oval shape, which *c.* 1600 was replaced by square toes. Throughout the second half of

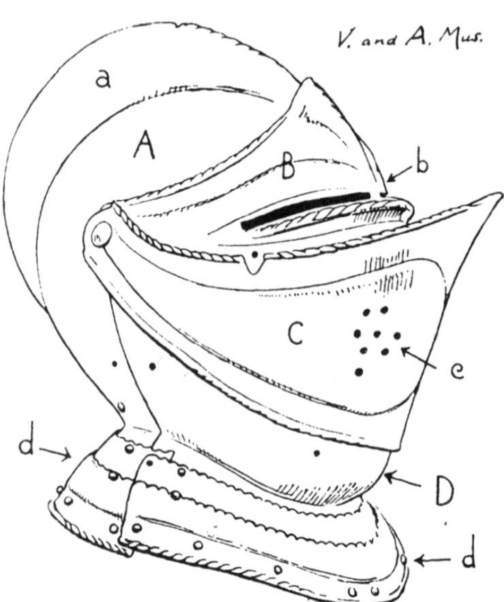

FIG. 51.—Close helmet *c.* 1560. A, Skull or basnet; *a*, Comb. B, Visor; *b*, Sights. C, Ventaille or upper-beaver; *c*, Breaths. D, Buffe or nether beaver; *d*, Gorget-plates.

[1] This rare term seems the only specific name for the variant arbitrarily mis-called "espaliers" in modern armour-jargon; most inventories refer merely to "pauldrons" *tout court*.

[2] Strictly speaking, it would seem, the movable front comprised:
(*a*) The VISOR proper, pierced for sight.
(*b*) The VENTAILLE (or upper beaver) with breathing-holes.
(*c*) The BUFFE (or nether beaver) covering the chin.

the century there was a tendency to "scrap" portions of the heavier harnesses. Not only English but French authors record this tendency, due to the intolerable weight of harness reasonably "proof" against anything more powerful than the pistol. It may, in fact, be said that, except for parade,[1] or in the case of the more conservative warriors, *cap-à-pie* lost favour by the last quarter of the sixteenth century. "Black-and-white" armour (*i.e.* black with white bands) of German importation had been known here from the earlier part of the epoch. Its objects were to diminish the conspicuousness of the burnished or "milled" steel, and to lessen the area liable to rust. In the period which we have reached russeted armour also appears, which, together with "sanguine" (blued) metal, becomes very popular among the leaders, when relieved with gilt bands of engraved ornament.

The average battle-sword, while slightly more developed as to its guard than hitherto, has not the complicated hilt of that worn in civil life. The very heavy lances and the lance-rests henceforth belong to the lists—consequently pauldrons definitely become symmetrical and lance-rests vanish—and the men-at-arms are replaced by *lanciers* and *cuirassiers.* Barret, in 1596, arms the man-at-arms in complete steel to mid-thigh (unless the tasses he names are, as is likely, intended to reach over the knee), with close helmet, strong lance, sword, and mace, and would have his thighs further protected by a pistol-proof saddle-bow (*cuissets* of proof). The defensive armour of the lancier was to be similar, but very lightly and partially proofed, and he was to have a "cask" (here=*burgonet*) and bear lance, "curtilace" (*cutlass*),[2] dagger, and pistol. When we come to examine the equipment of the various classes of light cavalry, the contemporary military writers seem at some variance among themselves and with the orders issued in emergencies to the actual troops. It is hard to get any hard-and-fast individual impressions of the different troops termed pistoliers, hargolets, petronels, and carbines, except that they were all "shot on horseback." Barret classes petronels and pistoliers together, and gives them a pistol-proof cuirass, burgonet, pauldrons (probably MONNIONS), and a single gauntlet ("bridle-" or "elbow"-gauntlet) for the more exposed left hand and forearm, and either a pistol (*petronel* with *snaphaunce*[3] lock or a long pistol *à la française*), or else a case of pistols. The hargolet and mounted arquebusier (the later dragoon) were armed with a headpiece (morion?) only, and a snaphaunce *caliver.*

The "armed" pikes (who occupied the front ranks) wore "corslets complete"[4] at first with a burgonet, but from the late 'nineties with a

[1] It is too readily assumed that every highly ornate armour is intended solely for parade: careful inspection shows many of them carefully designed for use. It is impossible to lay down a clearly defined line of demarcation.

[2] A broadsword or sabre of the *faulchion* family.

[3] The earliest form of flint-lock; the caliver is a light standard arquebus.

[4] The sixteenth-century corslet, when complete, comprised back, breast, collar, pauldrons, vambraces, tasses, and open headpiece. Gauntlets from 1557–1558 were more or less optional.

morion;[1] the lighter-armed "dry pikes," had *brigandines*, jacks, and mail-sleeves, with headpiece as the "armed." The actual pikes were at times 16 to 18 feet in length. The arquebusier, besides a *buff-coat*, *jack*, or the like, and portions of mail, wore a morion, and, with sword and dagger, had the necessary "furniture" (ammunition, tools), etc., required by his weapon. The musketeer by the close of the century had renounced any better headgear than "a fair hat with a feather." He had a *bandileer* whence hung his *charges*, also a powder-flask, *touch-box*, bullet-bag, and tools, with sword and dagger; in action his musket-rest was looped to his left wrist.

The infantry-captain, when not actually in action, bore a *leading-staff* (or *feather-staff*), *i.e.* a miniature *partizan* as a mere mark of office. He was further distinguished by a scarf.[2] In action, officers of foot bore *partizans*; sergeants carried *halberds*. From 1570 onwards there are various marks of the decadence of the armourer's craft. The slipshod bands of decoration that characterize so-called "Pisan" armour, the making of the short *tasses* in one plate apiece (though marked to suggest laminations), the forging of the open helmet, and the skull of the close headpiece in two halves are significant. A notable innovation in the early sixteenth century was the prominent *cabled* edging of the principal portions of the harness. This cabling down to the 'fifties is bold and dashing; afterwards it becomes trivial and meaningless.

> *P.S.*—To describe the precise arming of each category of troops is hardly practicable, except for the offensive weapon peculiar to certain of them. Very clear rules are laid down by the military writers of the day—Garrard, Styward, Barwick, Sir Roger Williams, and Sir John Smythe. It would appear that in practice the soldiery were apt to depart widely from these counsels of perfection, and to omit, for comfort, as much of the heavy armour as they could surreptitiously contrive. Smythe, for instance, a "stickler" for the complete corslet, laments that though such were supplied for overseas service, "certain captains" therein engaged were content to have their "footman piquers" discard pauldrons, vambraces, gauntlets,[3] and tasses.

STUART (1600–1650)

Long before 1600 it had been evident to thinking men that armour was doomed. Not that armour of "proof" would have been impossible even now, but the consequent weight would have immobilized and

[1] This was the infantry-helmet *par excellence*, and seems to have had several variants, of which we can only identify the "comb" and "Spanish" forms [Figs. 48A and 49 are typical].

[2] Off duty or when not on active service he wore a *buff-coat*, steel collar, and scarf; the first garnished with *arming points* at the shoulder—these were for the attachment of the *vambraces*—also a walking cane or *brandistock* (a sword-stick).

[3] Smythe is for "the whole hog." The gauntlet, as it happened, had been authoritatively pronounced a non-essential of the corslet as early as 4 and 5, Philip and Mary.

i. CUIRASSIER, *c.* 1620
Wash-drawing by Van Dyck.

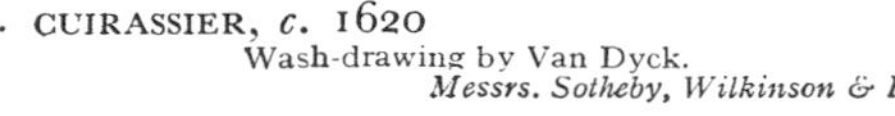

ii. CUIRASSIER, *c.* 1620
Wash-drawing by Van Dyck.
Messrs. Sotheby, Wilkinson & Hodge.

PLATE XXXVI.

i. A PIKEMAN, *c.* 1630
[Note headpiece hung behind hip.]

ii. MUSKETEER, *c.* 1620
From portrait of Sir Nicholas Crispe.
Penes F. H. Cripps-Day, Esq.

iii. ARQUEBUSIER, *c.* 1610

crippled the wearer. The characteristics of this last period are easily summed up. The heavy cavalry were for the most part pretty thoroughly armed. The *Undertaking of London Armourers' Co.*, 1618, had for the lancier "breast, back, gorget, close headpiece, pauldrons, vambraces, gushes (=*cuishes*), and one *gauntlet* (for the left hand; the right, defended by the sword-guard, being covered with a buff glove), to be coloured russet." The "gushes" or cuishes here described are a hybrid between the original cuishes (unconnected with the body-armour) and the older form of *tasses*, which they resemble in that they are attached (buckled or *screwed*) directly to the *skirt* or to the flanged base of the breastplate. They reached to below the knees where they formed KNEE-COPS,[1] and were shaped to cover the full knickers now worn. The cuirassier was armed very similarly, but generally had a distinctive variety of headpiece specifically called a "cuirassier's headpiece" (Plate XXXV.) as against the "field (=battle) headpiece" of the other (see below). The light horseman's armour, likewise russeted, comprised cuirass, collar, pauldrons [*monnions*], and an "elbow-gauntlet" for the left hand, also a "barred headpiece" (*Lobster-tail helmet*) [Fig. 52]. The *dragoon* (or what we should call "mounted infantry") wore merely a *buff-coat* and headpiece (either of the *lobster-tail* or *morion* kind), together with his "piece" (*arquebus* or *carbine*) and its appurtenances. Unlike other horsemen he at first wore shoes and stockings instead of boots, being in fact mounted infantry.[2]

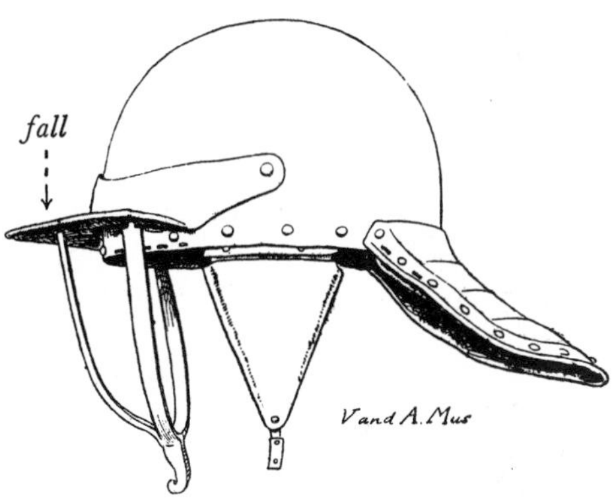

FIG. 52.—"Lobster-tail" casque (burgonet).

The cavalry cuirass of this period has a very sharp medial ridge. In front it sinks to the fork in a sharp point, whence the corset-like waist-line curved up on the hips and behind to a level approaching that of an "Empire" waist. Back and breast are from now on joined at shoulders and sides by plated straps and catches. The long tasset-cuishes are often affixed direct to the rim of the breastplate by screws and nuts. The *gorget-plates* of the helmet are deep, and the *collar* of the harness markedly so, especially where intended for wear with a mere buff-coat. The old *culet* returns to favour in a deep and spreading form, and the pauldrons have markedly angular wings at back and front. Since the cavalry had begun to discard armour below the knees (from mid-sixteenth

[1] Similar long tasses occur for light-horse and mounted infantry officers from the last third of the sixteenth century.

[2] In fact, in the later sixteenth century, some dragoons appear to have been "mounted" pikemen, and armed accordingly.

century), high boots had replaced greaves and sabatons. The helmets of the sixteenth century (whether *close helmets*, *burgonets*, or *morions*) *c.* 1560–1585 had had the *comb* from nape to brow of notable height. Subsequently they shrink (except in the later *comb-cap*) and now have no comb or a very slight one.

By this time the " comb morion " (Fig. 49) had gradually lost favour and been supplemented by the " Spanish " kind (Fig. 48, A). The pikes now wore this latter, crowning a *corslet* which had shed successively its *vambraces* and *pauldrons* (the latter were abandoned between 1622 and 1625). The so-called *comb-cap* was apparently an alternative head-gear for pikes, and by the Civil Wars they wore a *pot.*[1] The *tasses*, of one plate each, ribbed to suggest laminations and meeting in the centre, were *hinged* to the breast. On the march, the headpiece of these troops was suspended by a ring [2] to a hook on the back-plate over the right hip. The arquebusier continued to be limited in armour to a morion; the musketeer had no armour. Their respective weapons were as heretofore.

Armour was probably worn on an increasingly limited scale from the outset of the Civil War. It remained for some considerable time the fashion for generals and great nobles to be *painted* in armour (generally so-called " half suits " or " three-quarter suits "), but these mostly reveal themselves as late Greenwich suits of the close of the sixteenth or early seventeenth century, and are akin to the fancy-dress photographs till recently a speciality of the popular " while-you-wait " studio. The short *tasses* of these Greenwich harnesses often had the lower edge " invecked " or wrought in an escalloped pattern. Apart from this, Greenwich suits have several common features by which they can be recognized, *e.g.* the *separate* plate riveted to the elbow-guard for the protection of the bend of the arm, the broad *square* shoulders, the narrow waist and " flaring " hips, and the pattern of the *cabling* of the margins (note interruption at centre), also the sharply concave profile of the beaver (or ventaille) of the close helmet [Plate XXXIII.]; [3] whereas from *c.* 1600 the profile of the beaver in ordinary close helmets begins to be much straighter and more vertical.

Another form of vambrace, of which examples appear in England increasingly from the middle of the sixteenth century, has a small " cop " over the elbow, the bend of the arm being wholly covered by narrow articulated lames. This type was never common, and seems always of foreign make.

Despite the improvements in firearms, the old English long-bow continued in favour with the native infantry till nearly the close of the sixteenth century. At St. Quentin, in 1557, the bowmen far outnumbered the " shot."

[1] A term of varied import: it appears in cavalry use to denote the "lobster-tail." The " comb-cap " was probably more popular in Holland than England; the broad-brimmed " pikeman's pot " seems distinctively native.

[2] Or it had the brim pierced for the purpose (Plate XXXVI. i).

[3] Cf. MANN, F. G.; *Greenwich Armour and Sculptured Tombes* (*The Connoisseur*, August, 1931).

BIBLIOGRAPHY

THE following list makes no claims to completeness. Indeed, many of the books here given contain far fuller bibliographies. Our modest aim has been to give a working selection of books which the average reader may consult with profit, thereby adding—especially on the pictorial side—to such information as he can extract from our present volume. They have been chosen as referring specifically, though not necessarily exclusively, to its subject-matter. The books are arranged : (1) English ; (2) French ; (3) German ; (4) Spanish.

From the present bibliography first-hand authorities contemporary with the fashions described are omitted of set purpose : they are apt to be none too easy of reference (and perhaps understanding) by the average reader. A number of the most important passages are quoted in many of the books specified below. It is worth while here referring again to DÉ MÉLY AND BISHOP's *Répertoire des inventaires imprimés.*

[*N.B.*—Where any of the following are cited in our main text, quotation is made under the author's name alone if but one work is given here, but where several works by the same writer are included, the particular work is indicated by the abbreviated title indicated *in square brackets* at the end of that item : *e.g.* FAIRHOLT = *Costume in England,* by F. W. Fairholt ; but C. Buttin's *Notes sur les Armures à l'Épreuve* is quoted as BUTTIN : *Épreuve.*]

In conjunction with the present work we would specially commend :

FAIRHOLT, F. W. : *Costume in England* (Lord Dillon's edition of 1896) ; and
HEWITT, JOHN : *Ancient Armour and Weapons,* 1859–1861.

Still, on the whole, far the best *general* English text-books of their respective subjects. The illustrations, unfortunately, are mostly very unsatisfactory and require verifying or supplementing from other sources.

COSTUME AND GENERAL WORKS

CALTHROP, D. C. : *English Costume.*
HEATH, RICHARD : "Studies in English Costume" (in *Magazine of Art,* vols. xi. and xii.).
KELLY, F. M., & R. SCHWABE : *Historic Costume . . .* 1490–1790. [K. and S.]
PLANCHÉ, J. R. : *British Costume.*
,, ,, *Cyclopædia of Costume.* [*Cyclopædia*]

BLUM, A. : *Histoire du Costume.*
GAY, VICTOR : *Glossaire archéologique.* [GAY]
JACQUEMIN, R. : *Iconographie du Costume* (plates only).

LECHEVALLIER-CHEVIGNARD : *Costumes des XVIe, XVIIe et XVIIIe siècles.*
PITON, C. : *Le Costume civil en France.*
QUICHERAT, J. : *Le Costume en France.*
RACINET, A. : *Le Costume.*
RENAN, ARY : *Le Costume.*
ROY, HIPPOLYTE : *La vie . . . au XVIIe siècle. Epoque Louis XIII.*
PARIS—SOCIÉTÉ DE L'HISTOIRE DU COSTUME. *Publications.*

BOEHN, M. VON : *Die Mode . . . im XVI^en^ Jahrhundert.* [*XVI*]
„ „ „ „ *XVII^en^* „ [*XVII*]
„ „ „ „ *XVIII^en^* „ [*XVIII*]
HEFNER-ALTENECK, J. VON : *Trachten* . . . etc. [HEFNER]
HOTTENROTH, F. : *Handbuch der deutschen Tracht.*
„ „ *Tracht*, etc.
KÖHLER, BRUNO : *Allgemeine Trachtenkunde.*
KÖHLER, KARL : *Trachten der Völker in Bild und Schnitt.*
MASNER, KARL : *Kostümausstellung.*
MÜTZEL, HANS : *Vom Lendenschurz zur Modetracht.*
QUINCKE, W. : *Handbuch der Kostümkunde.*
ROSENBERG, C. A. : *Geschichte des Kostüms.*
WEISS, HERMANN : *Kostümkunde.*
Zur Geschichte des Kostüms (in Series " Münchner Bilderbogen ").
Zeitschrift [des Vereins] für historische Waffen-[und Kostüm]kunde : Leipzig and Dresden. (*In progress.*) [*Z.H.W.K.*]

ARMOUR

CAMP, S. J. : *Catalogue . . . Armour . . . Wallace Collection.*
COSSON, C. A. DE, and W. BURGES : *Ancient Helmets and Mail* (*Archæol. Journ.*, 1880). [*Helmets*]
DEMMIN, A. : *Arms and Armour* (transl. by C. C. Black).
FFOULKES, C. C. : *The Armourer and his Craft.* [FFOULKES]
LAKING, G. F. : *Record of European Armour.* [LAKING]
MANN, J. G. : *Notes on Armour of the Maximilian Period and the Italian Wars* (*Archæologia*, lxxix. 1929). [MANN]
TRAPP, OSWALD GRAF : *The Armoury of the Castle of Churburg* (transl., with a Preface, by James G. Mann). [TRAPP]

BUTTIN, CHARLES : *Le Guet de Genève*, etc. [*Guet*]
„ „ *Le Musée Stibbert.* [*Stibbert*]
„ „ *Notes sur les Armures à l'Épreuve.* [*Épreuve*]
COSSON, C. A. : *Cabinet d'Armes du Duc de Dino.* [*Dino*]
DUYSE, H. VAN : *Catalogue . . . Porte de Hal* (Introduction).
MAINDRON, M. : *Les Armes.*

BOHEIM, WENDELIN : *Handbuch der Waffenkunde.*
HEFNER-ALTENECK, J. VON : *Die Waffen.*

LEGUINA, ENRIQUE DE : *Glosario de Voces de Armeria.*
VALENCIA DE DON JUAN, Count de : *Catalogo de la Real Armeria.* [VALENCIA]

ICONOGRAPHY

LODGE's *Portraits* of illustrious Personages, Harding's book with the same title, and Hailstones' *Yorkshire Worthies* may still be consulted with advantage. So, where a copy is available, may the albums of the National Portrait Exhibitions at South Kensington in 1866, 1867, and 1868, despite a number of preposterous attributions. To all serious students, who happen to be in London, there is happily accessible probably the richest existing collection of pictorial documents in the Witt Library of photographs and reproductions of paintings and drawings of all schools (32 Portman Square, W.1). Intended primarily for the illustration of the history of Art, they are no less valuable for the study of costume and armour. Such books as C. H. Collins Baker's *Lely and the Stuart Portrait Painters,* and illustrated catalogue of the Petworth collections, and his and W. G. Constable's *English Painting in the Sixteenth and Seventeenth Centuries,* are full of good stuff, finely presented. In France, Dimier's *Histoire de la peinture de portrait en France au XVIe siècle* and E. Moreau-Nélaton's *Les Clouet et leurs émules* are excellent to consult. Hirth's *Les grands Illustrateurs* is another work of capital importance. Mr. Goulding's catalogue of the Welbeck miniatures is no less valuable (as are generally the Walpole Society annuals in which it originally appeared). Among periodicals which should be profitably explored for material are *Apollo,* the *Burlington Magazine,* and the *Connoisseur,* among English magazines; among French, the *Revue de l'Art, Les Arts,* the *Gazette des Beaux Arts*; among German, *Belvedere* and *Pantheon.* It may not be out of place to refer to the excellent examples of *English* costume (sixteenth to eighteenth centuries) included in the illustrations to Kelly and Schwabe's *Historic Costume.*

But the material is endless, and fresh stores become available every day in the form of reproductions of every form of art: illustrated *catalogues raisonnés* of collections public and private, of exhibitions and sales, monographs on artists, schools and periods. Even dealers' advertisements repay attention.

POSTSCRIPT.—A study (preferably from originals) of historic ornament and design, with special reference to textiles, is in a measure indispensable; to say nothing of the materials, dyes and "cut" favoured in the costumes of different epochs.

INDEX AND GLOSSARY

Reference to the page is made in ordinary Arabic numerals, to the inset line illustrations in italicized Arabic figures, and to plates in Roman numerals.*

Items of such general character as boots, stockings, cloaks, hairdressing, etc., being duly discussed under their appropriate headings in the text, have been ignored here.

In the interests of the general reader we have endeavoured throughout the book to avoid too lavish a use of technical terminology.

* Where followed by an asterisk (*) the reference is to a *footnote*.

† It is, so far as I know, not current in old English texts.

† PANES—or, better, PAIR OF PANES—also denotes paned trunk-hose.
‡ Do not confuse the *Restoration* "pantaloons" with the close trousers of a later age and same name.